AMERICA THROUGH EUROPEAN EYES

ON AMERICA
VOLUME II

THE COMMERCE
OF
AMERICA WITH EUROPE

JACQUES PIERRE BRISSOT DE WARVILLE

ON AMERICA

VOLUME II

THE

COMMERCE

OF

AMERICA WITH EUROPE

[1794]

AUGUSTUS M. KELLEY · PUBLISHERS
NEW YORK 1970

First Edition 1794

(London: *Printed for* J. S. Jordan, *No. 166 Fleet-Street,* 1794)

Reprinted 1970 by
AUGUSTUS M. KELLEY · PUBLISHERS
REPRINTS OF ECONOMIC CLASSICS
New York New York 10001

· · · · · · · · · · · · · · · ·

S B N 678-00598-2
Volume II 678 04029 X

L C N 67-30855

· · · · · · · · · · · · · · · ·

PRINTED IN THE UNITED STATES OF AMERICA
by SENTRY PRESS, NEW YORK, N. Y. 10019

THE

COMMERCE

OF

AMERICA with EUROPE;

PARTICULARLY WITH

FRANCE AND GREAT BRITAIN;

COMPARATIVELY STATED, AND EXPLAINED.

SHEWING

THE IMPORTANCE OF THE AMERICAN REVOLUTION
TO THE INTERESTS OF FRANCE,

AND POINTING OUT THE ACTUAL SITUATION

OF THE

UNITED STATES of NORTH AMERICA,

IN REGARD TO

TRADE, MANUFACTURES, AND POPULATION.

―――――

By J. P. BRISSOT DE WARVILLE,
AND
ETIENNE CLAVIERE.

―――――

TRANSLATED FROM THE LAST FRENCH EDITION,
Revised by BRISSOT, and called the SECOND VOLUME of his View of America.

WITH THE LIFE OF BRISSOT, AND AN APPENDIX,
BY THE TRANSLATOR.

―――――

LONDON:

PRINTED FOR J. S. JORDAN, N° 166, FLEET-STREET.

M DCC XCIV.

A SKETCH

OF THE

LIFE

OF

J. P. BRISSOT.

BY THE EDITOR.

———

H E was born at the village of Ouarville, near Chatres, in Orleannois, on the 14th of January 1754. His father was what the French called a *Traiteur*; that is, keeper of an eating houfe or an ordinary. He was intended for the profeffion of the law, and was articled to an attorney for that purpofe. But he grew difgufted with the chicane and turpitude he was daily obliged to witnefs, and therefore, after the five years of his articlefhip were expired, he left Chatres, and went to Paris.

An

An accident one night at the theatre at Paris placed him in the company of an Englifh gentleman. They became intimate, and from this gentleman he obtained fome knowledge of the Englifh language; which he afterwards improved by a refidence in London.

He had received a regular claffical education, and acquired, by ftrict application, a tolerable knowledge of the German, Italian, and Spanifh languages, fufficient to confult the authors who have written in thofe languages. On his arrival at Paris his firft ftudy was jurifprudence, with an intention of becoming an advocate in parliament. No fcience however efcaped his attention. He attended lectures and experiments in every branch of fcience; wherein his active genius found ample exercife. Chymiftry was his favourite object of purfuit; but his circumftances were too limited to indulge much in it. The fmall patrimony which he inherited from his father did not exceed forty pounds per annum.

In

In the year 1777 he made his firſt tour to London. During his ſtay in London he became engaged in the conduct of a French newſpaper, at that time called the *Courier de l'Europe*, but ſince the *Courier de Londres*. Some miſunderſtanding having happened concerning the ſtamps (at the ſtamp-office in London) for this paper, the proprietor took a reſolution of printing it at Boulogne ſur-mer; and Briſſot was appointed the Editor, and reſided at Boulogne for that purpoſe. He continued in this capacity at Boulogne about two years. From thence he went to Paris; and was admitted Counſellor in Parliament.—Early in the year 1782 he went to Neufchatel to ſuperintend the printing of one of his books (mentioned hereafter). This was the memorable period of the revolution at Geneva. Here he became acquainted with M. Claviere and M. du Rovray, who, with a numerous party, were expelled that city, and ſought an aſylum in Ireland.

In the autumn of this year, he married a

daughter

daughter of Madame Dupont of Boulogne.
This young lady had been recommended to the
celebrated Madame de Genlis, who obtained a
fituation for her in the nurfery of the Duke de
Chartres, late Duke of Orleans, who fuffered
under the guilotine; in which fituation fhe
continued fome time after her marriage.

At the beginning of the year 1783 he vifited
London a fecond time. His view in this journey was to eftablifh in London a Lyceum, or
Academy of Arts and Sciences, together with
an office of general correfpondence. In this
undertaking he was encouraged by fome of the
firft literary men in France; and a Monfieur
du Forge, mufician at Paris, was fo captivated
with the fcheme, that he advanced four thoufand
livres (1661.) for one third fhare of the profits.
Briffot was to have the fole management, and
the other two thirds of the profits. He took a
houfe in Newman Street, Oxford Street; and
publifhed a profpectus of his undertaking. He
fent for his wife and his youngeft brother (his
eldeft

eldeſt brother was a prieſt). At this time he commenced his defcription of the fciences in England (mentioned hereafter), to be publiſhed monthly. Having in one of his publications taken occaſion to vindicate the Chevalier de Launay, editor of the *Courier du Nord,* printed at Maeſtricht, the editor of the *Courier de l'Europe,* now M. du Morande, was ſo highly offended by it, that he became from that time Briſſot's moſt determined enemy. It is to be obſerved, that the Courier du Nord and the Courier de l'Europe were rival newſpapers. De Launay quitted Maeſtricht, and went to Paris, where he was immediately put into the Baſtile, and was never more heard of.

In the month of May, 1784, Briſſot was arreſted by his printer in London. Although he was at this time very well known to ſeveral perſons of rank and fortune, yet he was too delicate to apply to any of them for pecuniary aſſiſtance. But after remaining a day or two in a lock-up houſe in Gray's Inn Lane, he ſent

his

his brother to an intimate friend, who inftantly paid the printer his bill, and liberated him.

The next morning Briffot fet out for France, leaving his wife and brother in England, affuring them he would quickly return, which he certainly intended. But in this he was feverely difappointed. Thus ended his literary enterprife of eftablifhing a Lyceum in London, in which he embarked his whole property with a degree of infatuation and zeal that feemed to border upon infanity. During his refidence in London he became acquainted with one Count de Pelleport, author of feveral pamphlets againft the principal perfons of the French Court, particularly of one called *Soirees d' Antoinette,* for the apprehenfion of the author of which the French Court offered a thoufand pounds (1000 Louis) reward. Briffot, inftead of proceeding directly to Paris, ftopped at Boulogne, and refided there with his mother-in-law; here he refolved to continue his publication on the original plan. Du M—— knowing that Pelleport

was

was the author of the offenfive pamphlet, and
that Briffot and Pelleport were intimate, refolved to obtain the reward, and gratify his refentment. He applied to Pelleport, offering
him the fuperintendance of a publication to be
carried on at Bruges (near Oftend), the falary
of which was to be two hundred pounds per
annum. Pelleport accepted the offer. But it
was neceffary to ftop at Boulogne, where fome
final arrangements were to be made. In the
month of July Pelleport embarked for Boulogne
with Captain Meredith. But the moment he
landed, he was feized by the officers of the
Police, who put him in chains and carried him
to Paris, where he was fent to the Baftile.
Du M——— was an agent of the Police of Paris.
Information being given to the Police, that
Briffot was at Boulogne, and that he was the
intimate friend of Pelleport, he was immediately taken into cuftody, carried to Paris, and
committed to the Baftile. However, it is certain that Briffot never wrote any thing againft
                                        either

either the King or Queen of France. He was fincere in his abhorrence of the arbitrary and defpotic principles of the French government, but with refpect to the private conduct of the King and Queen he never beftowed the fmalleft attention upon it. In this magazine of human victims he continued about fix weeks. His wife applied to Madame Genlis in his favour, and Madame Genlis moft generoufly made a point of it with the Duke de Chartres to obtain his liberty. The Duke de Chartres's interference does not appear by any document; but Briffot's acquittal of the charge brought againft him, appears in the following report of his examination, made to the French minifter, M. Breteuil, on the 5th of September.

" The Sieur Briffot de Warville was convey-
" ed to the Baftile on the day after the Sieur
" de Pelleport, who was arrefted at Boulogne
" fur-mer, arrived at Paris. In confequence of
" his connections with this man, guilty of
" writing libels, he was fufpected of having
                                        " been

" been his coadjutor. The atteftation of a boy
" in the printing office, from whence one of
" thefe libels iffued, gave ftrength to fufpicions;
" but this atteftation, tranfmitted from Lon-
" don, is deftitute of authenticity; and the
" Sieur Briffot de Warville, who has very fa-
" tisfactorily anfwered to the interrogatories
" which were put to him, attributes his crimi-
" nation to the animofity of enemies whom he
" conceives to have plotted againft him in
" London. The Sieur Briffot de Warville is a
" man of talents, and of letters; he appears to
" have formed fyftems, and to entertain extra-
" ordinary principles; but it is certain that, for
" the laft feven or eight months, his connec-
" tions with the Sieur de Pelleport had ceafed,
" and that he employed himfelf folely upon a
" periodical paper, which he obtained permif-
" fion to circulate and fell in France, after
" having fubmitted it to the examination of a
" licenfer."

It is proper to obferve, that the addition of

de

de Warville, which Briſſot made to his name (to diſtinguiſh himſelf from his eldeſt brother) is a kind of local deſignation, not uncommon in many countries. William of Malmſbury, Geoffry of Monmouth, Rapin de Thoyras, Joan d'Arc, &c. &c. But in the orthography he ſubſtituted the Engliſh *W* for the French dipthong *Ou*; the ſound of that dipthong being ſimilar to our W. Thus *Ouarville* is pronounced *Warville* in both languages.

In a very ſhort time after his releaſe from the Baſtile he very honourably diſcharged his pecuniary obligation to his friend in London.

In the year 1787, which was the era of the foundation of the French revolution, the Duke de Chartres, now become Duke of Orleans by the death of his father, embraced the party of the Parliament againſt the Court. Upon the principle of gratitude Briſſot attached himſelf to the Duke of Orleans. As an honeſt man he could not do otherwiſe.

We

We shall here pass by his tour to America, and some other circumstances, because they are intimately connected with the account of his writings, which is subjoined.

Upon his return to France he found that his celebrity had not been diminished by his absence. He was elected a member of the Constituent Assembly, and was much engaged in the committees of research, of which he was the reporter. He was also elected a member of the Legislative Assembly for the department of Paris. It must be observed, that the revolution cast a veil over the crimes of all those who had been obliged to leave their country. In this group who returned to France was Du M——. He opposed Brissot in his election for Paris, but Brissot was elected by a majority of more than three to one. However Du M——'s party were excessively mortified; and they unceasingly calumniated Brissot in the most opprobrious terms. M. Petion, mayor of Paris, and who was Brissot's friend and townsman, contributed

contributed much to ftrengthen his intereft and afcendancy.

Briffot now diftinguifhed himfelf as one of the *Amis des Noirs* (friend of the Negroes), of whom he was a moft zealous advocate. In a fpeech which he delivered in the Affembly in the year 1791, there is a ftrong trait of philanthropy.

Of this fpeech the following is a fhort extract: " You have heard of enormities that freeze you with horror ; but Phalaris fpoke not of his brazen bull, he lamented only the dagger that his own cruelty had raifed againft him. The colonifts have related inftances of ferocity ; but give me, faid he, an informed brute, and I will foon make a ferocious monfter of him. It was a white man who firft threw a negro into a burning oven ; who dafhed out the brains of a child in the prefence of its father ; who fed a flave with its own proper flefh. Thefe are the monfters that have to account for the barbarity of the revolted favages.—Millions of Africans have

perifhed

periſhed on this ſoil of blood. You break, at every ſtep, the bones of the inhabitants, that nature has given to theſe iſlands; and you ſhudder at the relation of their vengeance. In this dreadful ſtruggle the crimes of the Whites are yet the moſt horrible. They are the off-ſpring of deſpotiſm : whilſt thoſe of the Blacks originate in the hatred of ſlavery, and the thirſt of revenge. Is philoſophy chargeable with theſe horrors ? Does ſhe require the blood of the coloniſts ? Brethren, ſhe cries, be juſt; be beneficent ; and you will proſper.—Eternal ſla-very muſt be an eternal ſource of crimes ;—diveſt it at leaſt of the epithet *eternal*; for an-guiſh that knows no limitation of period can only produce deſpair."

Upon the abolition of the French monarchy, in the month of September 1792, the Legiſla-tive Aſſembly diſſolved itſelf. The conſtitu-tion being diſſolved by the abolition of the King, they conceived that it was the inherent right of the people to chooſe a new repreſentation, in

order

order to frame a new conftitution, fuited to the wifhes of the people, and to the neceffity of the exifting circumftances of the times. In this general election Briffot was elected one of the deputies from the department of Eure and Loire. His abilities and talents became every day more confpicuous. He was chofen the Reporter of the Committee of Public Safety; in which fituation he conducted himfelf without reproach, until the treacherous conduct of Dumourier threw a fufpicion on the whole of the Gironde party.

Although affailed on all fides by his enemies, his character afperfed and depreciated by the bafeft of calumnies, Briffot fhewed himfelf confiftent with his public principles of philanthropy.

In the dreadful maffacre of the 3d of September, his opponents, particularly Du M——, fought every opportunity to accomplifh his deftruction, by accufing him of being a principal inftigator of thofe horrors. And it muft be owned,

owned, that thefe repeated and continued ca-
lumnies weakened him in the public efteem.
Du M——— was perfectly acquainted with the
Englifh method of writing a man down.

When Condorcet moved for the abolition of
royalty, Briffot was filent.

When the motion was made to pafs fentence
of death on the King, Briffot fpoke and voted
for the appeal to the primary affemblies.

When Fayette was cenfured, Briffot defended him.

When the Duke of Orleans (M d' Egalité)
was cenfured, Briffot defended him.

The two firft feem to have arifen in principles of humanity.

The two laft, unqueftionably, arofe in the
ftrongeft ties of gratitude and friendfhip.

A confcientious man cannot fuffer a more fevere affliction, than when his private honour
places him againft his public duty.

Of

Of BRISSOT's WRITINGS;

AND PARTICULARLY OF THIS WORK.

Upon the settlement of the American government after the war, he became an enthusiastic admirer of the new constitution of that great country. But some French persons, who had been in America, and were returned to France, had published their thoughts and opinions of America, in a manner that was nothing short of illiberality. The reader will find the principal names of these writers in the thirty-second chapter of the first volume. Brissot was fired with indignation at this treatment of a people, whom he conceived could not in anywise have deserved such reproach; and, imagining that the general peace of 1783 had opened an honourable and free commuication of reciprocal commercial advantages between America and France, he wrote *this volume* with the view of supporting and establishing that primary idea,

or

or *theory* of a French commerce with the United States.

Upon this point it is no more than ordinary can-dour to obferve, that all which Briffot recommends, explains, or relates, concerning a French commerce with the United States, applies equal-ly, and in fome points more than equally, to the Britifh commerce with them. Every Britifh merchant and trader may derive fome advantage from a general view of the principles which he has laid down for the eftablifhment and regulation of a reciprocal commerce between France and America. The produce and manufactures of England are infinitely better fuited to the wants of America ; and therefore all his theory, which is directed to the welfare and improvement of France, muft ftrongly attach the attention of the Britifh merchant and mechanic ; who, in this great point, have not at prefent any fuperiors, but have feveral rivals. Briffot's ambition was to make France the greateft and moft powerful rival. And every candid perfon

muft

muſt allow that he deſerved much credit of his countrymen for the progreſs he made, in this firſt attempt, to open the eyes of the French nation to proſpects of new ſources of advantage. All that is further neceſſary to ſay of this work, is ſaid by Briſſot himſelf in the introduction, from the tenth to the twentieth pages. In the laſt French edition of Briſſot's Travels in America, publiſhed by himſelf, about ſeven or eight months before his decapitation, this volume is placed the laſt of that work. We have followed the Author's arrangement, and collated the whole by the laſt Paris edition.

Of the preceding volume, entitled " New Travels in the United States of America," we have nothing to add : the whole of the French edition is now before the reader.

Of Briſſot's other works it is proper to mention the following.

The Theory of Criminal Laws, in two volumes.—Although M. la Cretelle, at the concluſion of his Eſſay on the Prejudices attached to Infamy,

Infamy, fpeaks in flattering terms of this work, for he fays, that it exhibits an extenfible knowledge, and fhews the writer's ambition afcends to great principles ; yet to thofe perfons who have read Beccaria's Effay on Crimes and Punifhments, it will not appear that Briffot has added much novelty to the fubject.

The Neceffity of a Reform of the Criminal Laws.

What Reparation is due to innocent Perfons unjuftly accufed.

Thefe were two difcourfes which were crowned by the Academy of Chalons fur Marne, and were printed in the form of two pamphlets. The minifters of Louis XVI. were a good deal offended at the principles they contained, and they forbid the Academy propofing the difcuffion of fimilar fubjects at any of their future meetings.

This check ferved but as a ftimulus to Briffot to continue his fubject. He therefore, in two years afterwards, publifhed his *Philofophical Library of the Criminal Laws.* This work is

now

now *ten volumes*. Briffot's view in this work was, to diffufe and explain thofe grand principles of freedom which produced the revolution in England in the year 1688, and the revolution in America in the year 1775. Before the diffolution of the monarchy in France thofe principles were almoft unknown to the French, and are ftill almoft unknown to the other parts of Europe. But as feveral of the monarchs of Europe approved of the American revolution, it may be prefumed that their fubjeCts will not long continue ignorant of the motives and grounds of a meafure which was honoured with the patronage of their fovereigns. This circumftance alone fhould convince the Englifh, that many of the powers of Europe behold with pleafure the diminution of their greatnefs and confequence, and that very few of thofe powers are ever friendly to them, except during the time they are receiving a bribe, by virtue of an inftrument, commonly called *a fubfidiary treaty*.

Of

Of Dr. Price of London he was an admirer ; but of Dr. Prieftley he was alfo an imitator for he amufed himfelf frequently with chymif- try, phyfics, anatomy, and religion. On the laft fubject there is a prefumption that he wrote but little ; for in his *Letter to the Archbifhop of Sens* (the only tract on religion, by him, that has come to the Editor's knowledge) he fays, " That religious tyranny had been proftrated " by the blows of Voltaire, Rouffeau, D'Alem- " bert, and D'Iderot." His mind was capaci- ous, and his comprehenfion extenfive. In his zeal to become an imitator of Prieftley, he publifhed a volume *Concerning Truth, or Thoughts on the Means of attaining Truth, in all the Branches of Human Knowledge.* Here was a wide field for the difplay of Briffot's talents and induftry. His defign was to have carried on the work to feveral volumes, and to have invited the com- munications of the literati of all Europe, in all the different *fciences,* and, it may be added, *fpeculations.* But there was fuch a freedom of

fentiment

fentiment manifefted in the firft volume, that
both the author and printer were alarmed with
the terrors of the Baftile.   Filled with thefe
apprehenfions, he left Paris, and went to Neufchatel.   There he printed his profpectus, and
he caufed it to be alfo printed in London.   But
when thefe copies were attempted to be circulated in France they were feized.   Not a fingle
number was permitted to be feen in any book-
feller's fhop in France.

Finding the execution of his project thus
rendered impracticable, he left Néufchatel, and
went to London ; where, in order to give cur-
rency to his free opinions, he altered the title
of his book.   He propofed to publifh the remaining part periodically, under the name of
A Defcription of the Sciences and Arts in England;
great part of which was intended to be devoted
to an examination of, and to obfervations on, the
Englifh conftitution.   His friends folicited the
French miniftry to permit this work to be reprinted at Paris.   At firft they obtained this
favour ;

favour; and the work went on as far as twelve numbers, or two volumes. After which it was prohibited; not more to the author's mortification than to the injury of his pocket. M. de Vergennes, who was at that time minifter of France, had fo ftrong a diflike to every thing that was Englifh, that he would not endure the fmalleft commendation upon any part of the Englifh conftitution, or commerce, to be promulgated in France. He had begun to difcover, that the favourite idea of his mafter, of feparating the Britifh colonies from the Britifh empire, might lead to an inveftigation of the principles of government at home, and prove extremely dangerous to a defpotic monarchy.

Notwithftanding he was thus difappointed a fecond time, he ftill purfued his defign; but under a fecond change of title. He publifhed two volumes under the title of *Philofophical Letters on the Hiftory of England.* The title did not attach the public attention; becaufe two volumes under a fimilar name had been

publifhed

publifhed in London, and had with fome *art* been impofed on the public, as the production of Lord Lyttelton ; but they were written by Goldfmith, in fupport of tyranny and arifto-cracy.

Every circumftance of cruelty and oppref-fion met with the obfervation of Briffot. When the late Emperor Jofeph was punifhing Horiah, the leader of the revolt in Walachia, and iffu-ing his fhocking edict againft emigration, Brif-fot addreffed *two letters to him* upon thofe fub-jects, which were read throughout Germany. In one letter he affirmed, that Horiah was juf-tified in his revolt : in the other he held, that a privilege to emigrate from one country to another was a facred right derived from na-ture.

He was an enthufiaft in his admiration of the American revolution, and of the conduct of the Americans in rifking every thing to eman-cipate themfelves from the tyranny of Great Britain. Upon comparing the new conftitu-tion

tion of America with that of England, he changed his opinion of the latter—*he ceafed to approve of it.*

Some French gentlemen, who had vifited America, having, when they returned to France, written fome fevere remarks on the Americans, Briffot defended the Americans, particularly in his book called *A Critical Examination of the Travels of the Marquis of Chatelleux.* But as this work has been already mentioned in the preceding volume (fee chapters 31 and 32), it is not neceffary to fay any thing more of it here.

It muft never be forgot, that during the period of the French monarchy there were more intrigues always going on in the French court than in any court in Europe. At this time (the year 1787) the court was full of intrigues—libidinous as well as political; for though the King had no miftreffes, the Queen had her favourites, and her party. Necker was difmiffed, and Calonne was appointed by her influence.

fluence. Montmorin fucceeded Vergennes, and
the Duke of Orleans was at the head of the
party that fought the overthrow of the new miniftry. When Calonne affembled the Nota-
bles at Verfailles, Briffot publifhed a pamphlet
entitled *No Bankruptcy; or Letters to a Creditor
of the State concerning the Impoffibilty of a National Bankruptcy, and the Means of reftoring Credit and Peace.* This pamphlet, which contained many fevere obfervations on Calonne's meafures and plans, and fome arguments in fupport of certain privileges claimed by the people,
the Duke of Orleans was highly pleafed with.
He made inquiry after the author, for the tract
was anonymous, and having difcovered him,
he ordered his chancellor to provide a fituation
for him. He was made fecretary-general of
the Duke's chancery. This did not fave him
from minifterial refentment. A lettre de ca-
chet was made out againft him, but having
notice of it, he inftantly efcaped to the Netherlands. He was for feveral months editor of the
Courier

Courier Belgique, printed at Mechlin. It was during this voluntary exile that he formed his project of vifiting America. He communicated his defign to the Philanthropic Society of the Friends of the Negroes at Paris, and was by them affifted and recommended to feveral perfons in America. The produce of this vifit to America was the firft volume of this work, written upon his return to France. The French miniftry being changed before he left Europe, he embarked at Havre de Grace in the month of June 1788.

Intelligence having reached him in America of the rapid progrefs liberty was making in France, he returned to his native country in 1789, in a confidence that his labours might become ufeful to the general intereft.

His firft publication after his return (except the preceding volume of his Travels in America) was *A Plan of Conduct for the Deputies of the People.*

His knowledge and admiration of America naturally

naturally produced a friendſhip with the Marquis de la Fayette, who introduced him into the club of the Jacobins.

We ſhall paſs by the ſeveral ſteps and meaſures of the revolution ; for to give an account of all Briſſot's concern therein, would be to write a large volume upon that event only. But the mention of a few circumſtances which are attached to Briſſot peculiarly, is indiſpenſable.

By the intereſt, or rather influence, of Fayette he was made a member of the Commune of Paris.   He was agent of the Police, and a member of the Committee of Inſpection at Paris ; and afterwards a repreſentative for the department of Eure and Loire.

He commenced a newſpaper, which he called *Patriote Français* ; in which he conſtantly defended the conduct of la Fayette.   He atached himſelf to the party called the Girondiſts.

To the Engliſh reader this name may require ſome explanation.   The warm and moſt

violent

violent of the National Convention, having
gained the confidence and fupport of the city
of Paris by various arts, but principally by de-
claring, upon every opportunity, that Paris
muft conftantly be the place in which the National Reprefentation muft hold their delibera-
rations; to balance againft this power of Paris, Condorcet, Petion, Vergniaux, Briffot,
Ifnard, and others, all members of the Convention, endeavoured to gain the commercial
cities in their intereft. Bourdeaux was the principal of thofe cities which joined them ; it is
fituated on the river Garonne, locally pronounced *Gironde*, which being the center of a department, named from the river, the appellation of Girondifts was given to the whole party.

The whole was a ftruggle for power : there
was no other object whatever. It is a foolifh,
and an idle affertion, in thofe who fay, that
Briffot and the party had engaged in a plot to
reftore the monarchy of France. Whatever
their opinions might have been in fome of the
early

early ftages of the revolution, perhaps from an
apprehenfion that the people of France might
hefitate at an abrupt propofition of a republican
government, they were unqueftionably innocent of the charge, at the time it was made.
Here follow, however, the documents as publifhed by authority, in juftification of the execution; which, like all other ftate papers, in
every country, confifts of the beft apology, or
moft colourable pretence, for a thing that has
been done by order of government.

REPORT *againft* BRISSOT, *and the other arrefted*
Deputies; made October 3, 1793.

THE Citizens of Paris, being informed that
Amar was to prefent his Report from the Committee of General Safety this day, filled the
galleries at a very early hour.

As foon as he appeared at the Bar, the applaufes were fo loud and continued that he was
unable

unable to begin for more than a quarter of an hour.

At length, amidft the moft profound filence, he read his report.

He began by ftating, that, before he proceeded to the report which had been expected with fuch impatience, and would amply recompenfe the unavoidable delay that had prevented a more fpeedy gratification of the wifhes of the people, he was commanded by the Committee of General Safety to requeft that none of the members of the Convention fhould be allowed to go out till the Decree of Accufation had been adopted. This requeft was immediately complied with, and a decree being paffed, the Prefident gave orders to the Commander of the National Guards to allow no Members to go beyond the Bar.

Amar then affirmed that the gigantic arm of treafon had been uplifted to ftrike the reprefentative majefty of the people, and to level with the ground the unity and indivifibility of the

French

French Republic.—The arm of treaſon had been nerved and ſupported by the united energies of Briſſot, Condorcet, Guadet, Vergniaud, and the other Deputies.

Briſſot, the leader of this traitorous band, commenced his political career by being a Member of the Commune of Paris, to which he was introduced by La Fayette, to whoſe deſigns he had proſtituted his pen.—At this æra of his life he made his appearance three times in the Jacobin Club.—In the firſt viſit he propoſed thoſe meaſures which have proved ſo diſaſtrous to the Colonies; in the ſecond, he attempted to produce the aſſaſſination of the people in the Champ de Mars; and in the third viſit he moved the declaration of war againſt Great Britain.

Introduced into the Legiſlative Aſſembly, he immediately entered into a coalition with Condorcet and the Girondine faction, whoſe deſigns he approved and ſupported. The conſummation of the object of this coalition was to have
been

been produced by the furrender of the Republican body to the violation of the Allied Powers, and by the deftruction of that unity and indivifibility which can alone be expected to combat with effect the tyrants who would undermine the proud pillar of Liberty', and deftroy even the veftige of freedom from the face of the earth.

The Court made ufe of their influence to declare war at a moment when the armies and the fortified places were in a ftate of abfolute want, or entrufted to traitors chofen by a perjured King. They protected Narbonne, the minifter, whom all France accufed of the meafures taken to render this war fatal to liberty; and in their Journals they calumniated the Patriots who had the courage to refift them. They defended Dietrifch, convicted of being an accomplice with La Fayette, and of having offered to give up Strafbourg; and while the chiefs of that faction protected the confpirators and traitorous Generals, the patriotic foldiers were proscribed, fcribed, and the volunteers of Paris fent to be butchered.

During the time we were furrounded by the fatellites of defpots, when the Court was going to open the gates of France to them, after having caufed the intrepid defenders of liberty to be murdered at Paris, Briffot and his accomplices did all they could to counteract the generous efforts of the people, and to fave the tyrant. During and after the unhappy infurrection of the 10th of Auguft, they endeavoured to prevent the abdication of Louis the XVI. and to preferve to him the Crown.

In the night of the 10th of Auguft, Petion, fhut up in the Thuilleries, confulted with the fatellites of tyrants the plan to maffacre the people, and gave orders to Mandat, Commander of the National Guards, to let the people come in, and then to cannonade them in the rear. A few days before, Genfonne and Vergniaud engaged to defend Louis XVI. on condition that
                                                    the

the three minifters, Roland, Claviere, and Ser-
van, were recalled.

Petion and La Source made ufe of all their
means to fend the federates from Paris. Briffot, Kerfaint, and Rouyer, according to the letters found in the Thuilleries, gave bad advice
to the tyrant, and, in defiance of the laws, they
dared to folicit places in the miniftry, under a
promife to extend the deftructive authorities of
the defpot.

The project to overturn the foundatiou of the
Republic, and to murder the friends of Liberty,
was put in practice in the Legiflative Affembly,
by Briffot, in his infidious harangue on the
20th of July 1792, oppofing the abdication of
the throne. We have feen Briffot and his accomplices Republicans under Monarchy, and
Royalifts under the Republic; always conftant
in their defigns to ruin the French nation, and
to abandon it to its enemies. At the time the
hypocritical tyrant, Louis the XVI. came into
the Affembly to accufe the people, whofe maf-

facre

facre he had prepared,—Vergniaud, like a true accomplice of the tyrant, told him—" That the Affembly held it to be one of their moft facred duties to maintain all conftituted authorities, and confequently that of Royalty,"

When the Attorney General, Raderer, came to announce, with the accent of grief, that the citizens in infurrection had taken the refolution not to feparate till the Affembly had pronounced the forfeiture of the Crown, Prefident Vergniaud filenced the applaufes from the galleries by telling them, that they violated the laws in obftructing the freedom of opinion; and he told Raderer, that the Affembly was going to take into immediate confideration the propofal which he, Vergniaud, had made, fhewing the neceffity of preferving the exiftence of the King.

Kerfaint feconded the motion. Geradet propofed to liberate Mandat, who was arrefted for having given orders to fire on the people; or, in the event that that commander was no more, to fend a deputation of twelve Girondift Members,

Members, authorifed to choofe his fucceffor, in order by this means to keep the public force at the difpofition of that mifchievous faction.

In that memorable fitting of the 10th of Auguft, the Girondift chiefs, Vergniaud, Guadet, and Genfonne, took by turns the chair, and went to the galleries to flacken the energy of the people, and to fave Royalty, under the fhield of the pretended conftitution. They fpoke of nothing but obedience to the conftitutional laws to thofe citizens that came to the bar to protect their newly acquired liberty.

When the municipality came to invite the Affembly to fend the *proces-verbal* of the great operations of the 10th of Auguft, in order to prevent the calumnies of the enemies of liberty, Guadet interrupted the members who made that demand, by making a motion to recommend anew to the magiftrates the execution of the laws.—He blamed the Council of the Commune for having confined Petion in his own houfe: though they did it in order to render it

impoffible

impoffible for that impoftor to make even infurrection fubfervient to act againft liberty.

When a deputation from the fuburb St. An-
toine came to announce the civic affliction of the
widows and children maffacred on that day, the
perfidious Guadet coolly anfwered them, "That
the Affembly hoped to reftore public tranquillity and the reign of the laws."

Vergniaud, in the name of the extraordinary commiffion directed by that faction, propofed
the fufpenfion of the King, who had been
dethroned by the people, as a fimple conferva-
tory act of royalty ; and feemed greatly affected
at the events which had faved the country, and
operated the ruin of the tyrants. He oppofed
Choudieu's motion, tending to exclude from the
Convention the Members of both the Legiflative
and Conftituent Affemblies ; and with the fame
cunning he prevented the regifters of the civil
lift from being depofited on the table.

Guadet wifhed to have a governor named to the
fon of the late King, whom he called the Prince
Royal.

Royal. Briffot and his accomplices always affected to invoke the literal execution of the
Conftitution, while the people, in the name of
the martyrs who fell before the caftle of the
Thuilleries, demanded the complete overthrow
of the tyrant.

Vergniaud oppofed this demand, faying, that
the people of Paris were but a fection of the
empire, and affected to oppofe it in this manner
to the departments.—He likewife refifted the
petition made by the Commons to put the tyrant
under arreft. He ufed all his efforts with Briffot, Petion, and Manuel, to get Louis XVI.
confined in the Luxembourg, from whence it
would have been eafier for him to efcape than
out of the tower of the temple.

Genfonne and Guadet had the fervility to
publifh, at different times, that Louis XVI.
had commanded the Swifs not to fire upon the
people. From that time, the leaders of the
Girondifts (Department of Bourdeaux), compelled to praife the events of the 10th of Auguft,
continued

continued, notwithftanding, to undermine the
Republic.   They publifhed the fevereft fatires
againft the Jacobins, againft the Commons and
people of Paris, and in general againft all thofe
who contributed to the deftruction of monarchy.
Roland's houfe was filled with packets of libels,
which were to be diftributed among the people,
and fent into the departments.

Thefe guilty men protected all the confpirators, favoured the progrefs of Brunfwick with
all their power, and were the agents of the
Englifh faction which has exerted fo fatal an
influence during the courfe of our revolution.
Carra was in league with certain characters of
the Court of Berlin.   In his Journal Politique
of the 25th of Auguft, 1791, he formed a wifh,
on account of the marriage of the Duke of
York with the Princefs of Pruffia, " that the
Duke might become Grand Duke of Belgium,
with all the powers of the King of the French."
While Brunfwick was preparing to decide the
fate of the French nation by the force of arms,

Carra

Carra in the fame Journal reprefented him as a great commander, the greateft politician, the moft amiable Prince in Europe, formed to be the reftorer of liberty in all nations.—He publifhed, that this Duke, on his arrival at Paris, would go to the Jacobins, and put on the red cap, in order to intereft the people in favour of this fatellite of tyrants. Finally, Carra was fo audacious as to propofe openly to the Jacobins, for the Duke of York to be King of the French.

From thefe and many other facts, too tedious to mention, there refults, that Carra and his affociate were iniquitous and deep diffemblers, penfioned by England, Pruffia, and Holland, to enable a Prince of that family which rules over thofe countries to obtain the crown of France. This fame Carra, together with Sillery, the difhonoured confidant of a contemptible Prince, was fent by the then reigning faction to Dumourier, to complete that treafon which faved the almoft ruined army of the Pruffian defpot. Dumourier came fuddenly to Paris to concert with Briffot, Petion, Guadet, Genfonne, and Carra, the

the perfidious expedition into the Auftrian Ne-.
therlands, which he undertook when the Pruffian army, wafting away by contagious diforders, was peaceably retiring—while the French
army was burning with indignation at the inaction in which they were kept.

It was not the fault of this faction, if the
motion often made by Carra to receive Brunfwick at Paris was not realized. He meditated, in the beginning of September 1792, to deliver up this city, without means of defence, by
flying beyond the river Loire, with the Legiflative Affembly, with the Executive Council,
and with the captive King. He was fupported
in it by Roland, Claviere, and le Brun, the
creatures and inftruments of Briffot and his accomplices.

But thefe perfidious minifters, having been
threatened by one of their colleagues to be denounced to the people, it was then that Carra
and Sillery were fent to Dumourier, to autho-
rife this General to negociate with Frederick
William,

William, to enable this Prince to get out of the kingdom, on condition that he fhould leave the Netherlands without the fufficient means of defence, and deliver them up to the numerous and triumphant armies of France.

The calumnious harangues that were made in the Tribunes were prepared or fanctioned at Roland's, or in the meetings that were held at Valaze's and Petion's. They propofed to furround the Convention with a pretorian guard, under the name of Departmental Force, which was to be the bafis of their fœderal fyftem. In the Legiflative Affembly they meditated a flight beyond the Loire, with the Affembly, the Executive Council, the Royal Family, and the public treafure. Kerfaint, at his return from Sedan, dared to propofe this project to the Executive Council; and it was fupported by Roland, Claviere, and le Brun, the creatures and inftruments of Briffot.

The faction ftrove to put off the judgment of the tyrant by impeding the difcuffion. They
appointed

appointed a commiſſion of twenty-four members to examine the papers found in the Thuilleres, in the guilt of which ſome of theſe members were implicated; and they endeavoured, in concert with Roland, to conceal thoſe which tended to diſcover their tranſaction with the court. They voted for the appeal to the people, which would have been a germ of civil war, and afterwards wanted a reſpite to the judgment.

They inceſſantly repeated, that the Convention could do no good, and that it was not free. Theſe declamations miſled the departments, and induced them to form a coalition, which was near being fatal to France.

They patronized an incivic piece, entitled *L'ami des Loix.*

On the 14th of January, Barbaroux and his friends had given orders to the battalion of Marſeillois to ſurround the Convention.

On the 20th, Valadi wrote to the other Deputies—" To-morrow in arms to the Convention—

tion—he is a coward who does not appear there."

Briffot, after the condemnation of Louis Capet, cenfured the Convention and threatened France with the vengeance of the European Kings. When it was his object to bring on war, he fpoke in an oppofite fenfe, and treated the downfal of all thrones, and the conqueft of the univerfe, as the fport of the French nation. Being the organ of the Diplomatic Committee, compofed almoft entirely of the fame faction, he propofed war fuddenly againft England, Holland, and all the powers that had not then declared themfelves.

This faction acted in coalition with perfidious Generals, particularly with Dumourier. Genfonnet held a daily correfpondence with him: Petion was his friend. He avowed himfelf the Counfellor of the Orleans party, and had connection with Sillery and his wife.

After the revolt of Dumourier, Vergniaud, Guadet, Briffot, and Genfonne, wifhed to

juftify

juſtify his conduct to the Committee of General
Defence, aſſerting that the denunciations made
againſt him by the Jacobins and the Mountain
were the cauſe of his conduct ; and that Dumourier was the protector of the *ſound* part of
the Convention.   This was the party of which
Petion, Briſſot, Vergniaud, &c. were the chiefs
and the orators.

When Dumourier was declared a traitor by the
Convention, Briſſot, in the *Patriote Françoiſe*,
as well as other writers, who were his accomplices, praiſed him, in defiance of the law.   As
members of the Committee of General Defence,
they ought to have given information relative to
the preparations that were making in La Vendee.
The Convention, however, was not made acquainted with them till the war became ſerious.

They armed the Sections where Ariſtocracy
reigned, againſt thoſe where public ſpirit was
triumphant.

They affected to believe that a plot was meditated by the Republicans againſt the National
Convention,

Convention, for the purpofe of naming the commiffion of twelve, who, in an arbitrary manner, imprifoned the, magiftrates of the people, and made war againft the patriots.

Ifnard developed the views of the confpiracy, when he ufed this atrocious expreffion : " The aftonifhed traveller will feek on what banks of the Seine Paris once ftood." The Convention diffolved the commiffion, which, however, refumed its functions on its own authority, and continued to act.

The faction, by the addreffes which it fent to the departments, armed them againft Paris and the Convention. The death of numbers of patriots in the fouthern departments, and particularly at Marfeilles, where they perifhed on the fcaffold, was the confequence of thofe fatal divifions in the Convention, of which they were the authors.—The defection of Marfeilles foon produced that of Lyons. This important city became the central point of the counter-revolution in the South. The republican municipality

lity was difperfed by the rebels, and good citizens were maffacred.—Every punifhment that
cruelty could devife to increafe the torments of
death was put in execution. The adminiftrative
bodies were leagued partly with Lyons, and
partly with foreign Ariftocrats, and with
the Emigrants difperfed through the Swifs
Cantons.

The cabinet of London afforded life and
energy to this rebellious league. Its pretext
was the anarchy that reigned at Paris— its
leaders, the traitorous deputies of the Convention.

Whilft they made this powerful diverfion in
favour of the tyrants united againft us, La Vendee continued to drink the blood of the patriots.

Carra and Duchatel were fent to this department in quality of Deputies from the National
Convention.

Carra publicly exhorted the adminiftrators
of the Maine and Loire to fend troops againft
Paris. Both thefe deputies were at the fame
time

time connected with the Generals of the combined armies.

Couflard, fent alfo as a commiffioner, carried his treafonable projects to fuch a length, as even to furnifh fupplies of provifions and ftores to the rebels.—The miffion of the agents of this faction, fent to different parts of the republic, was marked by fimilar traitorous meafures.

Perhaps the column of republican power would ere this have meafured its length upon the ground, if the confpirators had preferved much longer their inordinate power.—On the 10th of Auguft the foundation of the column was laid, on the 31ft of May it was preferved from deftruction. The accufed publifhed a thoufand feditious addreffes, a thoufand counter-revolutionary libels, fuch as that addreffed by Condorcet to the department of the Aifne. They are the difgraceful monuments of the treafon by which they hoped to involve France in ruin.

Ducc

Ducos and Fonfrede formed the flame of the rebellion, by their correfpondence and their fpeeches, in which they celebrated the virtues of the confpirators.

Several of thefe confpirators fled, and difperfed themfelves through the departments—They eftablifhed there a kind of National Convention, and invefted the adminiftration with independent powers—they encircled themfelves with guards and cannon, pillaged the public treafuries, intercepted provifions that were on the road to Paris, and fent them to the revolted inhabitants of the former provinces of Britanny. They levied a new army, and gave Wimpfen, degraded by his attachment to tyranny, the command of this army.

They attempted to effect a junction with the rebels of la Vendee, and to furrender to the enemy the provinces of Britanny and Normandy.

They deputed affaffins to Paris, to murder the members of the Convention, and particular-

ly

ly Marat, whofe deftruction they had folemnly fworn to accomplifh.—They put a poignard into the hands of a woman who was recommended to Duperret by Barbaroux and his accomplices. She was conveyed into the gallery of the Convention by Fauchet.—The enemies of France exalted her as a heroine. Petion pronounced her apotheofis at Caen, and threw over the blood-ftained form of affaffination the fnowy robe of virtue.

Girey Dupre, the colleague of Briffot, in the publication of the *Patriote Français*, printed at Caen feveral fongs, which invited, in a formal manner, the citizens of Caen to arm themfelves with poignards, for the purpofe of ftabbing three deputies of the Convention, who were pointed out by name.

Briffot fled with a lie added to his other crimes. Had he gone to Switzerland, as the falfe paffport ftated, it would have been for the purpofe of exciting a new enemy againft France.

Rabaud

Rabaud St. Etierre, Rebecqui, Duprat, and Antiboul, carried the torch of fedition into the department of le Gard and the neighbouring departments.—Biroteau, Rouger, and Roland, projected their terrible plots in Lyons, where they poured the ample ftream of patriotic blood, by attaching to the friends of their country the appellation of anarchifts and monopolizers.

At Toulon thefe endeavours were fuccefsful, and Toulon is now in the hands of the Englifh. The fame lot was referved for Bourdeaux and Marfeilles.—The reigning faction had made fome overtures to Lord Hood, whofe fleet they expected. The entire execution of the confpiracy in the South waited only for the junction of the Marfeillefe and Lyonefe, which was prevented by the victory gained by the Republican army which produced the reduction of Marfeilles.

The meafures of the confpirators were exactly fimilar to thofe of the enemies of France, and particularly of the Englifh.—Their writings differed

differed in nothing from thofe of the Englifh minifters, and libellers in the pay of the Englifh minifters.

Mr. PITT	The DEPUTIES
Wifhed to degrade and to diffolve the Convention.	Attempted to do the fame.
He wifhed to affaffinate the members of the Convention.	The deputies procured the affaffination of Marat and Le Pelletier.
He wifhed to deftroy Paris.	The deputies did all in their power to produce this effect.
He wifhed to arm all nations againft France.	The deputies obtained a declaration of war againft all nations.
In the intended partition of France, Mr. Pitt wifhed to procure a part for the Duke of York or fome other branch of his mafter's family.	Carra and Briffot entered into a panegyric of the Dukes of York and Brunfwick, and even went fo far as to propofe them for Kings.
He endeavoured to deftroy our colonies.	The deputies have produced the deftruction of the colonies.
	Briffot, Petion, Guadet, Genfonne, Vergniaud, Ducos, and Fonfrede, directed the meafures relative to the colonies, which meafures reduced them to the moft lamentable fituation.

Santhonax

Santhonax and Polverel, the guilty Commiſſioners who ravaged the colonies with fire and
ſword, are their accomplices. Proofs of their
corruption exiſt in the correſpondence of Rai-
mond, their creature.

Of the numerous facts of which the faction
are accuſed, ſome relate only to particular individuals: the general conſpiracy, however, is attached to all.

Upon this act of accuſation they were tried
before the Revolutionary Tribunal, on the 30th
day of October, 1793. When the act of accuſation was read to them in the Court, they
refuſed to make any anſwer to it, unleſs Ro-
berſpierre, Barrere, and other members of the
Committee of Safety, were preſent, and interrogated: they inſiſted upon thoſe members being ſent for; which being refuſed, and they ſtill
refuſing to make any anſwer, the Judge ſtated
to the Jury, that from the act of accuſation it
reſulted that,

I. There

I. There exifted a confpiracy againft the unity and indivifibility of the Republic, the liberty and fafety of the French People.

II. That all the individuals denounced in the act of accufation are guilty of this confpiracy, as being either the authors of, or the accomplices in, it.

The Jury of the Revolutionary Tribunal, to whom thefe facts were fubmitted, brought in their verdict at eleven o'clock at night, on the 30th of October, againft

BRISSOT,

Vergniaud	Sillery
Genfonee	Fauchet
Duprat	Duperret
Valaze	Lafource
Lehardi	Carra
Ducos	Beauvais
Fonfrede	Mainvielle
Borleau	Antiboul
Gardien	Vigee, and
Duchatel	Lacaze,

who were declared to be the authors and accomplices of a confpiracy which had exifted againft the unity and indivifibility of the Republic,

public, and againſt the liberty and ſecurity of the French people.

The Preſident of the Revolutionary Tribunal immediately pronounced the ſentence decreed by the conſtitution :—That they ſhould ſuffer the puniſhment of death—that their execution ſhould take place on the ſubſequent day, on the *Place de la Revolution*—that their property ſhould be confiſcated, and that this ſentence ſhould be printed and poſted up throughout the whole extent of the republic.

As ſoon as the ſentence was pronounced, Valaze pulled a dagger from his pocket and ſtabbed himſelf.—The Tribunal immediately ordered that the body ſhould be conveyed on the morrow to the *Place de la Revolution*, with the other deputies.

At eleven o'clock in the forenoon, on the 31ſt, the execution took place.—The ſtreets were lined with ſoldiers, and every precaution taken to prevent the diſturbance of the public tranquillity.

Duchatel,

Duchatel, it was faid, had obtained a vial of poifon, by means of a friend from *Rochecoul*, of which place he was a native; but it does not appear that he made any ufe of it.

CAUSE *of the* LOSS *of* POPULARITY, *and of the* FALL *of* BRISSOT *and his once powerful Party.*

IT has been obferved in fpeaking of the conteft between the party of the *Gironde* and that of the *Mountain*, that it was merely a ftruggle for power; but it may be not unfatis-factory to the reader to receive fuch further information as fubfequent events and difcoveries have afforded, to qualify him to judge of the value the contending parties fat upon their power, and the ufe they defigned to make of it.

There can be no queftion of the whole party attached to Briffot being republicans to a man, as has been already faid. Even though they voted for the appeal to the primary affemblies upon the condemnation of the king, they were

not

not lefs averfe to royalty. But their objeĉt
was to gain time, hoping thereby to give pre-
valence to their own opinion, that fo violent a
meafure as putting him to death would chill
the ardour in many of the warm friends of the
revolution in their own country, and confiderably increafe the number of their enemies
without.

Although this party might be faid to declare
war againft England, yet they did not wifh it
to continue for any length of time ; they were
provoked to it in honour by the conduĉt of the
Britifh miniftry towards their ambaffador. They
mifcalculated the amount of the fupport that
miniftry were likely to receive from the arifto-
cracy of the nation ; and they over-rated, not
the talents, but the ftrength of the oppofition.

Though there were not many of the **Girondifts** who could be called rich, yet all of them
had fomething to lofe (Briffot, perhaps, as
little as any) they had neverthelefs a confiderable portion of fame and reputation, which
they valued and reckoned upon as the foundation

tion of their future fortunes; and this, they were fensible, was liable to be shaken or over-turned by those accidents, which popular commotions attendant on revolutions, give rise to; and they were not less fensible how much war and its viciffitudes increase that hazard.

Their first hope then was, by their moderate behaviour towards the dethroned king, to blunt the refentment of thofe powers which had taken up arms against France, and to prevent it from rifing up in others, whofe neutrality they had reafon to defire. Once compelled to hoftility against England, they confoled themfelves that the English people would confider their ministers as the aggreffors, and that the oppofition, urging that circumftance with as much fuccefs as truth, would foon be able to deftroy the credit of the then administration, and by fupplanting it, pave the way for fuch pacific arrangements as would be gratifying to the ambition of the leaders of both nations. The failure in thefe particulars appears to have thrown

thrown the Girondifts into a great dilemma, and to have been the principal caufe of their ruin.

They were difappointed from feeing the additional vigour which the Cabinet of St. James's infufed into the coalition, and that the allied armies were fo fuccefsful after the junction of the Britifh forces. The people became furious a fecond time; they beheld their country almoft wholly furrounded by powerful enemies, and even that fmall portion of it which connected it with Geneva and the Swifs Cantons was *flippery ground*. The point of honour, which had prompted to the war with England, was forgotten, and the recourfe to it was now declared to be a rafh meafure, and, as has been feen, was made a capital charge of, againft the leader of the party, on his trial. The revolution in France was in many refpects new in its nature; it promifed to embrace the intereft and mend the condition of the loweft claffes of its citizens. The vaft weight of op-

preffion

preffion now fuddenly thrown off the people's minds, left them unfteady and ungovernable; a mixed fentiment of joy and revenge filled their breafts, and all who did not partake of it, were confidered either as enemies, or fufpefted perfons. A man who had been perfecuted by the violent among the Royalifts, and fcoffed at by the moderate of the Revolutionifts, diftinguifhed himfelf in an extraordinary manner about this time, and whofe popularity had a great and decifive influence over the fate of the whole Girondift party. Two of this party, not the leaft fenfible among them, were heard to confefs, on the morning of their execution, that to the perfonal virulence direfted againft *Marat*, was to be imputed the cataftrophe about to take place. They had endeared him to a certain numerous and now moft powerful clafs of men, by their fatires, invefives, and perfecutions; and Icilius, the Roman tribune, in the early part of that republic, could not have had more fway over the difpofitions of

his

his conftituents, than had this furious democrat
over the moft enraged and moft formidable of
the Parifians. So much did they fix their faith
on the juftnefs of his notions and fuggeftions,
that, upon his reproaching in the Convention,
the rich merchants and traders of Paris with
egotifm and monopoly, in engroffing the firft
neceffaries of life, enhancing their price and
aggravating the fufferings of the poor, and upon
his obferving that the hanging one or two of
thefe trading ariftocrats· at their own doors,
could alone exhibit a proper example to the
reft; the facile people were prompted to
force their way into the fhops and warehoufes
of fuch as dealt in the neceffaries of life,
obliging the owners to fell their goods at a
reduced price, which they themfelves fixed.
Thefe tranfactions greatly inftigated the law of
the *maximun*, and while they expofed their
author to the merited opprobrium and cenfure
of the refpecters of the laws and the haters of
its tranfgreffors, they hurried the enemies of
the

the demagogue into indifcretions and incon-
fiftencies, which evidently cleared the way to
their own downfal.

A revolutionary tribunal had juft been eftablifhed for the fpeedy trial of offenders againft
the new government; and to this court of
juftice did the unwife of the Briffotins cite
Marat, as a *counter-revolutionift*.

The indictment, or act of accufation, al-
ledged the accufed to have endangered the
Revolution, by ftirring up the people to pillage, through his inflammatory fpeeches in the
National Convention, with other charges of a
like nature. It required but little difcernment
to forefee how fuch a proceeding muft end,
fince, whatever criminality was contained in
his harangues and conduct, it could not be
qualified with the epithet *counter-revolutionary*,
the *mens confcia* was wanting to authorize the
conviction. Had he been tried for the mif-
demeanor in the ordinary courts, it was fuppofed, he would have been convicted, and
probably, have been expelled the Convention.

This

This erroneous proceeding, this overcharged weapon, on the contrary, raifed the object aimed at, higher in the efteem of his followers and abettors : upon his acquittal, he was carried, crowned with a wreath of oak leaves, upon the people's fhoulders, and placed on his feat in the fenate ; while one of its members was eloquently condemning the procedure of his enemies, and judicioufly remarking, that they ought to have difcerned the difference between a *counter*-revolutionary and an *ultra*-revolutionary conduct.

A deadly combat between thefe inveterate parties immediately commenced, and many, who had ftill lefs efteem for Marat than for his adverfaries, neverthelefs encouraged him to thofe meafures which haftened the overthrow of the Girondifts. In the collifion of paffions and confufion of interefts, which take place in the revolution of a great nation, it is, perhaps, impoffible ftrictly to analyfe thofe which actuate the principal movers of it; there

there are, however, well founded reasons to
believe, that those early revolutionists had
raised what they considered *a devil*, and which
they were desirous, but unable, to allay. The
velocity of the revolutionary machine, which
had made many others giddy, now made these
nice observers of it tremble; they essayed to
moderate its rapid movement, in doing of
which they made more than one false step,
they fell under its cumbrous weight, and were
crushed to death.

The falling away of LA FAYETTE; the
defection of DUMOURIER; the inroads of the
Austrians and English upon the French territory, with many other calamities, especially
that of the scarcity of bread, were all charged
upon the influence the Girondists had in the
sea-ports, and the ill effects of their *moderantism*
upon the whole republic. The irascible and
over-heated imaginations in the Convention
flew to the uppermost seats of that assembly,
which they termed the *Mountain*, and urged
their

their complaints againſt their enemies, with the ſame vehemence the Roman people did when they betook themſelves to the *Mons Sacer.* While they complained that the Girondiſts had failed to bring forward the plan of a conſtitution, as had been promiſed, they reſolved to receive nothing of that ſhape from their hands. The Mountain excited a general indignation and fermentation againſt their adverſaries, and by the inſurrection of the 31ſt of May 1793, obtained a complete victory over them. The vanquiſhed were all either impriſoned or diſperſed, except a few of them, who took to arms and headed a number of inſurgents in the ancient province of Normandy; but theſe were ſoon after obliged to ſubmit. Our author was making the beſt of his way to Switzerland, under a feigned name and ſurreptitious paſſport, when he was taken within a day's journey of the frontiers; brought back to Paris, and impriſoned in the *Abbaye.* The victors loſt no time in producing a democratic conſtitution, conftitution, which increafed their credit with the now ftrongeft party ; and when the opportunity offered, they ftruck the blow fo fatal to the Girondifts within their power, and to the hopes of all thofe who had attached themfelves to them, either for intereft or through efteem.

Such was the fate of Briffot and his chief adherents, and fuch appear to be the only vifible means which led to it. There were among them men of rare talents, profound learning, and accurate obfervation ; all cherifhed great ambition, in fome it was more open, in others more concealed ; but to acquit them of the fufpicion of *royalifm*, or the accufation of feeking to throw the French nation back again into defpotifm or bondage ; it is fufficient to pourtray their behaviour in the laft few hours of their life, which were occupied in reciting, or finging thofe civic odes and enthufiaftic hymns, that had fo efpecially conduced to animate the country,

Briffot

Briſſot ſung the Marſeillois air in his way to
the place of execution, and was joined in
chorus by five others of the unhappy ſufferers.

In every point of view, this great revolution
is deſerving the ſtudy of ſurrounding nations,
and the lives of thoſe men who have acted
conſiderable parts in it, are entitled to particular regard.

There was not one among theſe diſtinguiſhed
victims who evinced the feebleſt ſymptom of
cowardice, when the carts ſtopped at the place
of execution ; and Duchatel, Ducos, Fonfrede,
and Lehardi, even exhibited a remarkably
firm and undaunted air, ſurveying the engine
of death with an unruffled countenance.

The deportment of Briſſot was not leſs
manly ; he preſerved a fixed ſilence, and, after
looking diſtinctly at every one of his colleagues, to whom he ſaid not a word, he ſub-
mitted his head to the axe of the guillotine.

Sillery ſaluted the people with an air of
reſpect, mixed with a tincture of that high
breeding

breeding now fo little cultivated; and, after converfing a fhort time with his confeffor who met him on the fcaffold, he bowed his neck to the fatal engine. Fauchet, who had been an Abbé, had his confeffor prefent alfo. Lafource was in appearance and deportment the moft grave of the whole; but Gardien, Carra, Vergniaud, Boileau, Antiboul, Vigée, Genfonné, Duperrêt, Beauvais, Lecaze, and Mainville, manifefted an uncommon refolution, exclaiming " *Vive la Republique*," till the deadly glaive fevered their heads from their bodies. The whole of this fhocking ceremony took up no more than thirty-feven minutes of time.

CONTENTS.

CONTENTS.

Section

C H A P.   VI.

Mr.

INTRODUCTION,

By J. P. BRISSOT de Warville.

———————

THE Court of Great-Britain had no fooner
figned the Treaty acknowledging the Independence of her late Colonies in North America,
than her merchants and political writers fought the
means of rendering to her by commerce an equivalent for her loffes by the war.

Lord Sheffield has predicted, in his Obfervations
on the Commerce of America, "that England would
always be the ftorehoufe of the United States ; that
the Americans, conftantly attracted by the excellence
of her manufactures, the long experienced integrity
of her merchants, and the length of credit, which
they only can give, would foon forget the wounds
which the minifterial defpotifm of London, as well
as the ferocity of the Englifh and German fatellites,
had given to America, to form with it new and durable connexions *."

* Thefe are not Lord Sheffield's words. They are M. Briffot's ;
and contain *his* defcription of Lord Sheffield's *fuppofed* fentiments,
from a perufal of that Nobleman's Obfervations on the Commerce
of America. *Edit.*

This

This politician was the only one who appeared in that career; others followed it [Dr Price, &c.]; and the debates, which the new regulations of commerce propofed for America, produced in Parliament, prove that the matter was known, difcuffed, and profoundly examined.

The Englifh nation refembled at that time a man who, coming out of a long delirium (wherein he had broken every thing that he ought to have held moft dear), eagerly ftrives to repair the ravages of his infanity.

As for us, we have triumphed, and the honour of the triumph is almoft the only benefit we have reaped. Tranquil under the fhade of our laurels, we fee with indifference the relations of commerce which na-nature has created between us and the *United States*; —whilft, to ufe the language of vulgar policy, the Englifh, of whom we are jealous as our rivals, whom we fear as our enemies, ufe the greateft efforts to make it impoffible for us to form new connexions with our new friends.

That the Englifh will fucceed, there is no doubt, if our languor be not foon replaced by activity; if the greateft and moft generous faculties, on our part, do not fmooth this commerce, new, and confequently eafy to be facilitated : finally, if our ignorance of the ftate of America be not fpeedily diffipated by the conftant ftudy of her refources of ter-

ritory,

ritory, commerce, finance, &c. and affinities they may have with thofe of their own.

Our ignorance! This word will undoubtedly fhock,—for we have the pride of an ancient people: We think we know every thing,—have exhaufted every thing:—Yes, we have exhaufted every thing; but in what? In futile fciences, in frivolous arts, in modes, in luxury, in the art of pleafing women, and the relaxation of morals. We make elegant courfes of chemiftry, charming experiments, delicious verfes, ftrangers at home, little informed of any thing abroad: this is what we are; that is, we know every thing, *except that which is proper for us to know* *.

It would be opening a vaft field to fhew what is proper for us to know, therefore I will not under-take it. I confine myfelf to a fingle point: I fay that it concerns us effentially to have a thorough knowledge of the ftate of America, and that, never-

---

* This affertion will perhaps appear fevere and falfe, even to perfons who think that we excel in phyfics and the exact fciences. But in granting this, is it thefe kinds of fciences to which a man who reflects ought at firft to give himfelf up? Does not the ftudy of his focial and civil ftate more nearly concern him? Ought not this to intereft him more than the number of ftars, or the order of chymical affinities?—It is, however, the fcience of which we think the leaft. We are paffionately fond of poetry: we difpute ferioufly about mufic; that is, we have a great confideration for playthings, and make a plaything of our affairs.

thelefs,

thelefs, we have fcarcely begun the alphabet which leads to it. What I advance has been faid before by Mr. Paine, a free American, and who has not a little contributed, by his patriotic writings, to fpread, fupport, and exalt, among his fellow countrymen, the enthufiafm of liberty. I will remark, fays he, in his judicious letter to the Abbé Raynal, *that I have not yet feen a defcription, given in Europe, of America, of which the fidelity can be relied on.*

In France, I fay it with forrow, the fcience of commerce is almoft unknown, becaufe its practice has long been difhonoured by prejudice ; which prevents the gentry from thinking of it. This prejudice, which is improperly thought indeftructible, becaufe the nobility are improperly thought one of the neceffary elements of a monarchical conftitution ; this would alone be capable of preventing French commerce from having activity, energy, and dignity, were it not to be hoped, that found philofophy, in deftroying it infenfibly, *would bring men to the* great idea *of eftimating individuals by their talents, and not by their birth:* without this idea there can be no great national commerce, but ariftocratical men will abound ; that is, men incapable of conceiving any elevated view ; and men contemptible, not in a ftate to produce them.

Finally, another prejudice, quite as abfurd, which has been combated a thoufand times, and is always predominant,

predominant in France, withholds from the eyes of
the public precious memoirs, and interefting difcuffions, which would inform France of her interefts.

Who is ignorant that it is to the freedom of debate and public difcuffion that England owes the
fingular profperity which, till lately, has followed
her every where, in commerce, in arts, in manufactures, as well abroad as at home ? a profperity which
fhe may enjoy in fpite of the faults of her minifters ;
for none but thefe have ever endangered it : and it is
to the freedom of debate that fhe has often owed her
falvation from ruin. Who doubts that this liberty
would not produce the fame happy effects in France ;
—that it would not deftroy falfe appearances ;—that
it would not prevent the deftructive enterprizes of
perfonal intereft ;—that it would not alarm mifchievous indulgence, or the coalition of people in
place with the enemies of the public welfare ? Government feems at prefent to do homage to this influence of the freedom of difcuffion. At length,
it appears to relax of its feverity in the laws of the
prefs ; it has fuffered fome fhackles, which reftrained difcuffion, to be broken, efpecially in political
matters. But how far are we ftill from feeling the
happy effects of the liberty of the prefs, rather granted to public opinion, than encouraged by a real love
of truth.

By what fatality are energetic difcourfes of truth
ineffectual ? This ought to be pointed out ; go-

vernment

vernment itself invites us to do it ; the abuses which render information useless in France, ought to be laid open.

It is because the liberty of thinking and writing on political matters is but of recent date.

Because the liberty of the press is environed with many disgusting circumstances ; and that an honest man who disdains libels, but loves frankness, is driven from the press by all those humiliating formalities which subject the fruit of his meditation and researches to a censure necessarily arising from ignorance.

It is because the censor, instituted to check the elevation of a generous liberty, thinks to flatter authority, by even exceeding the end proposed ; suppresses truths, which would frequently have been received ; for fear of letting too bold ones escape, with which he would have been reproached, multiplies objections, gives birth to fears, magnifies dangers, and thus discourages the man of probity, who would have enlightened his fellow citizens ; whilst this censor sanctions scandalous productions, wherein reason is sacrificed to sarcasms, and severe morality to amiable vices *.

It

* We may put in the rank of these productions which dishonour the censorship, the comedy of Figaro, a scandalous farce, wherein, under

It is becaufe there are but few writers virtuous enough, fufficiently organifed, or in proper fituations to combat and furmount thefe obftacles.

Becaufe thefe writers, few in number, have but little influence; abufes weakly attacked and ftrongly defended, refift every thing which is oppofed to them.

Becaufe the neceffity of getting works printed in foreign preffes, renders the publication difficult; but few of them efcape from the hands of greedy hawkers, who monopolize the fale, to fell at a dearer price, who poft the myftery, and a falfe rarity, to fell dear for a longer time.

Becaufe thefe books-are wanting in the moment when they would excite a happy fermentation, and direct it properly, in giving true principles.

Becaufe they fall but fucceffively into the hands of

under the appearance of defending morality, it is turned into ridicule, and wherein great truths are difparaged by the contemptible dialogift who prefents them; wherein the end feems to have been to parody the greateft writers of the age, in giving their language to a rafcally valet, and to encourage oppreffion, in bringing the people to laugh at their degradation, and to applaud themfelves for this mad laughter: finally, in giving, by culpable impofture, to the whole nation, that character of negligence and levity which belongs only to her capital.

well-

well-informed men, who are but few in number, in
the search of new truths.

Because the Journalists, who ought to render them
a public homage, are obliged, through fear, to keep
silence.

Because the general mass, abandoned to the torrent
of frivolous literature, loses the pleasure of meditation, and with it the love of profound truths.

Finally, because truth is by this fatal concurrence
of circumstances never sown in a favourable soil,
nor in a proper manner ; that it is often stifled in its
birth ; and if it survives all adverse manœuvres, it
gathers strength but slowly, and with difficulty ;
consequently its effects are too circumscribed for instruction to become popular and national.

Let government remove all these obstacles ; let it
have the courage, or rather the sound policy, to render to the press its liberty, and good works, such as
are really useful, will have more success ; from which
there will result much benefit.

Does it wish for an example ? I will quote one,
which is recent and well known : the law-suit of the
monopolising merchants against the colonists of the
sugar islands. Would not the last have, according
to custom, been crushed, if the dispute had been
carried

carried on in obfcurity? They had the liberty of fpeech, of writing, and of printing; the public voice was raifed in their favour, truth was triumphant; and the wife minifter, who had permitted a public difcuffion that he might gain information, pronounced for humanity in pronouncing in their favour.

Let us hope that this example will be followed; that government will more and more perceive the immenfe advantages which refult from the liberty of the prefs. There is one which, above all others, ought to induce it to accelerate this liberty, becaufe it nearly regards the intereft of the prefent moment: this liberty is a powerful means to eftablifh, fortify, and maintain public credit, which is become, more than ever, neceffary to great nations, fince they have ftood in need of loans. As long as the attempts of perfonal intereft are feared by the obfcurity which covers them, public credit is never firmly eftablifhed, nor does it rife to its true height. It is no longer calculated upon the intrinfic ftrength of its refources, but upon the probability, upon the fear of the diforder, which may either divert them from their real employ, or render them fterile. The liberty of the prefs keeps perfonal intereft too much in awe not to fetter its meafures; and then public credit fupports itfelf if it be eftablifhed, is formed if it be ftill to be conftituted, and fortifies itfelf if it has been weakened by error.

Full

Full of thefe ideas, as well as the love of my country, and furmounting the obftacles to the liberty of printing, I have undertaken to throw fome light upon our commercial affinities with the United States. This object is of the greateft importance : the queftion is, to develope the immenfe advantages which France may reap from the revolution which fhe has fo powerfully favoured, and to indicate the means of extending and confolidating them.

It appears to me that all the importance of this revolution has not been perceived ; that it has not been fufficiently confidered by men of underftanding. Let it, therefore, be permitted me to confider it at prefent.

I will not go into a detail of the advantages which the United States muft reap from the revolution, which affures them liberty. I will not fpeak of that regeneration of the phyfical and moral man, which muft be an infallible confequence of their conftitutions ; of that perfection to which free America, left to its energy, without other bounds but its own faculties, muft one day carry the arts and fciences. America enjoys already the right of free debate, and it cannot be too often repeated, that without this debate, perfection is but a mere chimera. In truth, almoft every thing is yet to be done in the United States, but almoft every thing is there underftood : the general good is the common end of every individual,—this end cherifhed, implanted, fo to fpeak,

by

by the conftitution in every heart. With this end, this intelligence, and this liberty, the greateft miracles muft be performed.

I will not fpeak of the advantages which all America muft one day reap from this revolution; nor of the impoffibility that abfurd defpotifm fhould reign for a long time in the neighbourhood of liberty.—I will confine myfelf to the examination of what advantages Europe, and France in particular, may draw from this change.—There are two, which are particularly ftriking: the firft, and greateft of the revolution, at leaft in the eyes of philofophy, is that of its falutary influence on human knowledge, and on the reform of local prejudices; for this war has occafioned difcuffions important to public happinefs,—the difcuffion of the focial compact,—of civil liberty,—of the means which can render a people independent,—of the circumftances which give fanction to its infurrection, and make it legal,—and which give this people a place among the powers of the earth.

What good has not refulted from the repeated defcription of the Englifh conftitution, and of its effects? What good has not refulted from the codes of Maffachufetts and New York, publifhed and fpread every where? And what benefits will they ftill produce? They will not be wholly taken for a model; but defpotifm will pay a greater refpect,

either

either from neceffity or reafon, to the rights of men,
which are fo well known and eftablifhed. Enlightened by this revolution, the governments of Europe
will be infenfibly obliged to reform their abufes, and
to diminifh their burdens, in the juft apprehenfion
that their fubjects, tired of bearing the weight, will
take refuge in the afylum offered to them by the
United States.

This revolution, favourable to the people, which
is preparing in the cabinets of Europe, will be undoubtedly accelerated, by that which its commerce
will experience, and which we owe to the enfran-
chifement of America. The war, which procured it
to her, has made known the influence of commerce
on power, the neceffity of public credit, and confequently of public virtue, without which it cannot
long fubfift : what raifed the Englifh to that height
of power, from whence, in fpite of the faults of their
Minifters, Generals, and Negociators, they braved,
for fo many years, the force of the moft powerful
nations ? Their commerce, and their credit ; which,
loaded as they were with an enormous debt, put
them in a ftate to ufe all the efforts which nations,
the moft rich by their foil and population, could not
have done in a like cafe.

Thefe are the advantages which France, the world,
and humanity, owe to the American Revolution ;
and when we confider them, and add thofe we are
obliged

obliged to let remain in obfcurity, we are far from regretting the expenees they occafioned us.

Were any thing to be regretted, ought not it to vanifh at the appearance of the new and immenfe commerce which this revolution opens to the French? This is the moft important point at prefent for us,— that on which we have the leaft information, which confequently makes it more neceffary to gain all we can upon the fubject; and fuch is the object of this work.

In what more favourable moment could it appear, when every nation is in a ferment to extend its commerce, feeks new information and fure principles? The mind is inceffantly recalled in this book to the *nature of things*, the fift principle of commerce.— At a time when people, which an ancient rivality, an antipathy, fo falfely and unhappily called natural, kept at a diftance one from the other, are inclined to approach each other, and to extinguifh in the connexions of commerce the fire of difcord; this work fhews that thefe rivalities muft be effaced by the immenfity of the career which is opened to all.—At a time when all the parts of univerfal policy are enlightened by the flambeau of philofophy, even in governments which have hitherto profeffed to be afraid of it, the author of this work has let flip no opportunity of attacking falfe notions and abufes of every kind.

Never

Never was there a moment more favourable for publishing useful truths. Every nation does not only do homage to commerce, as to the vivifying spirit of society ; but they employ in the examination of all these connexions and affinities,—that logic of facts, whose use characterizes the end of the present century,—that art truly philosophical, of considering objects in their nature, and in their necessary consequences :—never had well-informed men more contempt for those chimerical systems solely founded upon the fancies of pride, upon the little conceptions of vanity, and upon the presumption of the false political science, which has too long balanced the destiny of States. Never were so many men seen united by the same desire of an universal peace, and by the conviction of the misfortune and inutility of hateful rivalities. At length it appears, that men perceive that the field of industry is infinite ; that it is open to every state, whatever may be its absolute or relative positions ; that all states may thrive in it, provided that in each of them the support of individual liberty, and the preservation of property, be the principal end of legislation.

This work still concurs with the patriotic views which the Sovereign of France manifests at present : he meditates important reformations. He directs them towards the happiness of the people ; and consults the most respectable members of this people, whom he wishes to render happy, upon the means of
insuring

infuring the fuccefs of his good intentions. Therefore, could there be a more propitious moment, to
offer to the prefent arbitrators of the national profperity, a work written with deliberation, on the
means of eftablifhing a new commerce with a new
people, who unites to an extenfive foil, and proper
to nourifh an immenfe population, laws which are
the moft favourable to its rapid increafe ?

At firft I had alone undertaken this work, depending on my own ftrength and laborious refearches : I had collected all the facts,—all the books,—
all the proofs which could be certain guides to my
fteps ; but I foon perceived the impoffibility of raif-
ing upon objects of commerce a folid and ufeful
theory, if it were not directed by the fkill which
practice only can give, and poffeffed by a man
whofe judgment had been long exercifed by reflection, and whofe decided love of truth and the public
welfare, had accuftomed to generalize his ideas. I
found this man, this co operator, of whofe affiftance
I ftood in need, in a republican ; to whom I am
united by a fimilarity of ideas, as well as by the moft
tender attachment. I have permiffion to name him,
—he confents to it : I have conquered his modefty
by the confideration of his intereft, and of the law
which the particular circumftances of his fituation
impofes on him : I have perfuaded him, that the
beft means of deftroying calumny was to make
known his principles and opinions on public matters.

It

It is M. Claviere, a Genevefe, exiled without any form from his country, by the military ariftocracy; which has fubftituted its illegal and deftructive regimen to the reafonable and legitimate influence of a people, diftinguifhed by their natural good underftanding, their knowledge, and their more fimple manners. What was his crime? That of having defended the rights of thefe people, with a firmnefs and ability, which the implacable hatred of his enemies atteft! This part does too much honour to my friend, not to confine myfelf to defcribe him in this character, the only one which has ever been productive of public good.

M. Claviere has, during his abode in France, given proofs of his knowledge in the philofophical and political part of commerce. It is to his abode among us that the public is indebted for fome ufeful works on thefe abftract matters; works, as remarkable for their folidity of principle and truth of difcuffion, as for the clearnefs and precifion of ideas; works, whofe fuccefs proves that minds may be led to the contemplation of thefe matters, by fubftituting an exact and clear analyfis to the metaphyfical and obfcure jargon which reftrained them from it.

Finally, the prefent work will prove at once the extent of his knowledge, and that of the fincere philanthropy which animates him, even for the good of a country, where a man lefs generous would fee
nothing

nothing, perhaps, but the origin and caufe of his misfortunes. Oh! how happy am I, to have it in my power to defend my friend againft cowardly calumniators, in putting him under the fafeguard of his own talents and virtues ? And is it not a facred duty for me, as the calumny is public, to publifh the part he has taken in this work, wherein it is impoffible not to difcover the honeft man, in the man enlightened ? The friend of mankind in the propagation of the wifeft maxims ? In the thinking philofopher, accuftomed to a fevere logic, to purfue the interefts of public good, whenever the light of truth can clear up fome of its afpects ? This is not a vague eulogium ; people will be convinced of it in reading the two chapters which concern the principles of commerce ; a great number of notes in which he has had a part, and efpecially the article of tobacco, which is entirely his own. In general, he will be known in thofe new confiderations which the commercial man of reflection only can fuggeft to the philofophical politician.

The fame motive has guided us both in the compofition and publication of this work. It was the defire of being ufeful to France, to Free America, to Humanity ; for nothing which paffes in the United States, neither ought to, nor can in future, be indifferent to humanity. America has revenged it by her revolution : fhe ought to enlighten it by her legiflation,

giſlation, and become a perpetual leſſon to all governments, as a conſolation to individuals.

It remains to me now to ſpeak of the ſources to
which we have had recourſe, in the order of this
work, &c. &c.

We have joined the information of intelligent perſons, whoſe abode in America has given them an opportunity of gaining information, to that with which
the public papers, the acts of Congreſs, of different
legiſlatures, and the different works publiſhed in the
United States, have furniſhed us. Therefore credit
may be given to all the facts which we advance.

In aſſociating our ideas, we have ſtriven to give
them an uniformity : we have, above every thing,
endeavoured to expreſs them with that clearneſs
which is ſo difficult to introduce into matters of
commerce and finance. The poverty of our language, and the ſingularity of new circumſtances
which we had to deſcribe, has ſometimes led us to
what is called neology. We muſt create what we
have not, and of which we ſtand in need, without
giving ourſelves any trouble about thoſe gramma-
rians, but triflingly philoſophical, whom Cicero de-
ſcribes thus in his time : *Controverſies about words
torment theſe little Greeks, more deſirous of contention
than of truth* *.

* *Verbi controverſia torquet Græculos homines contentionis cupidiores
quam veritatis.*

We

We have carefully avoided certain words much ufed in vulgar politics, and which give and perpetuate falfe ideas and deceitful fyftems. Such are thefe expreffions; *powers fill the firft charaƈter*, *have the firft rank*, the balance of *trade*, *the political balance of Europe*, &c. Thefe words, which ftir up hatred and jealoufy, are only proper to feed petulant ambition, and, if I may ufe the expreffion, to put the *policy* of *difturbance* in the place of that happinefs. Minifters, wearied of thefe words and ideas, will attach a greater price to real glory,—that of making the people happy.

Many notes will be found in this work; we thought it neceffary to give this form to all the ideas, which, thrown into the text, might have obfcured the principal one.

A note relaxes the mind, in fufpending the chain of the principal thoughts; it excites curiofity, in announcing a new point of view; it forces the reader to a certain degree of attention, in obliging him to attach the note to the text, to reap any advantage from his reading.

We have in thefe notes indicated, as often as it has been poffible, the ideas of reform which may be ufeful to France. We have frequently quoted the Englifh nation and government. Let not our readers be furprifed at it. It is this nation which has made moft progrefs in the praƈtice of fome good principles

of

of political economy To what nation in Europe can we better compare France? If a rivality ought to exiſt between them, is it not in that which is good? Ought not we from that moment to know all the good meaſures taken in England? Ought people to be diſpleaſed with us for mentioning theſe meaſures? The example of thoſe who have already quoted England has encouraged us. They have naturalized in France, happy inſtitutions, imitated from her rival.

If our criticiſm appears ſometimes roughly expreſſed, our readers will be ſo good as to conſider, that friends to public welfare çan but with difficulty refrain from being moved by the aſpect of certain abuſes, and from ſuffering the ſentiment of indignation which it excites in them to break forth.

Notwithſtanding the numerous precautions we have taken to come at truth; notwithſtanding the extreme attention we have given to this work, errors will undoubtedly be found in ſome of the ſtatements, and perhaps in the reaſonings. Whether they be publicly diſcuſſed, or that we are privately informed of them, we ſhall ſee theſe refutations with pleaſure; we ſhall joyfully receive theſe obſervations, and if they be well founded, we ſhall be eager to retract. This is but a ſimple eſſay on an important ſubject. It may become a good work by the aid of a concourſe of lights.

PARIS, April 1, 1787.

THE

COMMERCE, &c.

CHAP. I.

OF EXTERNAL COMMERCE; THE CIRCUMSTANCES WHICH LEAD TO IT, AND THE MEANS OF ASSURING IT TO A NATION.

COMMERCE fignifies an exchange of productions, either by barter, or by reprefentative figns of their value.

External commerce is that carried on between two or more nations. It fuppofes in them mutual wants, and a furplus of productions correfpondent thereto.

Nations, which nature or the force of things invites to a commercial intercourfe, are thofe which have that correfpondence of wants, and furplus of productions.

This familiarity enables them to trade together, directly or indirectly; a direct commerce is that which exifts between two nations, without the intervention of a third.

Commerce

Commerce is indirect when one nation trades with another by way of a third. This is the cafe of ftates which have no fea-ports, and yet wifh to exchange their productions for thofe of the Indies.

That nation, which having it in its power to carry on a direct commerce with another, yet makes ufe of an intermediate one, is neceffarily obliged to divide its profits. However, this difadvantage may fometimes be compenfated by other confiderations.

Such, for inftance, is the cafe of a nation which, in want of hufbandmen and manufacturers, prefers that ftrangers fhould themfelves come in fearch of it's fuperfluities, and bring in exchange thofe of others : its wants of population impofes this law, and whilft thefe confiderations exift, it is both morally and phyfically better, that its inhabitants fhould be employed in cultivation, than become carriers of their own national productions, or of thofe of others.

It is impoffible that nations which already have communications with each other, fhould be ignorant of their mutual productions. Hence arifes the defire of acquiring them in thofe where they do not exift. Hence direct or indirect commerce, which is confequently the inevitable refult of the ftate of things.

From

From the fame principle, it is the intereft of each nation to render its exterior commerce direct as foon as poffible, without doing an injury to its interior trade.

Direct importations, not being fubject to the expences and commiffions of agents, procure things at a cheaper rate.

A moderate price is the fureft means of obtaining an exterior commerce, the beft reafon for preference and the guarantee of its continuation *.

The

* It is vulgarly faid that a thing is dear when once it is above the accuftomed price ; and it is efteemed cheap the moment that price is diminifhed.

By this it feems that the dearnefs of a thing is the comparifon of its ftated, with its ufual price. The laft is determined by five principal circumftances. 1ft. The coft of the raw material. 2d. That of the workmanfhip. 3d. The want the confumer has of the thing. 4th. The means he has of paying for it. 5th. The proportion of its quantity with the demand there is for it. Thefe circumftances increafe or diminifh the profit of the feller ; fometimes indeed they may prevent him from gaining at all. Circumftances which influence the moft are fcarcity and abundance, expreffions by which the proportion between the want and the quantity of productions are defignated.

If there be a furplus of them, they are naturally fold at a low price. Whence it appears, that nations having great quantities of raw materials, various manufactures and a numerous population, are more particularly invited to an exterior and

continued

The country which can produce and fell a thing at the cheapeſt rate, is that which unites the favourable advantages of that production, whether it be with reſpect to its quality, manufacture, or its low rate of carriage.

The advantages which render commodities and raw materials cheap, are a fertile ſoil, eaſy of cultivation, climate favourable to the production, a government which encourages induſtry, and facilitates carriage by the conſtruction of public roads and navigable canals: finally, a population not too numerous relative to the extent of country which offers itſelf to be cultivated *.

The

---

continued commerce, becauſe they have it in their power to carry it on upon better terms.

An article may be ſold at a low price, and enrich him who furniſhes it; as it may be ſold dear, and ruin the ſeller. This depends upon the relation there is between its value and the means of its production. Every nation diſpoſed to exterior commerce in whatſoever article it may be, ought therefore to conſider two things, the price at which it can afford ſuch an article, and that at which it is ſold by rival nations: if it cannot equal the laſt, it ought to abandon that part of its trade.

* The ſituation of the United States proves the laſt aſſertion, which may at firſt ſight appear paradoxical; things are cheap there, becauſe population is not in proportion to the extent of lands to be cultivated. In a good ſoil, a man may, by his labour, eaſily ſupply the conſumption of ten men, or even more.

The fame circumftances are ftill more favourable to the manufacture of things common,
fimple, or little charged with fafhion, if the
raw material be a natural production of the
country, in plenty, and eafy to be worked up;
becaufe thefe manufactures require but few
hands, or are carried on at that leifure which
agriculture affords. Nothing can equal the
cheapnefs of this workmanfhip, and in general
no induftry is more lucrative, or better fupported on eafy terms, than that which is employed
in the intervals of repofe from cultivation; in
that cafe cheapnefs is neither the product nor
the fign of mifery in the manufacturer: it is,
on the contrary, the proof and confequence of
his eafy circumftances *.

The moft neceffary conditions for manufacturing, at a cheap rate, articles complicated, or
extremely fine and perfect, or which require the

more. Thefe ten men may therefore be employed for exterior confumption.

* Switzerland, and certain parts of Germany, offer a ftriking example of this fact. Merchandife is fabricated there, at
a lower rate than in any other country of Europe, by means of
this employment of leifure hours, and is capable of being tranfported to diftant countries, without lofing its original advantage; even acrofs great ftates, where nature, left to her
own energy, would be ftill more favourable to the fame manufactures.

union

union of feveral kinds of workmanfhip, are a
conftant and affiduous application, and a numerous population ; one half of which muft be
at a diftance from the labours of the field, and
applied to manufacture alone.

Thefe manufactures ought, according to
natural order, to be the productions of an excefs
of population only, which cannot give its induftry to agriculture or fimple manufactures ;
but in general they are the refult of the gathering together of the poor and wretched in great
cities *.

Thefe

---

* Thefe manufactures are crowded with individuals, who
having no property, or hope of conftant employ in the country,
or who are reduced by the allurements of gain and luxury, run
into cities, and foon become obliged to fell their induftry at a
mean price, proportioned to the number of thofe who are in
want of employ. When cheapnefs of workmanfhip comes
from this afflicting concurrence of the want of money in men
without employ, it is not a fign of profperity. On the contrary, it is the refult and proof of a bad focial organization, of
too unequal a divifion of property, and confequently of an unjuft diftribution of neceffary employments, which compels induftry to change, from the fabrication of what is neceffary and
ufeful, to that which is fantaftic, forced, and pernicious. Hence
it follows that wretchednefs in any country is in proportion to
this cheapnefs of workmanfhip.

It is equally evident from thefe reafonings, that new
and well conftituted ftates ought not to defire manufactures
produced

Thefe manufactures cannot furnifh their productions but with difficulty and uncertainty for
exterior commerce, when they are eftablifhed
and fupported merely by forced means, fuch as
prohibitions, exclufive privileges, &c. by which
natural obftacles, not to be deftroyed, are pretended to be combated. Countries exempt
from them prevail in the end, and obtain a
preference.

It fometimes happens, that obftacles caufed
to manfactures by dearnefs of provifions, bur-
thenfome impofts, diftance from the raw material, and unfkilfulnefs, or fmall number of
hands, are furmounted by ingenuity, or the ufe
of machines; which make the work of one
man equal to that of many, and render a manufacture capable of fupporting the commerce of
populous countries, where fuch manœuvres and
machines are not made ufe of, or known.

But thefe means are precarious, and fooner

produced by things fo badly arranged : they ought not to be
anxious about them till the rate of population and excefs of
ufeful labour naturally incline induftry to apply itfelf to improve and carry them on. Thefe reafonings againft low
priced workmanfhip do not hinder us from agreeing, that
there is a real advantage in the means of exterior commerce ;
and that in the actual ftate of things manufacturing and commercial nations may perhaps be obliged to feek for it, although
it does not compenfate the interior evil by which it is produced.

or

or later give way to a more happy fituation, where climate, foil, and government efpecially, concur in favouring, without effort, all the activity and induftry of which men are fufceptible *.

Thus, in the final analyfis, the power of furnifhing at a low price belongs inconteftably to countries fo favoured, and they will obtain in all markets a fure preference to thofe to which nature has been lefs kind, let their induftry be ever fo great, becaufe the fame induftry may always be added to natural advantages.

Exterior commerce, more than any other, is intimidated by fhackles, cuftoms, vifits, chicaneries, and proceffes; by the manner of deciding them, and the folicitations and delays they bring on.

The ftate which would favour fuch a commerce fhould, in the firft place, deftroy all thefe obftacles. It is more to its intereft fo to do, as from exterior commerce refults an augmentation of the national revenue.

All things equal, relative to the price of mer-

---

* *Favouring*, in political economy, fignifies, for the moft part, not to fhackle induftry with too many regulations; however favourable certain of thefe may be, they reftrain it in fome refpect or other. Trade is never better encouraged than when left to itfelf.

chandife,

chandife, and to the facilities with which direct
exterior commerce can be carried on, it is more
readily eftablifhed between two nations which
have a fimilary of political and religious principles *, manners, cuftoms, and efpecially of language : thefe decifive means of connexion cannot be combated but by evident advantages from
which there refults lefs expence and more profit. Commercial people generally place profit
at the head of every thing.

Nations not having thefe affinities between
them, ought, in order to compenfate for their
deficiency, to give great encouragements, and
tolerate to the utmoft degree the religious and
political opinions of ftrangers, as well as their
manners and cuftoms.

To obtain the preference in exterior commerce, neither treaties, regulations, nor force
muft be depended upon. Force has but a mo-

* Religious confiderations had formerly a confiderable influence on civilifed men, and on commerce. The Catholic fled
from the Proteftant, the Puritan fufpected the Quaker. A reciprocal hatred reigned between the fects. To day, mankind
being more enlightened, all fects connected by commerce, and
experience having fhewn that probity has almoft always been
independent of religion, it is no more required to know whether a man goes to the temple, or to confeffion—It is afked if
he fulfils his engagements with honour. Yet this relation muft
ftill be counted among commercial connexions.

mentary

mentary effect.   It deftroys even that which it
means to protect.   Treaties and regulations are
ufelefs if the interefts of two nations do not invite them to a mutual intercourfe.   They are
ineffectual if that attraction does not exift.
Treaties, regulations, force, all yield to the im-
pulfe or nature of things*.

   This force of things in commerce, is but the
refult of the circumftances in which two nations are which attract one towards the other,
and oblige them to enter into an alliance, rather

---

   * *Force of things.*   The political law which governs all, in
politics as in phyfics.   There is a general force whofe action is manifeft, which, in fpite of wars, treaties, and the manœuvres of cabinets, governs all events, and carries away men
and nations in its courfe.   It is this force of things which
overturned the Roman empire, when it ftood upon a bafis difproportioned to its mafs ; which in the 14th century took from
the Englifh one half of France, and in the 18th, has taken
from them half of the new world ;—which delivered Holland
from the yoke of Spain, and Sweden from that of Denmark.
It is this force which deftroyed the projects of fuch conquerors as Charlemagne, Zengis, and Nadir.   They ran from
place to place ; they deftroyed mankind to build empires.
Thefe empires died with them.   This force acts upon commerce as upon revolutions.   It is that which, by the difcovery
of the Cape of Good Hope, bereaved the Venetians of their
trade to the Indies, and made it pafs over fucceffively to the
Portuguefe, the Dutch, the Englifh, and the French.   Finally,
it is the force of things which will decide the great queftion
of the commerce of America.

than

than with any other nation. Thefe terminate
in their mutual intereft : it is therefore neceffary, in order to create a perpetual commerce
between two countries, to give each of them a
preponderating intereft fo to do.

C H A P. II.

OF EXTERNAL COMMERCE, CONSIDERED IN ITS MEANS OF EXCHANGE, AND ITS BALANCE.

WE are deceived in believing that commerce cannot be eftablifhed between
two nations without gold or filver to balance
their accounts. It will be interefting to enter
into fome detail on this head, on account of the
deficiency of coin in the United States, and the
neceffity of reducing themfelves to the commerce of exchange, being the two principal objections ignorantly brought againft a trade with
them *.

It

* The fcarcity of money in the United States of America
has been greatly exaggerated in France. It muft be fcarce in
all new ftates, where nothing fhackles induftry, where fo many
things

It has been frequently afferted that the balance will be againſt them; that they can only offer an exchange in merchandiſe. It is therefore neceſſary to prove that this great word, balance, is inſignificant; that a great commerce may be carried on without money, and that one of exchange is the moſt advantageous of any.

When a nation pays with money the whole, or the balance of its importations, it is ſaid the balance of trade is againſt it, by which a diſadvantageous idea of its poſition is meant to be given. This is a prejudice eaſy to be overturn-

things are to be created, and where, in every quarter, there are ſuch quantities of lands to be cleared. In order that money ſhould be plenty in this ſtate of creation, mines would be neceſſary; and at the ſame time a want of hands, and induſtry clogged with impediments, circumſtances much more unfavourable to foreign commerce than the ſcarcity of money in an active and induſtrious country. One fact ſeems to prove to us, that in independent America, money is found in the moſt deſirable proportion to population, at leaſt by taking Europe for the term of compariſon. Contracts eſteemed good, and of which the intereſt is regularly paid, are ſold there at the rate of ſix per cent. per annum. Yet the clearing of lands muſt produce a much greater benefit; why then is not all the money ſwallowed up? why remains there enough of it to fulfil theſe contracts, which produce no more than five or ſix per cent? Is it not becauſe money is not ſo ſcarce there as people in France imagine?—where the actual ſtate of the Americans is confounded with the diſtreſs in which they were when they combated for their liberty.

ed,

ed, although entertained by men celebrated for their knowledge.

In effect, whence comes to this country the gold it pays? It is either from its mines, and in that cafe it pays with one of its own productions; or it owes it to artificers who exercife their functions in a foreign country, and even then it pays with a production which originates within its dominions. As long as a nation pays another, directly or indirectly, with its own productions, its pofition cannot be difadvantageous. Therefore, the unfavourable word balance, thus attached to the balance of an account paid in money, offers no exact and nice idea of the favourable or unfavourable ftate of a nation.

Gold is alfo a merchandife, and it may be convenient to one nation, according to its relations or connexions with another, to pay with money, without its having, for that reafon, an unfavourable balance againft it.

There is but one cafe wherein the balance againft a nation can be declared; it is, that when having exhaufted its money and treafures, it remains debtor to another nation. But things could not remain long in this ftate; fo wretched a foil, unequal to the confumption and exchange of its inhabitants, would foon be abandoned; this, however, cannot happen. Importation

tation prefently becomes in proportion to exportation ; an equilibrium is eftablifhed, and the
pretended unfavourable balance has not duration
enough to give a right of fuppofing even its exiftence.

There is as little truth and juftice in faying a
nation has the balance of trade in its favour,
when it receives in money balances due to it
upon the amount of its exportations. This balance, exifting for a certain time, would heap up
fpecie in the country, and at length render it
very miferable. This has never been the cafe,
yet it would have happened if this fyftem had
the leaft foundation.

The circulation of money depends on too
many caufes, to deduce from its abundance a
certain fign of a favourable commercial balance ;
a thoufand combinations and events, which have
no relation to that balance, draw money from
abroad or fend it there ; and in general, continued and various motions of commerce, the tables of exportation and importation, according
to which the fign of a favourable or unfavourable balance is regulated, are too uncertain and
defective for the purpofe, as well as for forming
a judgment of the quantities of coin or riches of
a nation *.

Let

* I will give a ftriking example of the deficiency of thefe
calculations,

Let the tables for comparing the exportation and importation of raw materials, and of manufactured articles, be encreafed to what they may; let

calculations, of the eftimation of a balance of trade and of the quantity of money. This example will prove that political calculators neglect, or are ignorant of foreign events which overturn their calculations.

M. Neckar wifhed to inform himfelf (Chap. IX. Vol. 3d, of his Treatife on the Adminiftration of Finance) what was the fum brought to and preferved in Europe from 1763 to 1777. He eftimates it at one thoufand eight hundred and fifty millions of livres, according to the regifter of Lifbon and Cadiz, comprehending that even which entered by contraband, and he values at 300 millions of livres that which went out of Europe during the fame interval.

It will only be neceffary to quote two or three authenticated facts, to prove the infufficiency of this calculation founded upon the regifters of Cuftom-houfes.

In ftating the fum of money entered into Europe, it does not appear that M. Neckar takes account of the gold and filver, which the conqueft and poffeffion of Bengal by the Englifh, and their eftablifhments in the Eaft-Indies, have caufed to pafs into this quarter of the world. But according to the calculation of the fecret committee, appointed by the Parliament of England, to examine the ftate of Englifh poffeffions in India, the fums drawn from Bengal from 1757 to 1·71, amount to 751,500,000 livres a. To what will it amount, if

a The detail of this calculation is given in The Defcription of the Indies, Vol. I. page 249. It is neceffary to take notice here of an error crept into that work, which is, that the fum total is there given in pounds fterling, inftead of livres tournois.

there

let the greateft care and fidelity be employed to
render them perfect, the refult will never be
more certain or decifive ; for as long as prohibitory

there be added to it thofe drawn from the Carnatic and from
Oude, of which the Nabobs have the fhadow only of the property, from the revenue of the northern Circars, from the theft
committed on the Emperor of Mogul, from 1771 to the prefent
day, of his twenty-fix millions, from the perpetual increafe of
territories and revenues, from the fale made in 1773 of the
Rohillas to the Nabob of Oude, which produced to the Englifh
upwards of fifty millions [b].

Finally, what will be the amount, if there be added to it the
enormous fums exported from the Indies by individuals, who
have there enriched themfelves ?   The fortune of Lord Clive
was beyond calculation ; that of Mr. Haftings, againft whom
a profecution is now carrying on, is calculated at thirty or forty millions.   Another Governor has, according to feveral
well-founded reports, recently paid upwards of two millions of
livres to filence his accufers.   It is true that a part of thefe
immenfe riches have been employed to defray the expences
incurred by the Englifh in guarding their poffeffions in India ;
that a more confiderable one has been fent into Europe under
the form of merchandize ; but it cannot be denied that a third
part has been brought in gold and filver to our continent.
What is the amount of it ? This is impoffible to ftate.   But
whatever it may be, it renders the calculation of Mr. Neckar
doubtful.—Let the inexhauftible riches of the Indies be judged
of by one fact, and confequently the immenfe fource from

[b] See Mackintofh's Voyage to the Eaft-Indies, Vol. I. page
340.

which

tory laws, which are always accompanied by illicit commerce, fhall exift, it will be impoffible

which the Europeans have drawn them, and by another confequence, the money which muft have come into Europe.
Nadir Schah, who conquered Delly in 1740, took from India
about forty millions fterling [c]. This money was circulated in
Perfia, and as that unhappy ftate is torn by defpotifm and continual wars [d], produces but little, manufactures nothing, and
is confequently debtor to exterior commerce, which comes almoft entirely into Europe, it follows that two-thirds of the
fums ftolen from India by the freebooter Nadir, have paffed
over to the fame quarter. Thefe events, unnoticed by political calculators, have certainly had great and univerfal influence
upon the fluctuation and circulation of money. That which
makes it fuppofed that no metals come from India, is the opinion that their importation is difadvantageous. But have the
freebooters who have pillaged that country for the laft thirty
years calculated this difadvantage? They ftrive to fecure
their thefts, and do not fpeculate like merchants : bulky merchandize would betray them.

With refpect to the ftated fums of money which pafs from
Europe to India, there is the fame defect in the calculations of
Mr. Neckar. He takes no notice of the events which obliged
the Englifh to remit confiderable fums to India : for inftance,
the two wars againft the Marrattas were prodigiously expenfive, that againft Hyder Ally in 1769 was not lefs fo. A fingle conflagration at Calcutta coft nearly twenty-four millions
of livres, which it was neceffary to replace, yet thefe fums are
far from balancing thofe which are exported from India.

[c] See Mackintofh's Voyages, Vol. I. page 341.
[d] See Mr. Capper's Voyage, at the end of that of Mackintofh, Vol. II. page 454.

to know and ftate exactly what comes in and goes out *; and if there be a country where no fuch laws exift †, are exact reg fters of the exports and imports to be found in it? And if they were, would it not be a conftraint which the private interefts of merchants would frequently oblige them to avoid?

Moreover, does it appear that, in thefe general balances, which are fuppofed to be paid in money, notice is taken of the operation of bankers, foreign government, and thofe who go abroad, in exporting the public fpecie ‡. Knowledge

---

* This is a ftrong objection made by the adverfaries of Lord Sheffield, to which his Lordfhip has not fatisfactorily replied.

Nothing can be more impofing than the tables of importation and exportation, and of the balance of trade in Great-Britain, publifhed by Sir Charles Whitworth. Yet fee with what facility the Count de Mirabeau reduces to twenty millions of livres tournois, the ninety millions which Sir Charles Whitworth eftimates to be the annual balance of Englifh commerce; and truft after this to cuftom-houfe calculations.—See Confiderations on the Order of Cincinnatus, in this volume.

† Such a country does exift. There are many States among the new Republics of America, which regifter veffels as they enter, becaufe duties are paid on importation; but there are none on exportation.

‡ It is very probable there are a number of particular caufes
which

ledge is deceitful which is acquired from such consequences.

But how appreciate—how estimate the increase of the riches and commerce of a nation ? —By its population. If this sensibly augments, if ease and the conveniencies of life become more general, if the causes of indigence in an increasing people be seen to diminish, or are confined to inability to work, occasioned by accidental illnesses ; it is evident, that the revenues of that nation exceed its expences, and that the balance of trade is in its favour ; for if the value of its exportation were inferior to that

which insensibly diminish the quantity of coin in those nations which have the balance of trade constantly in their favour, Were no such causes to exist, the consequence will be that such nations would be obliged to bury their gold and silver in the earth, to prevent its falling into disuse ; yet neither of these cases happen. Therefore money necessarily passes from such countries to others,

M. Casaux has proved this to be true, with respect to England, in his Considerations on *the Mechanism of Society*. He there explains, that if the calculations of Sir Charles Whitworth be true, England ought to possess at this moment about four hundred thousand millions of livres in gold and silver, as the sole balance of her commerce from 1700 to 1775. Yet it is certain that she is far from having that enormous sum, She has not even a sum in proportion to her population and contingencies. She supplies that deficiency by an immense circulation of her bank-paper.

of

of its importation, a confiderable debt and impoverifhment would foon be the confequences :
and impoverifhment falls immediately upon population.   It is therefore by rational and well
compofed tables upon this fubject only, that a
minifter of found judgment, profound and extended in his plans, will be prevailed upon to
govern himfelf.   It is by them he will judge of
the increafe and advantages of exterior commerce, as well as of national riches.

He will be very cautious of decorating with
this title the amaffing of gold and filver, and
equally fo of making it the token of riches,
or of judging of their extent by the quantity of
thofe metals.   All fuch ideas are fordid, dangerous, and falfe ; fordid, becaufe they attach to
this fign the reprefentation of productions, and
confequently the extenfion of commerce ;   dangerous, becaufe they accuftom men to look
upon gold as real riches, to neglect the thing
for its fhadow *, and make them ftrangers to
their

---

* Could gold and filver be preferved from adulteration and
the attempts of tyranny and ignorance, they would have a
much better title to be confidered as real riches.   Gold being
an univerfal agent, he who poffeffes it may emigrate to where-
ever he pleafes, and take his gold with him.   This metal is
therefore every thing, with nations unhappy enough to make
arbitrary

their country; falfe, becaufe that difplay of figures announces the quantity only of money which continually difappears; and which, when carried to a certain degree, is of no farther confideration *.

Enquiries

arbitrary exceptions to general maxims, upon which public credit is founded. But how dearly do they pay for their ignorance of the advantages of public credit! How dearly do governments themfelves pay for their errors and outrages! All their meafures are forced—nature is liberal in vain; inceffantly employed in repairing evils which continually prefent themfelves, fhe has not time enough allowed her to add to our happinefs. When it was faid that money had no particular country, governments were emphatically told, that it was neceffary to do without great quantities of it: it will never be rejected till the ineftimable advantages refulting from a refpect for public credit fhall be properly known. The lefs individuals love and heap up money, the richer, more enlightened, and better governed will a nation be. To be attached to money, to hoard it up, is a fign of an alarming crifis, of a deficiency of judgment and faith in adminiftration; from whence comes the proof of what has been faid in the text, that 'a writer who extols gold as a fign of riches, and recommends it to his fellow citizens, is deceived, or has a bad idea of their fituation.' In the laft cafe he would do much better, if, inftead of preaching this pernicious doctrine, he encouraged government to give an immoveable ftability to national credit.

* It has not yet been remarked, that thoufands of millions is a vague expreffion, and does not furnifh a complete idea. The imagination cannot exactly conceive for fuch a fum an employ which would ferve as the meafure of its power and effect. It

is

Enquiries on the quantity of coin are like thofe on the balance of trade. To eftablifh both one and the other with fome degree of certainty, it is neceffary to affemble notions and details, of which the elementary principles vanifh, or inceffantly vary*.

The

is known what could be done with twenty or an hundred millions of men, but it is not known what could be effected with an hundred thoufand millions of crowns ; yet they are heaped upon paper to give an idea of power.

* In general, the mafs of gold or filver is divided into three principal parts.—The firft under the form of money, ferves for daily and unavoidable expences. Each individual, as foon as he is charged with the fupport of himfelf and family, muft have at leaft fome pieces of money for daily exigencies, and the payment of impofts. To this muft be added that fum which is referved for cafualties.—This cuftom is more or lefs obferved in all countries, in proportion to the probability of difaftrous events. It is impoffible to calculate this firft part—It is however evident, that it ought to be in proportion to the population, and to increafe with it ; and that a decreafe of population would foon take place, were many individuals totally deprived of a pecuniary contingency fufficient to procure them fuch neceffaries as cannot be difpenfed with, and which they neither make nor receive themfelves. It appears alfo, that this part of the coin remains in the country by reafon of its continued application in little fums to daily wants, and of the abfolute ftagnation of that which is laid up in referve.

The fecond part is deftined, under the fame form, to the great operations of commerce. It is equally impoffible to fix its quantity, on account of an infinity of combinations which

continually

The proceedings in the adminiftration of fi-
nances are more ufeful and certain ; by laying
afide the pomp of falfe riches, and by confidering gold and fiver in a point of view relative to
their

continually change and caufe thefe metals to pafs from one
country to another. Daily charges, cuftoms, &c. retain a part;
but thefe objects belong equally to our firft divifion.

The third part contains uncoined gold and filver, under
whatever form they may have : it is, like the fecond, fubject to
numbers of continual variations, which leave no fatisfactory
means of determining its quantity.

To pretend to afcertain the quantity in the mafs, by payments of uncertain commercial balances, and by the addition
of fpecie produced from mints fince a new coinage has taken
place, is not a more certain means, becaufe it would be equally neceffary to obferve the continual action of commerce upon
thefe metals, under all their forms, and of the combinations it
produces, which fucceffively arife from one another. In thus
eftimating money it is forgotten, that it is an univerfal agent,
which, by that character alone, muft neceffarily change its fituation perpetually ; fince commerce has produced an affinity
among men, by wants, which they have created to themfelves,
of their reciprocal productions. It is equally unobferved, that
different circumftances reduce gold to the ftate of an ingot ;
that confequently the fame piece may pafs feveral times under
the die in the courfe of a certain number of years. This is a
reflection which M. Neckar feems not to have made when he
ftated the money exifting in France at fo confiderable a fum. It
will be known when the recoinage of the old Louis is finifhed,
what we ought to think of his calculations. But the fum is far
fhort of 957 millions, as eftimated by that minifter. It is more
than

their particular properties. They supply our wants as means of exchange only; they are notes to the bearer, which having every where the same value, are every where negociable. Thus they are ambulatory; they pass, repass, are accumulated or disperfed like the waves of the fea, continually agitated by fuccessive winds blowing from every point of the compass. To undertake to make them stationary, would be striving to change their nature, to deprive them of that property from which they derive their value : this ridiculous enterprife is, notwith-standing, a consequence of the system which causes them to be looked upon as real treasures. Their difappearance is dreaded, and yet their circulation is clogged, and the mind lofes fight of the ufe of the most fimple and univerfal means of creating real riches, without which metals would be ufelefs, and consequently of no value.

On the contrary, difdaining vulgar opinions, and feeing nothing in gold and filver but the means of exchange, but proper agents to faci-

than probable, that it will never amount to more than two thirds of it.

At this moment, fourteen months after the arret for a new coinage, it amounts to no more than 550 millions, and every thing indicates a rapid decline.

litate

litate it ; the mind, freed from the fear of the want of them *as riches*, conceives the idea of doing without them *as agents*, at leaft about man's perfon *. What a vaft field is this opened to induftry ! Thefe metals are in that cafe referved for the beft ufes to which nations who obtain them from abroad can put them to. They are fent out to feek materials for induftry, new commodities, and efpecially increafe the number of ci-

---

* It is aftonifhing, that among fo many travellers who have gone over the United States of America, not one of them has given a detail of the manner of exchanging feveral neceffaries of life ; they are reciprocally furnifhed in the country with what they are in want of, without the interference of money. The taylor, fhoe-maker, &c. exercife their profeffions in the houfe of the hufbandman who has occafion for their commodities, and who, for the moft part, furnifhes materials, and pays for the workmanfhip in provifions, &c.—This kind of exchange extends to many objects ; each of thefe people write down what they receive and give, and at the end of the year they clofe an account confifting of an infinity of articles, with a very fmall fum ; this could not be effected in Europe but with a great deal of money. Thus it appears, that an eafy means of doing without great fums of money is given to country people by inftructing them in writing and arithmetic ; that confequently the fovereign who fhould eftablifh fchools for the purpofe of teaching this moft neceffary art and fcience, would create a confiderable means of circulation without the ufe of coin, and that this expence, which feems to alarm fo many governments, is in fact one of the moft lucrative fpeculations which the treafury could make.

tizens ;

tizens; of every fpecies of riches this is the
moft fure and fruitful. Thus when gold is reduced to its exact value, that its real ufe is
known, the advantageous purpofes to which it
is proper, are more juftly calculated. It is then
perceived that paper credit may have the fame
properties as gold itfelf; and to fucceed in giving them to it, nothing more is neceffary than
to preferve the moft inviolable refpect for the
principles which fupport public confidence; for
upon what bafis refts the value and general ufe
of money, if it be not upon the certitude that
it will be received every where in payment for
things which men's wants may require, becaufe of its conventional value? why fhould a
paper which prefents the fame conventional value, the fame certitude and folidity, be refufed
in payment? I will add more—A more folid
bafis than gold and filver has, may be given to
paper money * : for we have no guarantee that
the value of thefe metals will not be all at once
diminifhed by the difcovery of new and rich

---

* I fay, paper-money, without attaching to this expreffion
the idea of conftraint to receive it as fuch ; this obligation diminifhes its value—I would fay paper credit, if the word credit did not feem to exclude its principal quality, that of being
always fufceptible, and in an inftant, of being converted into
money without the leaft lofs.

mines ;

mines; we cannot calculate their quantities
concealed in the earth, and men inceffantly rake
up its bowels in fearch of them *. Therefore
in countries where precious metals are fcarce,
but where lands may be fuccefsfully cultivated,
banks fhould be formed, whofe operations fhould
chiefly reft upon title deeds and productions depofited ; in a word, upon fuch objects only as
gold and filver fhould reprefent †.

In

* Why fhould not difcoveries be made in other countries,
like that in the laft century by two fhepherds in Norway, of
the rich mines of Konfberg, where very confiderable maffes
of filver are found? The King of Denmark has one of 560lb.
weight in his cabinet.

† It is not true that much gold and filver are neceffary to
eftablifh banks, or create notes which may be thrown into
circulation. A proof of the contrary arifes from facts continually before our eyes. The multitude of bills of exchange
which circulate and crofs each other in every direction, have
not all of them, for origin and fecurity, a depofit of gold and
filver. Neither are they all paid when due with thefe metals.
Commerce produces an abundance of fuch papers, which falling due on the fame day are difcharged by each other without
the intervention of fpecie ; efpecially in cities where public
banks are eftablifhed to facilitate this kind of payment. Thefe
are called transfers, and the principal object of Caiffes d'Efcomptes and banks is to facilitate them by the payment of bills
fallen due by thofe who have ftill fome time to run. In fine,
thefe Caiffes d'Efcomptes and banks, are themfelves caufes
and ftriking proofs of the little difficulty there is in fupplying,

by

In countries where thefe metals are already
in circulation, but are ftill foreign productions,
eafy and certain means fhould be fought after to
render exchanges lefs dependent on the fecurity
or abundance of fpecie. Paper credit fhould be
naturalized there, becaufe its infallible effect is
to double or treble the quantity of current coin,
and even to replace it entirely, where, as in
England, public confidence has never received a
wound. Thefe obfervations might be more
extended if a treatife on the nature of banks
and Caiffes d'Efcompte were in queftion. But
this is not my prefent object ; I have confidered
exterior commerce in its means of exchange
only, like metals and paper credit, and in its balance for the purpofe of applying thefe principles to the relations and commerce of France
and the United States : and more efpecially to
clear up fome difficulties to the French, who
feem to have a bad opinion of this commercial
intercourfe, on account of the want of money

by confidence, the places of gold and filver. Firft eftablifhed
by depofits in fpecie, they foon circulate their notes for fums
more confiderable than thofe depofited : and what furety is
there for the payment of fuch notes if it be not by other bills
not due, which the Caiffes and banks receive in exchange for
their own notes payable at fight, to which public confidence
give the fame value as to gold and filver.

in America, and to encourage the independent Americans, who feem to dread the pretended inconveniencies arifing from its deficiency.

I think I have proved :

1ft. That the balance of trade is but an infignificant word : that the balance paid in fpecie is no proof of a difadvantageous commerce on the part of the nation which pays it, nor advantageous to the nation which receives it *.

2d. That the tables of that commercial balance deferve no faith, and that the only me-

---

* Obferve what a refpectable author, well verfed in the matter, and whom we fhall hereafter have occafion to quote, thinks of it.

" Thefe commercial balances, calculated in different ftates, are pitiful ; when I fee confequences drawn from ridiculous and laboured official accounts, *mi fanno dal rifo crepare.*

" To confider France and England only, the two principal manufacturing countries, and the moft commercial ones in the world, what omiffions, negligencies, double employs, errors, corruptions, nocturnal expeditions, duties evaded, and contraband trade ! The prodigious quantity of wool which is fent from England is certainly not regiftered, no more than the filks, gold laces, gauzes, blondes, cambrics, brandies, and many other articles which are fraudulently introduced there. The fame in France : no account can be taken of the immenfe quantities of drapery, hofiery, and fmall hardware, which the Englifh fend in exchange. Voy. en Italie, de M. Roland de la Palatiere, tom. i. p. 352.

thod

thod of eftimating the increafe of trade, is by the increafe of population *.

3d. That it is impoffible to judge exactly of the quantity of money exifting in a country, and that all calculations on that head are founded upon an uncertain and defective bafis, becaufe it is impoffible to collect all their elementary principles.

4th. That metals are not real riches.

5th. That confidered as agents of exchange, it would be more advantageous to fubftitute pa-

---

* The errors in thefe pretended balances muft be continually infifted upon : confequences dangerous to the people are frequently drawn from them.

Financiers who pillage the kingdom, fay to Princes on prefenting them thefe fallacious calculations, " that things are in a profperous way ; that commerce flourifhes, that impofts may be laid on, loans negociated, &c. Thefe fophifms are feducing : let Princes accuftom themfelves to judge of public profperity by population, and the general eafe of the people ; let them be eye-witneffes of this, and miftruft a momentary appearance of profperity, which frequently covers profound mifery, and they will not be fo often deceived.

A King of Sardinia paid a vifit to a part of Savoy, the nobility of which had been reprefented to him as being poor and miferable : they came to him elegantly dreffed in ciothes of ceremony, to make him their court. At this the King expreffed his furprife to one of the gentlemen, who faid to him, *Sire, nous faifons pour votre Majefté tout ce que nous devons, mais nous devons tout ce que nous faifons.*

per

per credit in interior commerce, and to apply them to ufes for which paper is unfit, to wit, all the purpofes of exterior commerce. There refults from thefe demonftrations, that commerce may be begun between two nations without the aid of money; that the quantity a nation has of it to exchange for foreign productions is in proportion to its confidential interior eftablifhments, which advantageoufly fupply its place.

In three words, a good foil, paper credit, and a government anxious to fupport it, are the true means of opening the refources of a nation, of procuring abundance of fpecie, as well as an extenfive exterior commerce.

I have not confidered this commerce in its influence upon the manners of the people; fuch a difcuffion would here be ufelefs, becaufe whatever that influence may be, exterior commerce is a forced effect of the refpective fituations of France and the United States, as will hereafter be made appear. I examine this matter as a politician, not as a philofopher, and I pray the reader not to forget the diftinction.

C H A P.

C H A P. III.

APPLICATION OF THE FOREGOING GENERAL
PRINCIPLES TO THE RECIPROCAL COM-
MERCE OF FRANCE AND THE UNITED
STATES :

That France has every Means of procuring a great Commerce, and thofe which muft affure it to her in the United
States ; that her Productions are proper for them ; and that
her particular interior Circumftances oblige her to engage
in this Commerce.

THESE truths will not be contefted when
the fertility of the foil of France fhall be
confidered, her various and particular productions, and the temperature of her climate, which
favours thofe the moft fimple and neceffary.

Thefe advantages conftantly affure her workmanfhip at a lower price than thofe of nations
endowed with the fame activity, but which
have not the advantages of fuch favourable circumftances.

Her manufactures are numerous, and her population is confiderable in comparifon with that
of moft other nations. Yet thefe are far from
the

the degree to which they may be extended ; for in confidering France, room for a more exten-five population is foon difcovered, and an im-menfity of means for a great number of manu-factures, which only wait for the will of go-vernment to be eftablifhed.

What other nation has more activity ? more induftry ? or unites to fo great a degree, all the advantages of civilization, and the matter and means of the moft varied and extenfive interior and exterior commerce, independent of comple-tion ? What other would have been able to refift, for fo long a time, the chain of misfor-tunes, and repeated faults of which fhe has been the victim ? The force of her conftitu-tion, rather than her apparent profperity, ought to be calculated by this refiftance. France is not what fhe might and ought to be. There is no doubt but fhe will become fo if fhe opens her eyes to her true interefts, if unfhackling her interior fhe does not neglect her exterior com-merce, and particularly that which the United States wifh to open with her. The produc-tions of her foil and induftry are proper for them. She can export in exchange from inde-pendent America the raw materials for which fhe may have occafion. Thefe two countries may therefore carry on a *direct* commerce of *ex-*

change

change between them, and fo much the more advantageous, as the raw materials, which muft conftitute it, would coft them more in any other place. Thefe truths will not be doubted when the double catalogue of the refpective wants of France and the United States, or of their importation and exportation, fhall have been examined.

Intelligent patriots are of opinion, that it cannot be advantageous to France, in her prefent fituation, to engage in the commerce of the United States.—They obferve, that her manufactures being inferior to thofe of the Englifh, fhe will be worfted in the American markets; they add, that inftead of encouraging this commerce, government would perhaps act more wifely by preventing the interior abufes which ftop the progrefs of cultivation and induftry.

I am far from denying the neceffity there may be of ftirring to reform fuch abufes, and to direct our efforts to culture and the improvement of manufactures ; but it is eafy to demonftate, that exterior commerce will in a very fhort time infallibly bring on fuch a reform, and that France in her prefent ftate is in the greateft need of this exterior trade.

In effect, an active and induftrious nation, whofe foil is fertile, ought always to have markets

kets for the fale of its commodities to animate
its induſtry. Its culture and manufactures
would languiſh if the limits of its confumption
were perceived. It is even neceſſary that thefe
markets ſhould be ſuperabundant; that one
may ſucceed the other, in cafe of unſuſpected
events, which might caufe a momentary change
in the ordinary courfe of things.

What caufe has thrown Ireland into fo continued a ſtate of languor, although one of thofe
countries the moſt favoured by nature, and the
beſt fituated for exterior commerce, if it is not
the deprivation of that commerce? An embarraffing exuberance of productions was feared;
the cultivation of them was prefently neglected,
and this negligence increafed waſte lands. This
iſland would at length have offered a fpectacle
of the moſt deplorable mifery, of a complete
depopulation, if, by a reſtitution of the liberty
of commerce, an end had not been put to fo
cruel a difcouragement which choaked induſtry,
by making it fear a want of markets for the vent
of its productions.

Let our patriots, therefore, ceafe to look upon
foreign commerce as contrary to the reforms
which are to revive our interior trade: to encourage the firſt is not to profcribe the fecond,
becaufe one cannot fucceed without the other.

But,

But, on the contrary, the feeds of activity are fown in the latter, by extending the boundaries of confumption.

Alas! is not France evidently in need of them? Are not her magazines crowded with a fuperfluity of the moſt neceſſary productions, for which ſhe has no market? Such as, amongſt others, her wines and brandies *. The United States offer to her an immenſe confumption; why does ſhe refuſe to fupply them?

Even if her wines and brandies were not in fuch fuperfluity, it would be prejudicial not to fupport the price of them by foreign confumptions. The greateſt ſcourge of induſtry, and eſpecially of manufactures, is the low price of thoſe liquors which are feducing by their ſtrength. On this account prudent manufacturers carefully avoid wine countries. It would be fuperfluous to give a detail of their reafons; but certainly the politician, the moſt jealous of a free extenſion of individual enjoyments, will never become an advocate for the indulgence of men in thoſe articles which deprive them of their faculties and reafon.

* Such is the fituation of Aunis and Saintonge—plentiful vintages are there literally feared, and theſe provinces are at this moment overcharged with wine, for which they have no exportation: the people are miſerable in the midſt of abundance. See Note, Chap. V. Sect. 1.

France

France ought to defire the commerce of the United States. She ought alfo to be anxious for it on account of her manufactures, to employ her population which is in want of work. Confequently workmanfhip is cheap; whence refults indigence, beggary, and ftrife *. Work and productions are increafed by opening new markets. Thus, for example, vineyards will remain, which a want of confumption would foon caufe to be deftroyed; thoufands of labourers, who languifh, will be employed, fociety will be increafed by thoufands of individuals; more corn, more cloth, &c. will be neceffary : hence an increafe of interior confumption and population.

When we examine the queftion, if exterior commerce be advantageous and neceffary to a nation; a newly conftituted ftate, whofe population is far from being in proportion to its foil, where there is fpace and property in land for every one, muft be diftinguifhed from that which is ancient, rich in productions as well as

---

* Means are every day fought to diminifh and prevent crimes—Let property or employ be given to thofe who are without them : this is the fecret—It muft notwithftanding be agreed, that property is preferable to employ in workfhops; under this point of view, commerce with the United States, in opening to us a great market, will be a means of diminifh-ing mendicity and vices in France.

in

in men; or, to fpeak with more precifion, a ftate
where the unequal diftribution of property
takes men from the fields, fhuts them up in
cities, and proftitutes their faculties to the fancies of the rich.

Certainly fuch a new ftate cannot increafe
its foreign commerce before it has cleared great
quantities of lands, and is become confiderably
peopled, and has a furplus of men and productions.

Such a ftate, while neceffary, will undoubtedly follow this counfel.

But this counfel would be improper to another ftate, which, advanced in its civilization,
covered with a population without property,
having manufactures and money in abundance ;
whofe induftry and territorial riches wait for
demands, and whofe culture languifhes for want
of markets. A foreign commerce is neceffary
to this ftate to vivify it.

Such is the fituation of France; neither foil,
induftry, activity, nor the thirft of gain, is there
wanting ; other pernicious caufes flacken her
interior commerce. If the merchant has not a
certainty of markets, he does not buy nor give
orders ; the manufacturer employs fewer hands,
has lefs occafion for the productions of the
                                                    earth.

earth. Languor then defcends from manufactures to cultivation, and diminifhes population.

The reverfe will be the cafe in the fuppofi-
tion of a vaft exterior commerce, and will lead
to the improvement even of our manufactures ;
for the neceffity of improving to obtain a preference will oblige manufacturers to ftudy the
tafte of the Americans, and to conform themfelves to it, to vary the productions of their induftry ; and will oblige them not to relax, that
they may not be furpaffed by rivals.

It is here neceffary to make fome reflections
on the general inferiority found in our manufactures, on comparing them with thofe of the
Englifh. This fact has furnifhed Lord Sheffield with his principal argument, to maintain
that America will always prefer the latter. It
is neceffary to clear up this point, which feems
not to be well underftood.

Manufactures of luxury, of conveniency, and
of neceffity, muft be diftinguifhed in a manner
hereafter pointed out. Lord Sheffield and all
foreigners agree, that France has the advantage
in the firft clafs of manufactures *. His Lordfhip

* Our manufactures of filk have proportionably a much
greater fale abroad than that of our woollens. It is that, independent of tafte, or, if we will, of fafhion, which we poffefs,
and

ſhip agrees even that France makes finer cloths
than thoſe of England ; but with reſpect to
manufactures of convenience, or ſuch as are intended for the conſumption of the people, we
muſt, in ſpite of patriotiſm, agree on our part,
that we are in many articles inferior to the
Engliſh. This will appear by the ſequel. It
would be ridiculous and even dangerous to flatter the nation in this particular ; the illuſion
would keep it in a ſtate of mediocrity. It is for
a better conſtituted patriotiſm to prove to the
nation, that it may riſe above mediocrity, and
to ſhew it by what means this is to be effected.
Should any body wiſh to know the cauſe of this
double difference between the French and Engliſh manufactures, it is as follows :

There is in England a greater number of
men, among the people, in eaſy circumſtances,
than in France, and who are conſequently in a
ſituation to chooſe and pay better for ſuch articles as they like. It is a known fact, that the
common people of England, although loaded

and which opens to us a great conſumption, the raw material
is in a great meaſure one of our own productions ; an advantage which puts it in our power to ſurmount many general inconveniencies, whoſe effects are more ſenſible upon our other
articles of exportation, ſuch as woollens, the production of
which has leſs relation with the manufacture.

with

with taxes, are well clothed and fed*; the rags of mifery are not found with the *poulle au pot* †. The Englifh manufacturer having a greater demand for articles of neceffity, and being better paid for them, can make improvements in his manufacture.

Should it be required to know from whence comes the eafinefs of circumftances fo general in England: independent of the foil and pofition, and the advantages of that liberty which

* The goodnefs of things manufactured is fo generally requifite in England, that merchandizes deftined for exportation are there diftinguifhed from thofe for interior confumption. There are great warehoufes wherein the fales are for exportation only; the object of others is interior confumption. People who judge haftily conclude from hence, that thofe for exportation are badly manufactured. They are deceived, the difference is in the choice of materials. *The Englifhman fpares nothing for that which he confumes.* The workmanfhip is the fame; it would coft in general more to manufacturers to have two forts of workmanfhip, a good and a bad one, than to have one only which is good, and a manufacture eftablifhed upon a bad kind of workmanfhip would foon be decried. A fhoe deftined to foreign commerce is as well made as another; but it does not laft fo long, becaufe the leather is not chofen from the beft kind; and fo of the reft.

† A memorable expreffion of Henry the fourth of France, who, in a converfation with his favourite Sully, faid, he hoped to fee the time when the pooreft of his fubjects would have it in their power to put a fowl into the pot for their Sunday's dinner.

reigns

reigns there, it refults from the confideration attached to induſtry in the opinion of the public ; from the laws fure protection accorded to every individual againſt the agents of government ; and the haughtinefs and infolence, to which they are naturally inclined (becaufe in men of flender education thefe are the effect of power), being continually repreſſed, and their being prevented from trampling upon the citizen, who muſt be obedient.—He is obedient to the law, and not to him who puts it in execution *. In fine, it is the confequence of not bluſhing to be a tradefman, artificer, or workman, from father to fon.

In France there are individuals exceſſively rich ; but the people are poor. The firſt have it in their power to pay extremely dear for arti-

---

* *Thee* and *Thou* as terms of contempt are unknown in England : *Sir* is the general defignation of every individual. A man accufed of the greateſt crimes, and who has the moſt miferable appearance, is never fpoken to in the fingular number when he is interrogated by his judges ; and as he becomes an object of pity when he is convicted, decent appellations, generally in ufe, are not changed with refpect to him. Can one fuppofe that this refpect for man is prejudicial to public profperity ? Man is elevated by it; it gives him energy, and inclines him to eafe. Contempt, which in other places is affected for the people, leads them to mifery, and retains them in it.

cles

cles of luxury and fancy, which caufe an improvement of manufactures of this kind. Finer cloths, as it has been before obferved, are to be found in France than in England; but their quantity is not great, becaufe there is not an extenfive demand for thofe of the firft quality.

On the other hand, the property of the people being very inconfiderable, they pay badly, and the confequence is, that things of conveniency or neceffity are badly manufactured for them.

I will not here enter into the examination of caufes which occafion fuch a ftate of things, nor of the means of changing it. I will leave the difcuffion of fuch means for another chapter, but the following conclufions muft neceffarily be drawn from thefe facts : the perfection of manufactures depends upon the demand, and the demand upon the means of payment. Now becaufe the French have not thofe means, they muft be fought after in a foreign country. Increafe foreign demands for French manufactures, and they will be feen to improve very rapidly. This is the effect which the commerce of the United States will produce in France. Thefe States contain a people accuftomed to be well clothed, to make ufe of well manufactured things only, and capable of paying for
good

good workmanfhip by their productions. Charged with the furnifhing of articles for American confumption, French manufacturers will
ftrive to outdo their rivals ; and they can eafily
accomplifh this *when Government fhall be wil-*
ling. Nature has given them the means. They
will become fuperior in almoft every thing
when once they fhall no longer be obftinately
counteracted.

Therefore the commerce with the United
States will be the caufe of improvement in
French cultivation and induftry. Confequently
it is neceffary to embrace and purfue it.

C H A P. IV.

THAT THE UNITED STATES ARE OBLIGED BY THEIR PRESENT NECESSITIES AND CIRCUM-STANCES TO ENGAGE IN FOREIGN COM-MERCE.

SOME writers, among whom are found the
celebrated Dr. Price and the Abbé Mably,
have exhorted the independent Americans, if
not to exclude exterior commerce entirely from
their ports, at leaft to keep it within very contracted bounds. They pretend, that the ruin
of

of republicanifm in the United States can happen only from exterior commerce; becaufe by
great quantities of articles of luxury and a frivolous tafte, that commerce would corrupt
their morals, and without pure morals a republic cannot exift.

" Alas ! What can the United States import
" from Europe, continues Dr. Price, except it
" be infection ?   I avow it, cries the Doctor, I
" tremble in thinking on the furor for exterior
" commerce, which is apparently going to turn
" the heads of the Americans.   Every nation
" fpreads nets around the United States, and ca-
" reffes them, in order to gain a preference;
" but their intereft cautions them to beware of
" thefe feductions *."

I am far from contradicting, *in its bafis*, the
opinion of thefe politicians.   Moreover, I think,
with Dr. Price, that the United States will one
day be able to produce every thing neceffary

---

* Price's Obfervations, page 76.   See the Abbé Mably,
what he fays of thefe obfervations, from page 146 to page 163.
See alfo what the Comte de Mirabeau has added to the Obfervations of Dr. Price, in his Reflections printed at the end of
his tranflation of this work, page 319. London edition, 1785.

He has, as a fevere philofopher, treated on exterior commerce, and made abftraction of the actual fituation of the
Americans.

and convenient, but I am alfo of opinion, that thefe two writers have confidered the indepen- dent Americans in a falfe point of view ; that they have not fufficiently obferved the ftate of their circumftances ; in fine, that *their circum- ftances and actual wants oblige them to have re- courfe to foreign commerce.* This is a truth which I propofe to demonftrate ; for I will prove that the independent Americans are in want of the neceffaries and conveniencies of life, and in fome ftates, of luxuries, and that their habits and nature, added to other circumftances, will always prevent their renouncing them en- tirely.

I will prove, that having no manufactures, they cannot themfelves fupply thefe wants, and that they can have no manufactures for a long time to come.

That although they already poffeffed them, they ought to prefer to national ones thofe of exterior commerce, and that they fhould rather invite Europeans to their ports than frequent thofe of the European ftates.

Finally, that by the fame reafon which makes it impoffible to exclude exterior commerce, in cafe of wants which alone it can fupply, it is equally fo to fix its boundaries.

When the nature of man is attentively con- fidered,

fidered, it is feen that it inceffantly difpofes him
to render his life agreeable. If he has a property, he ftrives to improve it ; if the foil he
cultivates be fruitful, and demands but little in
advance, the defire of increafing his enjoyments
ftimulates him to torture his land to draw from
it its various productions. One idea put in
practice gives birth to another ; one want fatif-
fied creates a fecond, to have the pleafure of fa-
tisfying this alfo. Such is the nature of man :
his activity, which leads him from defires to
enjoyments; from one change to another, is
the fource of what are called manufactures.
A manufacture is but the means of giving to
a production of the earth, a form which adds
to it a new degree of agreeablenefs and utility. Want and defire of manufactures are
therefore in the nature of man ; fo that if
we fuppofed Europe entirely annihilated, manufactures would foon rife up in America, becaufe each individual ftrives to render his exiftence agreeable by means the moft fpeedy and
efficacious *.

Manufactures,

* Perhaps the character and life of favages, who are fuppofed to have no manufacturers among them, will be oppofed
to thefe reafonings ? Men are deceived in judging thereby ;
for thefe people, which we look upon as only one degree removed

Manufactures, like the wants of civilized men, may (as was obferved in the laft chapter) be divided into three claffes : 1ft. Thofe of neceffity ; 2d. thofe of convenience ; 3d. thofe of fancy or luxury. Food, and the natural exigencies of mankind, are comprehended in the firft clafs.

It is from the wants of convenience efpecially, that manufactures have their origin. Without doubt, fkins of fheep were fufficient to defend men from the feverities of cold ; a cabin or a hut from the intemperature of the atmof-

moved from a ftate of nature, work up and manufacture the earth's productions. Thus from their corn, before it is ripe, they extract a gelatinous juice, with which they make palatable cakes. Therefore, before the arrival of Europeans, they knew how to make fermented liquors, tools, utenfils, arms, ornaments, &c. They confined themfelves to thefe ; hunting took them from a fedentary life, and did not give them time enough to extend their ideas.

The paftoral life of the Arabians has conducted them one or two degrees farther in the art of manufacturing, becaufe that kind of life affords greater leifure, and gives more uniform and conftant productions. Thofe fhepherds whofe riches confift but in their flocks, and who live on milk alone, and are clothed with their wool only, have a paffionate defire for coffee, fherbet, and fugar. The defire of increafing their enjoyments is the caufe. Let it be therefore agreed, that man by his nature is inclined to enjoyment, and confequently to manufactures.

phere ;

phere; but man is no fooner preferved from one evil, than he feeks to get rid of another. Skins are infufceptible of being well joined together, ufe makes them hard; a cabin is frequently thrown down, is confined and fmoaky; whence arife the wants of conveniency, which are transformed into enjoyments, whofe accuftomed ufe changes them into neceffities.

When man has every convenience, he then thinks of ornament. Hence the wants of luxury; they are entirely in the imagination, and procure imaginary pleafures only. Therefore to wear any laced clothes, or drink coffee out of a china rather than a delfen cup, is a want created by luxury or fancy.

The nature of thefe three kinds of want being pointed out, it is neceffary to know what thofe of the Americans are. They have the two firft of them. Their habitudes contracted in their infancy from European emigrants, and their commerce with the Englifh, have accuftomed them to the kind of life and tafte of the latter, and it is well known that Englifh induftry has been particularly directed to neceffary and ufeful arts.

The independent Americans, at leaft thofe who inhabit great maritime cities, have borrowed from the Englifh a tafte for luxuries; they

feek

feek for gauzes, blond lace, filks, &c. It is
however with pleafure I obferve, that if this
tafte of modes has infected London within thefe
few years, its ravages have not been extended
with the fame rapidity in the United States as
in Europe. Their fituation, auftere religion,
morals, and ancient habits, their rural or marine
life, prevent their feeking after elegance and
drefs, and keep them from oftentation and vo-
luptuoufnefs. Although they may perhaps be
changed a few degrees, the evil is not yet fenfible, at leaft in the Northern States *. Therefore our obfervations ought principally to reft
upon the two firft claffes of wants. Now it
is impoffible that the Americans fhould ever renounce them ; they will be perpetually led and
attached to them by their nature and habitudes,
and by the manner in which their population
is increafed.

By their nature, becaufe they are men; and
it has been proved, that man is endowed with

---

* Luxury is certainly to be found in Virginia ; and when
we fpeak of luxury with refpect to free America, it is neceffary
to diftinguifh carefully the Southern from the Northern States ;
cities from the country ; maritime cities from interior ones.
By thefe diftinctions many contrarieties in the accounts of fu-
perficial travellers may be explained.

that

that activity which perpetually difpofes him to add to his enjoyments.

By their habitudes, becaufe, as it has been obferved, they contracted that of all thofe wants, and it is well known, that a tafte for pleafure is not to be exterminated when rooted by habitude. How can it be required of man to deprive himfelf of wine and liquors to which he is accuftomed, and in which he places a part of his enjoyments, except we would render him unhappy? I will not quote hermits, fick perfons, or philofophers, who have had that empire over themfelves; but let not a like prodigy be expected in a whole nation. An affociation of three millions of philofophers has not yet been, nor will be feen to confine themfelves to the regimen of Pythagoras *, or the diet of Cornaro.

The fevere facrifice of tea, which the independent Americans made at the beginning of the war, will perhaps be alfo quoted. The enthufiafm of liberty and influence of example were able, during fome time, to overcome their

* It is not that we ought not to believe that one of the great means of regenerating the old people of the Continent, and of fupporting republicanifm in the United States, would be to give to children fuch an education as Pythagoras exercifed at Crotona.—*See the Life of Pythagoras.*

habitudes;

habitudes *; as religious enthusiasm has combated, sometimes successfully, the passions of an
hermit. But there is no cause powerful enough
to produce a like effect, except in the crisis
which makes the facrifice necessary and easy.
The reason of the dependence in which the
Americans would put themselves with respect
to the Europeans, and the fear of distant corruption, are motives too feeble to carry men to
that point of heroism ! It is not sufficiently de-
monstrated to them, that they cannot drink
wine from Madeira without being some day
corrupted by it, and without preparing the way
for great calamities.

The manner in which population is renewed
and increased in America, does not make it probable that its inhabitants will ever be able to renounce the want of European productions.

A prodigious number of individuals emigrate
every year from all parts of Europe to America,
who carry with them wants and inclinations

* It is assured that abstinence from tea was not every where
faithfully observed, which appears very probable on reflecting
that there was a party which fain would have violated it. I
have known several persons whom the deprivation of tea had
made ill for a long time, although they had tried illusive means,
by substituting the infusion of agreeable simples for that of the
tea-leaf.

which

which they have from education and habit. If
they find them in America, they continue to
gratify them ; if they are unknown there, they
naturalize them, and it is the firſt thing they
go about ; for they do not ſo much perceive the
new pleaſures they are going to enjoy, as thoſe
of which they are deprived ; ſo great is the
force of our firſt habits and cuſtoms. Remembrance, although frequently mixed with the
cruel idea of ſervitude, abandons man in the
grave only.

According to this inclination, natural to all
men, let the immenſe variety of wants and ap-
petites be calculated which are going to tranſ-
plant themſelves from Europe to the United
States ; and let it be judged, whether it be poſſible to put bounds to or deſtroy them.

To ſucceed in this, it would not only be neceſſary to ſhut out foreign commerce from all
the American ports : American induſtry muſt
be circumſcribed, and the ſource of their wants
ſtopped up ; it would be neceſſary to imitate the
Lacedemonian law, which ordained that nothing ſhould be worked up but with the heavy
hatchet, the more effectually to baniſh the luxury of elegant furniture. In a word, a miracle
muſt be operated upon the Americans, to take
from them all remembrance of what they have
been,

been, of all they have feen, fmelt, or tafted; and the fame enchantment muft deprive European emigrants of their ideas; as it would be abfurd to hope for a like prodigy, *the force of things*, which drags the independent Americans into exterior commerce, muft be fubmitted to*. All is reduced to two words; America has wants, and Europe has manufactures.

In the United States fome of the inhabitants fill up the leifure afforded by agriculture (in which the Europeans cannot hope to become their rivals) with an attention to manufactures. And they have others confined to the moft neceffary arts; connected with cultivation, fifheries, and the conftruction of veffels. But even thefe manufactures are but few in number, and infufficient for the wants of the United States. They are therefore obliged to have recourfe to Europe. It is not that they neither have, nor can have almoft all the raw materials employed

---

* It is with regret that I write this fact, on confidering it philofophically, but it appears to have been demonftrated politically. No perfon wifhes more than I do to fee the United States feparate themfelves from all the world, and in this fituation to find again the aufterity of the Spartan regimen, without its cruel principles of military difpofition. It would be a fmart ftroke in politics; but this unhappily is no more than a dream.

in

in our own manufactures. They have hemp,
flax, and cotton *.

But, if they had raw materials in plenty, they
ought to be advifed not to eftablifh manufactures ; or, to fpeak more juftly, *manufactures
could not be eftablifhed ; the nature of things or-
dains it fo*. Let us difcufs this queftion, as it
is an important one.

There are many reafons for men's engaging in
a new country in agriculture rather than in manufactures. There, where two individuals can
eafily live together, they marry, fays Montefquieu. The labour of the field offers to them
more means of living together, of augmenting
and fupporting their family, than working at

* The four Southern States gather great quantities of cotton. Their poor are clothed with it winter and fummer. In
winter they wear cotton fhirts, and clothes of wool and cotton
mixed. In fummer their fhirts are linen, and their outward
clothes of cotton. Women's drefs is entirely of cotton, and
made up by themfelves, women of the richeft clafs excepted ;
yet a woman of this clafs has a deal of cotton worked up in
her houfe, and this callico equals in beauty that of Europe.
Thofe from the South furnifh a deal of cotton to the States of
the North, which cannot grow it, the climate being too cold.

There is fcarcely any part of the United States without good
flour and faw mills. The Northern States have others for
flattening iron. It is in the conftruction of mills efpecially,
that the Americans diftinguifh themfelves, in varying their employ and utility, and in their diftribution.

manufac-

manufactures : in thefe the dependence of the workman, his precarious and changeable ftate, his moderate wages, and the high price of provifions in cities, where moft manufactures are eftablifhed, put it out of his power to think of having a companion, and if he has one, the profpect of mifery which fhe muft have before her eyes after his death, impofes on him a law contrary to propagation, to avoid the cruelty of caufing children to be brought into the world only to be unhappy *.

In a new country where land is not dear, where it requires not much in advance, or an expenfive cultivation, and is at the fame time fruitful, the number of little and happy families muft rapidly increafe.

What a difference in other refpects from this pure and fimple country life, where man is conftantly in the prefence of nature, where his foul is elevated by the fpectacle, where his phyfical principles continually regenerate by a fa-

---

* Journeymen manufacturers, and in general men in a ftate of dependence, whofe fubfiftence is precarious, and who have children, certainly love them lefs than the inhabitants of the country who have a fmall property. The paternity is a burthen, and confequently often odious to the firft ; their children are ignorant of the foft careffes of paternal love. What kind of generation muft arife from fuch a connexion !

lubrious air, and in reviving exercifes, where he lives in the midft of his relations and friends, whom he makes happy : what a difference from that to the life of manufacturers condemned to vegetate in difmal prifons, where they refpire infection, and where their minds are abforbed, as well as their lives abridged. This conduct alone ought to decide the Americans to reject the painful ftate of manufactures *.

Befides

---

* The idea of property is one of the ftrongeft ties by which man is attached to life, to his country, to virtue, and I will add even to health. The fatisfaction of a manufacturer, who at the end of the week has a guinea in his pocket, is far from that of the little country proprietor, who is feldom poffeffed of fuch a fum ; but who gathers in his own field every thing neceffary. He loves it, fees it always with pleafure, takes care of its cultivation, and, by a confequence of this foft difpofi-tion, he attaches himfelf to the animals which affift him in that cultivation.

The labourer fees, as he works, the poffibility of increafing the number of his children ; and he has the pleafing hope of leaving them after his death a little corner of earth which will keep them from indigence.

The labourer is happy becaufe his contracts are with the earth only, which gives liberally and difintereftedly, whilft the intereft of the mafter who pays the manufacturer embitters the wages which he receives.

The labourer is ftill happy, becaufe he is only amongft his equals ; inequality is the fource of malice. The fuperior is

malicious

Befides there will be, for a confiderable time to come, more to be gained in the United States, by

malicious to fupport his oppreffion. The flave is vindictive to deftroy and revenge it.

The labourer is amiable and generous, becaufe it would be neceffary to abandon all cultivation, if there were not between hufbandmen a reciprocity of fervices and confidence.

Perhaps it would not be difficult to prove that health and goodnefs are diminifhed in proportion to the increafe of manufactures, cities, property, and the defertion of rural life, and that vices and crimes are increafed in the fame proportion.

This is not the opinion of the fenfible and interefting author of the Study of Nature : " When I was at Mofcow," fays he, (Vol. III.) " an old Genevois, who was in that city, " in the time of Peter I. told me, that fince different means " of fubfiftence had been opened to the people by the eftab- " lifhment of manufactures and commerce, feditions, affaffina- " tions, robberies, and incendiaries, had been lefs frequent than " formerly."

But this would not have exifted, and there would have been the fame public and private virtue, if inftead of making the Ruffians manufacturers, they had been made proprietors of lands.   Hufbandmen are honeft people, fays M. de St. Perre himfelf.—And workfhops, as I have juft obferved, do not offer that neceffity of reciprocal fervice which gives the habitude of goodnefs ; they prefent intereft ftruggling againft intereft, rich and indolent ftupidity ftriving to cheat active indigence.   If workfhops do not make men rafcals, they difpofe them to become fo ; they make them egotifts, infenfible, uncouth, and bad fathers.

Therefore, the fact quoted by this author does not prove, that by the earth, which yields abundantly, than by manufactures—and man places himself in that fituation where the greateft and moft fpeedy gain is to be acquired.

As population muft, for many ages, be difproportioned to the extent of the United States, land will be cheap there during the fame length of time *, and confequently the inhabitants will for a long time be cultivators.

Thofe

---

that to prevent crimes, it is neceffary to eftablifh manufactures ; but that it is better to have manufactures peopled with degraded workmen, than forefts with banditti ; 'tis a leffer evil, but it is ftill an evil.

* An idea of the price of lands in the United States, may be formed from the following article taken from the Gazette of Philadelphia, of 9th of December 1784 : "Obferve that the "ground of Pennfylvania begins to be dear, and that the inha- "bitants begin to emigrate to Kentucky."—By this adver- tifement there are offered to fale, "25,000 acres of land, fitu- "ated in the county of Northampton, State of Pennfylvania, "upon the Delawar.—A public road, a navigable river, fertile "foil, excellent for culture—meadows—places for mills— "great forefts—plenty of fifh-ponds, &c. at half a guinea an "acre.

"Another quantity of 25,000 acres, upon the Sufquehan- "nah, with equal and even greater advantages, at the fame "price.—Good title deeds,—facilities of payment.—A referve "of three hundred acres only will be required in each diftrict "for the maintenance of the clergyman of the parifh ;—one "hundred

Thofe whom ambition, thirft of gain, or ignorance, fhould incline to eftablifh manufactures,
will, from that moment, be difbanded from it
by the dearnefs of workmanfhip. This dearnefs is already very confiderable *, and may become ftill more fo, as the caufe which occafions
it muft naturally become more extended.

What is the caufe? It has already been inti-
mated fo as to be forefeen.

Cities are built in all quarters †; lands are
cleared and eftablifhments made every where.
In the county of Kentucky, for inftance, where,
in 1771, there were fcarcely one hundred inhabitants, there are now nearly thirty thoufand;
and thefe men have emigrated from inhabited
coafts or countries. Thus hands are taken from
the commerce and agriculture of thefe laft;
which is confequently the caufe of the increafed price of workmanfhip.

" hundred guineas when there fhall be fifty families, to build a
" parfonage houfe—ten guineas a year for five years, and pro-
" vifion for the fchool-mafter."

    * Three, four, and five livres, are frequently paid in the
cities of the United States for the day's work of a carpenter,
lockfmith, &c.

    † This is a great evil, as will be hereafter proved, and
which will contribute more than any other to the ruin of republican fpirit.

From

From this dearnefs it has been concluded in Europe, that the people in America were wretched; a contrary conclufion ought to have been drawn. Wherever workmen govern; wherever they are paid a high price, the people are neceffarily happy; for it is of them that the various claffes of workmen are compofed.

On the contrary, wherever workmanfhip is at a low price, the people are wretched; for this cheapnefs proves, that there are more work-men than there is work to execute, more want of employ than can be fupplied. This is what the rich defire, that they may govern the work-men, and buy the fweat of their brows at the loweft rate poffible *.

It is the reverfe in America, the workman gives the law, and fo much the better, he re-ceives it too often every where elfe.

---

* To be convinced of this truth, look at England and France; workmanfhip is very dear in London but cheap in Paris. The workman in London is well fed, clothed and paid; in Paris he is quite the contrary.

" It frequently happens," faid an American one day to me, " that I meet in the United States a ploughman, conducting his " plough and horfes, and eating a wing of a turkey and a piece " of good white bread. I have feen, added he, a veffel arrive " at New York, full of Scotchmen, not one of whom was un- " employed the next day."

This

This dearnefs of workmanfhip is prejudicial to manufactures, and ftill fo much the better. Thefe eftablifhments are fo many tombs which fwallow up generations entire *. Agriculture, on the contrary, perpetually increafes population.

By preventing, or at leaft retarding the rife of manufactures within their provinces, the Americans will ftop the decadency of morals and public fpirit : for if manufactures bring gold into the States, they bring at the fame time a poifon which undermines them. They refemble a number of individuals whofe nature and morals are at once corrupted : they form and accuftom men to fervitude, and give in a republic a preponderance to ariftocratical principles, and by accumulating riches in a fmall number of hands, they caufe republics to incline to ariftocracy.

Therefore the independent Americans will do wifely to leave to Europe the care of manufac-

---

* There are feveral manufactures at Amiens, and it is remarked, that the hofpitals are more filled with manufacturers than with mafons or other like artizans. A manufacturing life makes more people ill and their complaints more dangerous; it is becaufe this kind of workmen becomes fooner debauched, and goes fooner to the hofpital, being moftly fingle, and without any domeftic attachment.

turing

turing for them, becaufe fhe is irrefiftibly drag-
ged into manufactures ; and as their population
and confumption muft rapidly increafe, it is not
impoffible that Europe may one day confine herfelf to this kind of occupation, and that America may one day become her ftorehoufe of
grain and raw materials, of which fhe will not
be in need. In this cafe, nothing will be feen
in Europe but cities and workfhops ; in independent America, nothing but fields well cultivated. I will leave it to be decided which country would have the moft happy fate.

Under the fame point of view, the independent Americans will ftill act wifely by leaving
it to the Europeans to furnifh them with neceffary articles; and in feldom frequenting the cities
and fea-ports of the ancient continent. In effect,
an European tranfported to independent America
is in the proportion of one to one hundred, and
fometimes to a thoufand.—His example has
therefore but very little influence ; the luxury
of which he makes a parade in paffing by, excites lefs confideration or refpect than contempt
and ridicule. If he leaves a remembrance of
himfelf, it is foon effaced by the general motion :
there are, moreover, fome Europeans, who,
ftruck and edified by the manners and cuftoms

of

of free America, have good fenfe enough to refpect and conform themfelves to them.

It is the reverfe when an American goes on
fhore in Europe, almoft alone, with his fimplicity of manners in the midft of a vortex of
men who efteem the eclat of exterior appearance
only ; who, agitated and led by the general ton,
facrifice every thing to the furor of making a
great figure by the brilliance of drefs, equipage,
and pomp : this American muft at firft be torn
down and tormented, becaufe he finds himfelf
thrown into a circle of habitudes contrary to his
own.   Afterwards he becomes familiarifed by
little and little, and if he does not quite get a
tafte for them, at leaft his attachment to a fimplicity of life and manners is neceffarily weakened.   Carrying back with him to his own
country this difpofition of mind, he introduces
it infenfibly into the minds of thofe who are
about him, upon which it has fome influence—
upon the minds of his children and friends.
Their tafte for fimplicity becomes lukewarm
by his example, and the following age fees public virtues fall into indifference.

It will be lefs dangerous to the public fpirit
of the independent Americans to admit the Europeans into theUnited States, than to go themfelves

felves into Europe; from which it refults that
it would be very impolitic to encourage the former to become the carriers of their exterior
commerce.

I have infifted upon this reflection becaufe
there feems to have appeared in fome States a
difpofition to give premiums for diftant navigation. They ought to reflect, that they have
but few hands, and that as few as poffible fhould
be taken from culture. They are in the fituation I have fpoken of in my principles of exterior commerce, where a nation gains by making carriers of others having lefs foil or employ.
They fhould alfo recollect, that republican morals are better preferved in the bofom of agriculture than upon the fea and in foreign voyages, which give to men communications with
other morals and governments.

It is a general queftion in the United States,
by what means it is poffible to put bounds to
exterior commerce, and ftop the progrefs of luxury: ftay at home,—cultivate, cultivate, I will
repeat to them; this is the fecret whereby you
will prevent the increafe of luxury; a fecret
much preferable to fumptuary laws and prohibitory regulations, which fome ftates have it in
contemplation to make.

There

There is no power great enough to fet, by regulations, fuch boundaries to exterior commerce as will not be exceeded: to circumfcribe it for inftance to merchandizes of convenience, without the importation of thofe of luxury. The nature or force of things only has fuch a power. That force has, as has been before explained, the union of the natural circumftances of a nation ; thefe circumftances alone mark the limits of commerce. A nation which cannot pay for luxuries with its own production, does not purchafe them. The favage can only procure with his furs, brandy, gunpowder, and woollen coverings; he buys neither filks nor laces.

If, therefore, the productions of the United States be fcarcely fufficient to pay for the importations of neceffity and convenience from Europe, merchandizes of luxury will not be imported: if thefe be carried to it, 'tis becaufe it can pay for them. There is no merchant who likes to ruin himfelf.

If, on the contrary, the United States have productions proper for the ancient continent, in quantities fufficient to procure, by their exchange, not only the moft neceffary and convenient things, but even thofe of luxury, nothing can hinder

hinder the latter from being fooner or later imported, by means of exterior commerce.

In truth, to increafe demands of this nature, the public opinion, which before treated opprobrioufly a tafte for modes, muft totally change, and the particular opinions of certain fects equally yield to it.

But notwithftanding the powerful influence of opinion upon merchandizes of luxury, the fate of this kind of commerce will be more particularly determined by the ftate of the independent Americans, for when rich they will adopt them. This fact will appear certain, if what has been faid on the nature of the human heart be recollected, and its inclination to improve man's fituation, and to increafe his enjoyments.

Tafte for a rural life alone, if the Americans preferve it, will retard the progrefs of luxury, which fprings up in cities, from fatiety, want of fomething to do, and from laffitude: employment preferves the country from thofe moral ills.

There is one laft confideration, which ought to perfuade the independent Americans to employ themfelves in cultivation, and reject both manufactures and exterior tranfports; which is, that

that in wifhing to undertake every thing at once, the fcarcity of money, neceffary at leaft for the mechanical part of thefe operations, will always be more perceived, whilft, by giving themfelves up entirely to cultivation, they will procure from their foil productions fufficient to pay for thefe manufactures from Europe, and to make up for the fcarcity of coin *.

They

* The independent Americans have but little money; this fcarcity arifes from two caufes; firft, from the kind of commerce they heretofore carried on with England, and afterwards from the ravages of a feven years war. As this commerce was purely one of exchange, and that in certain ftates, as Virginia, the importations always furpaffed the exportations; the refult was, that they could not but be debtors to England, and could not draw money from that ifland.

It was a kind of commercial fervitude, which the Englifh looked upon as the pledge and guarantee of the dependence of the Colonies upon the mother country.

The money they had came from their illicit commerce with the Sugar Iflands and European powers. The war, afterwards, by changing labourers into foldiers, caufed a part of their lands to remain without cultivation. From that time exchanges increafed and money decreafed. The little of it remaining in America, came firft from money carried and expended there by the Englifh and French armies, and afterwards by the loans negociated in Europe by Congrefs.

But it is eafy to conceive, after what has been faid upon the quantity of coin, how a nation, which, by an extraordinary revolution, is all at once widely developed, its population rapidly

They appear to be alarmed at this; what has been faid upon the fubject of money ought to remove their fears. It has been demonftrated that a nation may carry on a very confiderable commerce without its aid. It will hereafter be feen that the United States produce many raw materials effentially neceffary to France, and that fhe can make their exports with greater advantage than thofe of any other country.

Thus it appears that thefe two countries may carry on together a direct trade of exchange without money, confequently an advantageous one; for the exchange between them of pro- ductions is more lucrative than an exchange of productions for money; although this opinion may not be adopted by men in general, who at- tach a greater price to gold than to merchan- dize, and continually forget its reprefentative value, to fubftitute for it a real one. It muft be inceffantly repeated to them that money would be abfolutely nothing without produc-

---

pidly increafed, and is thereby obliged to continual advances, for clearing of lands, for building, making of roads and canals, to pay foreign debts, moftly in fpecie, and which has no mines, muft feel the fcarcity of money, and the reafon of it is clear: the want of it is at prefent fupplied, in Connecticut, by an ex- change of commodities, or thefe againft labour.

tions;

tions; that a rich people is that which, by its induſtry, increaſes population, and has conſequently an abundance of productions; that the ſecret of increaſing the quantity of coin conſiſts only in the art of multiplying neceſſary productions, and it is this to which the United States ought to incline, without being anxious about the money which they may have at preſent or in future.

Let us reſume the different queſtions contained in this chapter.

My object has been to make it appear that the United States were forced by their neceſſity and circumſtances to engage in exterior commerce.

To convince my readers of this, I have proved that the independent Americans had wants of neceſſity, of convenience, and even ſome of luxury, which they could neither renounce nor ſupply themſelves with.

That having no manufactures of their own, they were obliged to have recourſe to thoſe of Europe: that they could eſtabliſh none for a long time, having but few hands, and that cultivation ought to employ all their cares.

That according to phyſical, political, and moral relations, they ought to perſevere in applying

ing themfelves to agriculture alone, and even give up all thoughts of tranfporting to Europe, by their own means, their proper productions.

That this was the only means of preferving their republican morals, and of retarding the progrefs of luxury.

In fine, that by engaging in agriculture, and neglecting manufactures, they will lefs perceive the want of money, and will find the means of fupplying that want, and of carrying on a very advantageous exterior commerce of exchange of commodities.

Thefe different points being firmly eftablifh-ed, it is at prefent neceffary to prove, that of all the nations of Europe, France is the moft proper to enter into a commercial alliance with the United States, and that their neceffities and pro-ductions are correfpondent to each other. It is propofed to lay open this truth, by prefenting the double table of reciprocal importations and exportations, to be made between France and free America.

CHAP.

CHAP. V.

OF THE IMPORTATION TO BE MADE FROM
FRANCE INTO THE UNITED STATES, OR
OF THE WANTS OF THE UNITED STATES,
AND THE PRODUCTIONS OF FRANCE WHICH
CORRESPOND THERETO.

THE attentive reader will have already
been able to judge, that if the independent Americans do not deviate from the career
which is open to them, Europe will, for a long
time, have to furnish them with manufactured
merchandize. It has been made to appear, that
the clearing and cultivation of lands, and all that
relates to interior commerce, such as roads and
canals, offered to their industry the most favourable and useful employ, especially whilst imposts do not restrain their movements, and that
a free constitution equally honours every individual.

It is now necessary to take a cursory view of
their wants, and to point out those articles with
which France may pretend to furnish them in
competition

competition with other nations, if even fhe cannot do it more advantageoufly than her rivals.
I will follow, in this enumeration, the Englifh
publications which have treated upon the matter, and particularly that of *Lord Sheffield:* he
has omitted nothing, becaufe his country pretends to furnifh every thing *.

SECTION I.

WINES.

Wine becomes a real want of thofe who have
once been acquainted with it. Happy or miferable, rich or poor, every body makes ufe of
wine. Wine is the delight of the happy or of
the rich. It helps the unfortunate to fupport
his forrow; the poor think they find it an equivalent for the food they are without.

Eafe has lately been too general in the United
States, not to have introduced the ufe of wine;
and futurity, by augmenting their means, will
only increafe their want of this liquor.

---

* I will not defcend to the minutiæ his Lordfhip has done,
but I will prove, in every important article, the French, if
they know how to profit by their natural advantages, muft
obtain a preference.

The

The wines which were moſt generally conſumed in the United States, were, as in England, Oporto, Madeira, and ſome from Spain. French wines charged as in Britain, with enormous duties, were introduced by contraband only.

Liberty has cauſed thoſe Britannic ſhackles to diſappear. French wines are freely imported into the United States, and pay but little duty.

Such is the ſtate of things, and it leads me to the diſcuſſion of three queſtions:

Does it ſuit the United States to cultivate vines, and to make wine?

Ought they not, in renouncing this cultivation, to give the preference to French wines?

And what means ought the French to uſe, in order to obtain and preſerve this preference?

It would be abſurd to deny, that the United States can produce wine, becauſe the experiments hitherto made have been fruitleſs. Extended as they are, and having countries as ſouthern as Europe, it is impoſſible there ſhould not be, in many places, a ſoil proper for the vine.

The little ſucceſs of attempts may therefore, without hazarding too much, be attributed either

ther to the ignorance of the cultivator, his want
of perfeverance, or a bad choice of plants.

However that may be, if the Americans will
hearken to the counfels of able obfervers, and
reap advantage from the errors of other nations,
they will carefully avoid the cultivation of vines.
In every country where they have been cultivated, for one rich man, they have made a number wretched.

The long and confiderable advances which
vines require, the preparation, prefervation, and
fale, of their produce, have put all the good
vineyard plots into the hands of rich people,
who not cultivating thefe themfelves, pay the
real cultivator very badly. The falary of the
wretched vine-dreffer is every where inevitably
fixed; the time he does not work not being
calculated, and few wine countries offer any
employ by which loft time may be filled up;
and otherwife, the variations in the prices of the
moft neceffary commodities occafioned by a
thoufand caufes, by the abundance or even fcarcity of wine, are not confidered for him.

Would it be believed, that abundance is the
moft unfortunate thing that can happen, either
to the proprietor or the vine-dreffer? In fact,
the expence of gathering augments, and the

price

price of the thing diminifhes. There is more work to be done, more hands are neceffary, and they are paid more wages ; more hogfheads are wanted, the expences of carriage greater, more fpace is required, the fale is lefs, and confe-quently the income*.

The fcarcity of wines, or the fterility of the vineyard, is perhaps lefs unfortunate than the abundance, at leaft to the proprietor. But it is cruelly felt by the vine-dreffer, and thofe wandering troops of day labourers, whom the

---

* The day's work of a vintager varies according to the fcarcity or abundance of wine, from fix to fifty fols. The price of hogfheads has likewife variations in a different price, from three to fifteen livres. There are years wherein the price of the hogfhead is higher than that of the wine which it contains.

The proprietor who eftablifhes his expences upon his re-venues, is every year deceived by thofe of the vineyard. In one year he receives at the rate of 20 for 100 ; the fecond year his vineyard is perhaps deftroyed by hail ; the third he is ex-pofed to bankrupcy, or to fuffer by it, or his wines turn four ; the fourth he may have but a moderate produce, which will not compenfate for his preceding loffes. In ten years time a proprietor would fcarcely find an average year which was to-lerably good ; yet, as men love to exaggerate their riches and means, each proprietor calculates his revenue upon the higheft produce that his vineyard has ever yielded : the greateft part of them fpend in confequence, and are ruined.

ingratitude

ingratitude of their foil, or a bad government, forces to go from home in fearch of employ.

The numerous variations which have an influence upon the produce of the vineyard, make it very inconvenient property, and triflingly advantageous *. The return muft be waited for when much has been gathered; payments muft be made when there has been but little. The proprietor muft therefore have other refources, whether it be to wait or to pay. The vine-dreffer, unhappy enough to have a property †, without any of thefe refources, ruins himfelf fooner or later. He is obliged to fell at a low price ‡, or to confume his wines himfelf;

thence

---

* It is a proverb in France, that there is no property worfe conditioned than that of the vineyard.

† The fituation of a vine-dreffer is different according to the cuftom of countries. In fome he is hired only by the day, and there he is completely wretched. In others, as in Switzerland, he has half of the produce. But an unjuft and tyran-nical tax, laid on by the proprietors themfelves, reduces this half to a quarter part.

‡ Such is nearly the fituation of moft of the vine-dreffers of *Aunis*, who are proprietors. They are at the mercy of the rich farmers of that country. When winter comes, the vine-dreffer has neither bread nor money. He goes to the farmer,

afks

thence refults his ftupidity and idlenefs, his difcouragement, his dull and quarrelfome humour,
and efpecially the ruin of his health. Too much
wine in the time of abundance, no bread in that
of fcarcity; thefe are the two alternatives which
divide his life.

Therefore countries covered with vineyards,
are generally lefs peopled, and prefent a picture
of a degenerated, weak, and wretched population. For the moft part they want hands to
cultivate the vineyard in a feafon when work
cannot be delayed. It is done by thefe bands
of ftrangers, of whom I have already fpoken,
and who come to fell fome days work to the
poor vine-dreffer.

The cultivation of a vineyard cannot be better compared than to thofe manufactures, of

afks him for both : the farmer fays I will accommodate you,
give me your note.   The bufhel of wheat is worth fix livres,
oblige yourfelf to return me, at a certain epocha, the quantity
of wheat which fhall be fold for fix livres.   He always takes
care to fix the time when corn is at a low price.   The obligation is paffed, the moment of payment arrives ; the vine-
dreffer, who has corn, gives more than he has received.   If
he has none, he is ftill more embarraffed ; the farmer preffes
him, you have wine fays he, fell it me.   But at what price?
The farmer offers a very low one.   It is refufed, he threatens,
the poor vine-dreffer is obliged to ruin himfelf, and this fcene
is annually repeated.

which

which the hopes of fuccefs are founded, upon
the low price of workmanfhip, and which enrich none but the undertakers, and retailers or
fhopkeepers.

The pernicious influence of the vine is extended, in wine countries, to even thofe who
do not cultivate it ; for the cheapnefs of wine
leads to exceffes, and confequently it becomes
a poifón for all ranks of fociety, for thofe efpecially who find in it a means of forgetting their
forrows.

Therefore, as I have already remarked, induftry carefully avoids thefe dangerous vineyard plots.   None of the great manufactures,
whofe fuccefs is the confequence of order, affi-
duity, and labour, are feen in the neighbourhood
of them.

The refult of all thefe obfervations is, that
the Americans ought to profcribe the cultivation of the vine.

It would infallibly render miferable that clafs
of fociety which fhould apply itfelf to it, and in
a republic there fhould be none who are
wretched, becaufe want obliges them to difturb
civil order, or, what is worfe, becaufe they are
at the command of the rich by whom they are
                                        paid,

paid, and who may make ufe of them to deftroy republicanifm *.

Confidered with refpect to the proprietors, the
vine ought ftill to be profcribed by the United
States ; becaufe every profeffion or calling, fufceptible of too great a variation of fortune,
which fometimes heaps up riches to one perfon,
and at other reduces to indigence individuals in
eafy circumftances, ought carefully to be avoided.—Economy, fimplicity, private virtues, are
not attached to fuch changeablenefs.

They are found in the bofom of mediocrity
only, from eafinefs of circumftances, founded
upon that kind of toil whofe produce is conftant †.   Such is that of agriculture in general;
it embraces divers productions, which, in cafe
of accident, replace each other ‡.

Finally,

* The mean language of fhopkeepers, who humbly offer
their merchandize, has already begun to find its way into the
American papers.

† The Indians are almoft all cultivators or weavers, which
is the reafon why private morals have been better preferved
among thefe people than any where elfe, in fpite of the exceffes of defpotifm.

‡ What recompence would be confiderable enough for an
ingenious man, who fhould give to humanity the means of
preferving potatoes for feveral years, efpecially if the procefs
were

Finally, if it be infifted that wine is neceffary to man, let it not ftupify him ; it fhould
be ufed with moderation, and its dearnefs alone
may oblige men to be moderate in the ufe of
it.   It being greatly the intereft of the American Republics to remove all exceffes from individuals, in order to prevent this degeneracy,
they ought to keep perpetually at a diftance
from them a production, whofe dearnefs will
prevent the abufe of it, whofe cultivation would
render it cheap, and confequently bring on dangerous exceffes both to policy and morals *.

The catalogue which I have juft gone over,
of the evils and abufes occafioned by the culture of vines, will not induce the French to
pull up theirs.   But it ought at leaft to excite

were fimple and not expenfive ? In that cafe want would be
no longer feared.   The embarraffment about the legiflation
of corn would difappear, and mifery perhaps be driven from
among men.

  * It will be objected, that men employed in agriculture,
have need of wine to fupport them in their labour. This is
but an opinion : there are found, in countries where it is leaft
ufed, vigorous and indefatigable men.   In truth, wine contains an active fpirit which may fupply the want of fubftantial
aliment, and it is for this reafon the peafants have recourfe to
wine or brandy, which is more within their reach. Give
them meat and potatoes, and they will eafily do without wine.

them

them to increafe in foreign markets the confumption of wines, in order to keep up their
price, and confequently to diminifh a part of
the evils which they produce. This will be
doubly advantageous, by an additional exterior
profit, and a diminution of interior ill. Nobody
will deny that French wines muft obtain the
preference in the United States. They are the
moft agreeable, the moft varied, and wholefome,
if moderately ufed; the leaft prejudicial, if ufed
to excefs. They ought to be the bafis of our
exportations to America; no nation can raife a
competition with us. Lord Sheffield himfelf
pays this homage to our wines; but in order
to affure to them this advantage for ever, the
art of making, preferving, and tranfporting
them muft be improved.

In general we are at prefent far from this * :
ignorance,

---

* I will quote, for inftance, the wines of Provence, which
by their ftrength ought to be capable of fupporting the longeft
voyages; and by their analogy to the wines of Portugal, would
have the greateft fuccefs in the United States, if they were
properly prepared. Thefe wines have hitherto been in the
loweft repute in the North, in the Indian and American colonies; and that becaufe, on one hand, the fitters out of veffels
brought them without choofing, and on the other, the individual having no idea of the culture of vines, nor of the preparation

ignorance, old prejudices, difcouragement of the people, impoft on exportation; all concur to retard the progrefs of improvement.

The United States (thefe ftates of fo new a date) already furnifh us the model of an inftitution, which alone would encourage the culture of corn and vines, and make the momentary inconvenience of abundant vintages, which ruin the proprietor and farmer, difappear.

This inftitution, eafy to be naturalized in France, would have two branches, a depofit in the public magazines of the productions of the earth; certificate or billets of depofit which would form an authentic title for the difpofing proprietor, transferable without formalities at the current price, like all other public effects.

It is thus, that in Virginia means have been

paration of wine, mixed the white grape with the red, did not diftinguifh the plants, the foil, nor fituation; cured it by rote, without paying attention to the difference of years and qualities; put into his tubs, to give, as he pretended, a higher flavor to his wine, all forts of deteftable ingredients, fuch as falt, lime, plaifter, and pigeon's dung; put it into bad cafks of chefnut-tree; left in them a year's fediment, and never drew off the wine, fo that it was always more inclined to turn four then any other wine, and therefore became little fit for a foreign voyage.

found

found to fupply the want of money *, and to give, at the time of reaping, a real and ufeful value to tobacco, which, without that, waiting for a demand, lies heavy upon the proprietor.

This is not the place to examine this idea profoundly, neither to deftroy the objections which will be made againft it. This project may conftitute the matter of a memoir by itfelf. I give here nothing more than the title †.

People

* The Virginians have given another example which proves how eafy it is to do without money. Many countries near to the Ohio, having none of it, the general affembly refolved, they fhould pay their quota of imports in hemp and flax, which fhould be depofited in the public magazines.

† If it were wifhed that this project fhould fucceed, it would be abfolutely neceffary to put away all poffibility of an abufe unpunifhed. It would perhaps be neceffary, that government fhould take no part, nor have any influence in it. This precaution will be exclaimed againft, but let us once more caft our eyes upon England. If there be a government upon earth whofe hands are tied, whofe fteps are watched, whofe actions are brought to light, to public cenfure, and confequently, whofe fecret attempts are lefs to be feared by the people, it is that of England. See what the aftonifhing Minifter, who is now at the head of affairs, propofes to hinder the intervention and influence of the Englifh government in the new plan of redemption of the public effects and of their decreafe. He infifts, that the commiffioners who fhall be charged with it, fhall be always independent of government; that they fhall be public agents, and that no force fhall conftrain

People in the United States, complain of an abufe in the commerce of the French wines, which abufe, it is of importance to remedy in

ftrain them to alienate from its object the money deftined to pay off or leffen the public debt.

This minifter clearly perceived, that the confidence of the people ought to be gained at any price, for the eftablifhment which exifts but by confidence; and that in fuch a cafe, the facrifice of power would fignify nothing to a government which is really willing to prevent abufes.

The advantages refulting from a plan like this are vifible. Public depofitories would fupply the defect of ability in thofe who could not lay up the productions of the earth. They would prevent fquandering, loffes, and fcarcity, and eftablifh a more conftant uniformity in prices as well as in quantities: want of confidence would at firft perhaps hinder the ufe of thefe magazines, caves, or cellars of thefe public refervoirs. But this would not long be the cafe, if fincerity, order, and economy, reigned in thefe eftablifhments. It is an advantage which might have been procured by means of provincial ad-miniftrations, and which perhaps will never be enjoyed but under their aufpices.

With refpect to the *billets* or *notes of commodities or produc-tions*, it is feen how greatly they would increafe national riches, how quickly the mifery of the peafants would difappear, if thefe notes circulated as value in commerce, and if the vine-dreffer could change his note of depofit for productions of which he was in need. The monopoly of rich cultivators would then be overturned; of cultivators who fuck up the whole fubfiftence of the vine-dreffer, and, by avaricious ad-vances, reduces him to their will.

the

the moſt ſpeedy manner, if we would not deſtroy the commerce in its origin. Illicit commerce produced there before the revolution
good Bourdeaux wine, becauſe it *is a property of*
ſmuggling to give that which is of ſuperior quality,
and at a cheaper rate.

Now, ſince the peace, wines ſent from
France have not been, as it is aſſerted, of a
good quality. It is poſſible that from greedi-
neſs they may ſometimes have been adulterat-
ed. But this tranſient abuſe which the merchant may eaſily deſtroy whenever he pleaſes,
by chooſing in the United States commiſſioners
whoſe reputation is untouched ; this abuſe, I
ſay, ought not to ſtop the exportations of
France.—Wine, if it be good, will always find
conſumers.—Nothing but intelligence and ſin-
cerity are neceſſary to ſucceed in this, for nature has done the reſt for France.

The Americans prefer, in general, the wine
which is carried to them in bottles, becauſe
they believe it leſs ſubject to become ſharp, or
to change on the voyage. On the firſt view,
it ſeems advantageous to France to furniſh its
wines with this envelope, becauſe it is a new
opening for its glaſs-ware. But if it be recollected, what a prodigious quantity of combuſtibles

bles glafs manufactures require, to the fenfible
deftruction of forefts, it appears imprudent to
encourage a commerce which cannot but augment it rapidly.   At leaft, before it be encouraged, it would be neceffary to have very certain accounts of the number of glafs manufactories in the kingdom, of their confumption of
wood and charcoal, of their produce and exportation, and finally of our forefts and mines.

SECTION II.

BRANDY.

The rapid progrefs lately made in chymiftry,
has difcovered in moft of the fruits of the earth,
the falts and fpirits which conftitute the effence
of brandy ; this difcovery has been turned to
advantage ; there refults from it a confiderable
abatement in the price of that liquor, that is to
fay a very great evil ; this proves, by the way,
that there are difcoveries in phyfics which
fhould not be revealed without having firft confidered their moral and political effects, and having indicated to government the means of preventing their inconveniencies ; it alfo proves,
that

that a chymift ought not to be a chymift only, but a politician alfo.

The brandies of France are generally looked upon as the beft, that is to fay, the moft delicate and leaft pernicious : therefore they obtain the preference with people in eafy circumftances.

A great deal of brandy is confumed by the common people ; but this is counter-balanced at home and abroad by fpirits drawn from grain, fruit, or fugar:

Rum, which is produced from the latter, has had, and ever will have, in the United States, the preference over our brandies, by reafon of its cheapnefs. The Americans, efpecially the Boftonians, import melaffes from the fugar iflands and diftil it, and independently of their confumption, they re-fell a great part of it to the inhabitants of the fame iflands, who cannot diftil it for want of combuftibles.

Befide rum, the Americans make ftrong fpirits from grain, potatoes, &c. They are indebted for this to the Irifh and Germans who have gone to fettle in the United States. A pernicious prefent thofe emigrants have made them.

In Ireland the cheapnefs of fpirits made from grain,

grain, places them within the reach of the poorest man. The lowest classes of society use them to an incredible excess; and this excess contributes not a little to promote that quarrelsome humour which characterises the Irish, to plunge them into stupidity, and hinder them from rising to that degree of prosperity to which the liberty of commerce they have lately obtained ought to carry them.

The Americans would already have experienced a part of that degradation of which the excessive use of strong liquors is the cause, if they were not almost all proprietors, in easy circumstances, and fathers of families; if instruction and morals were not more generally propagated among them than among any other people; and, finally, if the quick and considerable profits which workmen there obtain by the high price of workmanship, did not give them a salutary ambition which keeps them from intemperance *.

Those

* The temperance of the Americans proves, *that a man is honest when he is happy.* He is neither vicious nor criminal, *except when he is wretched.* What therefore is the first cause of his vices and crimes? The cause of his wretchedness. The genealogy of almost all crimes is—no property or want of employ—cause of wretchedness of the people—wretchedness

the

Thofe of the United States *, where the people have gone from fimple and primitive manners, where luxury begins to reign, where fla-

the caufe of drunkennefs——drunkennefs the caufe of quarrels
—of idlenefs, of mifery, of thefts.——Thefts caufe imprifonment
and capital punifhments.

The firft link only to which a defe&t of property is attached, remains to be remarked. It is not neceffary to name it.
But it arifes from this genealogy, that in the a&tual order of
things, the people being drawn into vices and crimes, are lefs
culpable than they are imagined; confeqûently, they ought
not to be fo feverely punifhed, and that government fhould
fupprefs too fevere pains. This truth cannot be too often repeated, and it ought to be joined to every circumftance
when opportunity offers, feeing that the lift of bloody execu-
tions is every where augmented, and that narrow minds which
fee the atrocity only of the crime, without perceiving its caufe,
inceffantly demand blood for expiation. There would be
but few fcaffolds if none but real criminals mounted them.

* See Smith's Voyage to the Southern United States,
where a defcription of the life of the Carolinians is given.
This author makes it appear, that they drink to excefs the
ftrongeft liquors, although the climate be extremely hot.
By this they abridge their lives, and appear old in the flower
of youth. This is one of the caufes of the mortality among
the Englifh in the Eaft Indies; they have introduced there
the ufe of wines and ftrong liquors, and they are vi&tims to
them. The Indians make no ufe of thefe, and live to a great
age.

In quoting Smith, the European readers ought to be put
on their guard againft Englifh partiality, which reigns throughout the work.

very

very ftill exifts, are daily witneffes to the ravages caufed by the exceffive ufe of fpirits made from grain *.

A long habit is difficult, and often impoffible, to fhake off, efpecially when it procures enjoyments.   Therefore, it is not to be expected that the Americans will ever renounce the ufe of thefe liquors.   The philofopher fighs at this; commercial nations, which turn to profit the misfortunes and caprices of mankind, ftrive to take advantage of it.   France will have the advantage †, if fhe can reduce the price of brandies to the level of that of rum.   Government, in order to aim at this point, has already perceived the neceffity of lowering the duties on the exportation of thefe fpirits.

But ought it to favour, with fo much complaifance, the diftillation and exportation of brandies ?   I do not think fo ; this new opinion feems to be a paradox ;   it will ceafe to appear

* All brandies, except thofe from fugar and wine, are pernicious, efpecially when new.   They cannot be drank without immediately difordering the body.   The moft trifling excefs is fufficient to caufe death.

† Lord Sheffield agrees that the brandies of France are preferable to thofe of Spain and Portugal, of which there is neverthelefs fome confumption in the United States.

fo.

fo, when it ſhall have been examined with attention.

The diſtillation of brandies, cauſe a great decay of combuſtibles : one great evil in a country where combuſtibles daily become more rare *.

The exportation of brandy produces but little to the revenue. To encourage this article, it has been neceſſary to take off the impoſt, which at preſent is no more than five ſols per hogſhead, whilſt wine pays a duty of at leaſt an hundred ſols, and in the Bordelois from that ſum to twenty-eight livres †.

Government

* All the provinces of France, thoſe even to which nature has refuſed the means of tranſporting their wood to others, feel the ſcarcity of this article. Lorrain may be quoted as an inſtance. The foreſts of that province decay, as it is reported, in the proſpectus of a price upon pit-coal, propoſed by the academy of Nanci—the dearneſs of wood is exceſſive there. The cauſe of this inconvenience is not difficult to aſſign ; it is the neceſſary conſequence of forges, glaſs-houſes, ſalt-pits, &c. The academy requires pit-coal to be ſought for, to ſerve inſtead of wood. A more ſimple means would be to deſtroy forges and glaſs-houſes, and to get iron and glaſs from America.

† Government has, ſince this work has been written, ſuſpended the duties paid by the wines of Bourdeaux and Languedoc. This ſuſpenſion was granted upon a remonſtrance, importing

Government ought to have done the reverfe, to have reduced the duties on wines, and augmented thofe upon brandies.

The exportation of brandies is prejudicial to the confumption of our wines, for it is the bafis of all made wines in countries where wine is not produced.   It is put into a great quantity of water ; to which is added bay berries, every where to be found.   Wine brandies are indifpenfable in this fabrication, no other can fupply their place, becaufe they only can give to artificial wines the winy tafte which is effential to make them drinkable.

What immenfe gain to ftrangers in this procefs—and what lofs to France ! A barrel of brandy which pays a trifling duty on exportation, whofe tranfport cofts but little on account of its contracted bulk, may be added to five or fix barrels of water, which coft nothing, and by the aid of fugared ingredients, which give colours, may enter into competition with fix barrels of wine, that pay confiderable duties on

importing that there was an enormous quantity of wines at Bourdeaux, and which the holders dared not export, that they might not be obliged to advance the high duties. This proves, that impofts occafion a ftagnation.

exportation ;

exportation; and whofe exportation and tranf-port is very expenfive.

Therefore, in diftilling and exporting bran-dies, we work for the intereft of our rivals; we give them an eafy means of doing without our wines. What folly! What would people fay of an Alchymift, who having found the philofopher's ftone, fhould communicate his fe-cret to his rivals, who would make ufe of it to his prejudice.

And yet this operation fo prejudicial to France has been favoured by government. It encourages diftillers; that is, it raifes up ene-mies againft the meliorating vineyards and wines; and efpecially againft the art of pre-ferving the latter. It would be much more prudent and advantageous to difcourage diftille-ries. In fact, the diftillation of brandies is for the vineyard proprietor a laft refource, which proves his ruin *.

SECTION

* In the Orleanois, fix barrels at leaft of wine are neceffary to make one of brandy. The wine of this country, when it is drinkable, is fold on an average at thirty livres a barrel. The fix barrels produce one hundred and thirty livres, and reduced to brandy they fcarcely produce eighty. Thus the proprietor fuffers a lofs of one hundred. Brandies fent abroad, where they diminifh the fale of wine, can bear no exportation duty.

SECTION III.

OILS, OLIVES, DRY-FRUITS, &c.

Thefe articles are fo many wants with the Americans of eafy fortune, and efpecially thofe in the northern States. Our fouthern Provinces, which produce fuch delicious fruits, cannot in this refpeft fear any competition. They are alfo articles which have hitherto beft fucceeded in adventures made from Marfeilles.

Moreover, all that Europe will be able to furnifh of them, will find room in the United States ; they will accompany our wines, and we can join with the fame eafe and certainty of fale, perfumeries, anchovies, verdigrife, &c. as well as an hundred other little things taken by the Englifh from Marfeilles, and of which they have created a want to the Americans.

duty. Wines, on the contrary, pay a confiderable one. Let thefe calculations be anfwered. The Englifh themfelves ought not to admit the brandies of France, becaufe, in filling England with artificial wines, they are prejudicial to their wine duty. The prohibition of brandies would, under this double afpeft, be advantageous to both countries.

Lord

Lord Sheffield, in his work, makes Spain, Portugal, and Italy, furnish the United States with thefe commodities. I wifh he had been fincere enough to give the advantage to France. France is fo generally known to fell thefe productions in the States of America, that it is equally aftonifhing this writer fhould have been ignorant of it, or filent upon the fubject. This fact, by proving his partiality, ought to put readers upon their guard againft his affertions.

SECTION IV.

CLOTHS.

People governed by a free conftitution are naturally grave and deliberate. They prefer, in every thing they ufe, goodnefs to elegance, what is folid to that which is fubject to the caprices of mode. Therefore as long as the independent Americans enjoy their excellent conftitution, they will prefer clothes of cloth to thofe of the moft brilliant ftuffs.

Moreover its beauty, pliancy, ftrength, and duration, render it more generally fit for this

ufe

ufe in any climate whatfoever : cloth fecures the body from the excefles of cold as well as from thofe of heat.   It refifts rain ; in a word it unites every convenience ; and if it be the univerfal clothing of people in a middling ftate, it offers equally to the rich, but reafonable man, a choice proper to fatisfy his tafte, and to proportion his expences to his means.

The manufacture of cloths is in the number of thofe complicated manufactures which employ throughout the year a great number of workmen by the day ; therefore it will not be fuitable to the Americans, fo long as that clafs of men which produces thefe workmen fhall be able to employ themfelves more ufefully in the clearing of lands, and in cultivation in general.

A manufacture of woollen ftuffs, proper for the clothing of the country proprietor, his family, and fervants, may, without doubt, be affociated into the labours of the field ; but manufactures of this kind, although very important in themfelves, can only be applied to coarfe and unfinifhed ftuffs.   The interrupted leifure of the peafant permits him to do nothing which is complicated.   Card, fpin, weave, and
bleach,

bleach, is all that he can do＊. If it be neceffary for him to go beyond thefe, he will find
a greater advantage in felling his raw materials,
or even with their firft preparations, if they be
fimple, and to draw from the manufactures,
properly fo called, the articles of which he is
in need.

We owe little gratitude to thofe of our fpeculators who immediately after the peace difperfed our cloths in the United States. If one
fpark of public fpirit had animated them, they
would have perceived the precious and honourable fervice which they were able to render to
their country in thefe firft adventures, by giving to the Americans a great idea of the ftate
of our manufactures. Thefe people were well
difpofed, by the fuccour France had given them,
to cherifh its inhabitants, to efteem their cha-

＊ As long as there are lands to be cleared, the leifure
which agriculture affords will be very fhort, becaufe every
feafon is proper for this employ, except when too great a
quantity of fnow ftops the work. The intervals of leifure
become regularly eftablifhed, when the fyftem of cultivation
is fixed, and the foil entirely difpofed thereto. Then undertakings are calculated upon their duration; but, in general,
fimple work, which requires no workfhop, no confiderable apparatus, is that only which agrees with agriculture.

racter,

racter, and receive their productions. They were well difpofed to abjure the contempt and averfion with which the Englifh had infpired them for their rivals and their productions, and to give France the preference in every thing. Why has avarice, by a miferable calculation, rendered thefe good difpofitions of no effect? Men were willing to gain, to gain greatly; to make what is called a good ftroke, in taking advantage of the diftrefs of the Americans, and forcing them to take thofe commodities which were unfit for every other market *.

This difhonefty has counterbalanced the fervice rendered them; for the imprudent and wretched young man, whofe throat is cut by an ufurer, owes him no acknowledgment. A greater evil to France has been the confequence —her cloths have loft their reputation in the

---

* I do not accufe any body; but I can certify, upon the authority of the moft refpectable eye witneffes, that fome of thefe outcaft cloths fell at the end of fix months wear into fhreds.

The Americans were fo ftruck by this, that Mr. Laurens, after having received two millions, which France lent to the United States, employed a part of that fum to buy Englifh cloths. Complaints were made; he anfwered that it was his duty to buy better and cheaper cloths.

United

United States. But let the Americans unde-
ceive themfelves; let them not attribute to the
nation the fault of a few individuals; let them
not have a bad opinion of our cloths, becaufe
fome bad ones have been fent to them. The
fame accident would have happened to Englifh
cloths if, in a like cafe, there had been Englifh
merchants avaricious enough, and fo far ftrangers
to the public good, as to fend their refufe to
the United States *.

* Englifh merchants love as well as others to get money,
and there are among them thofe who, for the love of gain,
would trample under foot every patriotic confideration. But
the public fpirit of the generality of them puts, in England
more than elfewhere, a check upon the fhameful enterprizes
of avarice; confequently the greater part of the merchants
never abandon the national interefts in their fpeculations, neither the honour of Englifh commerce, nor the reputation of
their manufactures. It is thus they are become the principal
agents for furnifhing every fpecies of manufacture to the
whole world. When it happens that any of them facrifice
national reputation to views of private intereft, honeft patriots
generally prefer accufations againft them before a public tribunal, and then the culprit is not fuffered to anfwer by clan-
deftine memoirs to public and fubftantial accufations; this obfcure and cowardly refource is held in too great contempt to
be made ufe of. There remains nothing to the culprit but
filence or falfehood; in both cafes he is difhonoured in the
opinion of the public, which affects and marks every individual, without refpect to rank, power, or riches

The

The Americans who come among us, ſtudy the nature of the intercourſe which we ſhall one day have with the United States ; they know that our manufacturers poſſeſs all the means which give to Engliſh cloths their reputation ; that they make them in the ſame manner, and that the ſuperfines are ſuperior to thoſe of England; that in general dying is better underſtood with us, and carried to a greater perfection : in ſhort, that it depends but on ſome circumſtances eaſy to be got over, to make the cheapneſs of our workmanſhip aſſure us the preference to the Engliſh with reſpect to cloths.

Lord Sheffield, in avowing the ſuperiority of our fine cloths, and of their cheapneſs, obſerves, that the greateſt conſumption of the Americans is of common cloths, with reſpect to which France cannot enter into a competition with England. And he draws from it this conſequence, that the inconvenience of dividing the demands to compoſe aſſortments, and the conſideration of the ſmall quantity of fine cloth neceſſary to form them, will cauſe theſe to be ordered in England, notwithſtanding the advantage there would be in getting them from France.

But

But why should we not furnish common cloths to the United States, since the labour of our manufacturers is cheaper than that of England? It is because the English wool is cheaper than ours. The English grow their own wool, and stand in no need of foreign wool, except a little Spanish, indispensable to superfine cloths. On the contrary, we import more than half of the wool we manufacture into cloth. M. la Platiere says there are thirty-five millions of sheep kept in Great Britain, each of which, he affirms, produces on an average at least six pounds of wool. It is the breed of sheep which gives to England such an amazing superiority over all other nations in her woollen manufactures. France ought to encourage the breed of sheep and the destruction of wolves*. M. la Platiere saw this evil, and had courage to publish it in the Encyclo-

---

* In the time of the monarchy there was an office called *Louveterie*, or Master of the French King's wolf-hounds, and his associates received a trifling recompence for the head of every wolf they killed: of whom this fact is well attested. There is a small district, the sub-delegate of which put into his account the price of ten thousand wolves heads. The quantity appeared extraordinary to the minister. The affair was examined. The sub-delegate was discharged. But he who prompted him to the act went unpunished.

pedic

pedie Methodique.   Platiere was called a man
of pretenfions.   The fame title was given to
Dr. Price in London when he predicted the
lofs of the Colonies.   The minifterial heads of
that country laughed at the prophet, but the
event proved he was right.

SECTION V.

LINENS.

There are two principal fpecies of linen-drapery, which are fubdivided into a multitude
of others.

The firft fpecies contains linen properly fo
called; that is to fay, linen which ferves to
make fhirts, fheets, table linen, and all the linen
made ufe of for every purpofe of cleanlinefs.

Thefe linens are made with hemp, flax, or
cotton ; this laft article is employed when the
two former ones are fcarce, it is fometimes
mixed with flax.

The manner of making thefe linens is very
fimple ; they are made in all parts of Europe *.

Thofe

* If there be a country where the manufacture of linens is
encouraged, it is in Ireland, particularly fince its refurrection
into the political world.   Parliament has eftablifhed a committee which is particularly employed about this manufacture,
and which grants very confiderable fuccours to manufacturers.

There

Thofe countries where religious or political defpotifm difcourages induftry; where the numerous inftitutions of charity, invented to divert the attention of defpair from mifery, nourifh idlenefs; thefe countries are the only ones wherein this manufacture does not merit the attention of the political obferver.

There is one who has obtained more than thirty thoufand pounds fterling from government, and whofe manufacture employs two thoufand men and women, and fix hundred children.

This committee names infpectors to examine the ftate of manufactures, and afterwards to make reports, or give a general defcription of their fituation, of the number of workmen they employ, of their produce, refources, wants, &c ‖.

Still more has been done in Ireland, to encourage the commerce of linen; great edifices have been built, and deftined to receive them, as well as thofe who come to offer them for fale. The moft confiderable market being at Dublin, three or four times a year, linen merchants from the North, who have bleach yards, come to Dublin with their affortments. They find in thefe edifices, places for their linens and for themfelves to lodge in, all at no expence.—They meet Englifh buyers or others, who go there to gather together all their purchafes.—Like depofitories are eftablifhed in the North; they are effentially neceffary to thofe manufactures, the articles of which are gathered in the country.—Where they exift, expences are lefs, and work is better paid for.

‖ When thefe infpectors are honeft, and men of underftanding, their reports are evidences of fuccefs. Then example has a fingular influence upon induftry.

Every

Every where elfe, the country people employ, more or lefs, the leifure which their
kind of life affords them to fpin and weave
linen.   Moft of the farmers and proprietors
who enjoy a little eafe, or who are not afraid
of letting it appear, fow hemp or flax, and draw
from their foil and the work of their hands the
linen which covers their bodies and fupplies
their family.

The Englifh have added other caufes to thofe
which produce low-priced workmanfhip : their
aftonifhing induftry, their obferving genius,
their ever calculating mind, have invented for
the fpinning, &c. of cotton, and for weaving,
feveral machines which ftill furpafs the cheapnefs to be expected from the leifure of the inhabitants of the country.

As thefe machines are infenfibly introduced
into countries, it may be expected that the low
price of linen-drapery will be every where eftablifhed.

But notwithftanding the multiplication of
thefe machines, nations which groan under a
bad government, or are grown rufty in old and
wretched habits, will always depend, for that
article of neceffity, upon thofe which have
eftablifhed bounds to their government, but
none

none for their induſtry, which muſt conſtantly increaſe.

It reſults from theſe facts, that the United States will always have, in proportion to the increaſe of their population and culture, leſs recourſe to ſtrangers for that principal kind of linen-drapery whoſe manufacture is ſo well aſſociated with the labours of the field*.

Very fine linens muſt be excepted; they are deſtined for luxury, and the individuals employed in manufacturing them are condemned to vegetate miſerably in cities, rolling perpetually in the ſame circle of mechanical labours †.

It

---

* The American women are renowned for their induſtry in the conduct of their houſes; they ſpin a great deal of wool or flax; they would loſe their reputation and be deſpiſed, if their whole family were not almoſt entirely clothed with the cloth and linen made in the houſe: if the whole interior of their ruſtic habitation did not bear evident marks of their cleanlineſs and induſtry.

† Manufactures are much boaſted of, becauſe children are employed therein from their moſt tender age; that is to ſay, that men congratulate themſelves upon making early martyrs of theſe innocent creatures; for is it not a torment to theſe poor little beings, whom nature commands us to permit to take the air and their ſports, until they are of riper years, and their ſtrength is become conſiderable—Is it not a torment to them to be a whole day, and almoſt every day of their lives, employed

It is the unhappy fate of all thofe who are born in Europe without property, and will not debafe themfelves by domeftic labour.

The United States, where laborious individuals may with fo much facility become proprietors, are far from that degradation ; and if they are wife, they will have, for a long time, the happinefs not to fee fpun or woven among them, any of thofe delicate kinds of thread and fine linens, which, fought after and bought up by the opulent, are the real productions of European mifery.

The fecond fpecies of linens contains what is more properly called linen-drapery ; that is

employed at the fame work, in an obfcure and infected prifon ? Muft not the wearinefs and vexation which they fuffer, obftruct the opening of their phyfical and intellectual faculties, and ftupify them ? Muft not there refult from this a degenerate race, inclined to automatonifm and flavery ? For moft manufactures require no other than mechanical labours, which a machine would perform as well as a man. It is therefore impoffible that a man condemned to this kind of employ fhould not become a machine ; and ftupidity and fervitude are joined to each other.—Thefe truths cannot be too often repeated, not to difguft the Europeans with the mania of manufactures ; they are too far advanced to retract ; but to hinder the Americans from ever following the fame career.

to fay, cloth made of thread of different colours, whether flax or cotton ; or thefe two fubftances mixed with others.

The greater part of this drapery requires too complicated a procefs, too varied an apparatus, too continued a labour, to be manufactured otherways than in thofe particular eftablifh-ments, fituated from neceffity in the neigh-bourhood of cities, and which have no affinity with a rural life.

The art of making well the tiffue, of mixing the colours, of contrafting them, of imaginary agreeable defigns, of preparing the linen when it is finifhed, &c. this art extenfive, varied, and delicate, requires the greateft attention. The moft important thing is to do a great deal in it at a little expence, and it is the point to which the Englifh are arrived, with refpect to that kind generally known under the name of print-ed callico.

This will be for a long time a confiderable article of commerce, between Europe and the United States, which confumes a great deal of it ; and it is an article wherein French induftry, left to its natural force, and not being reftrained by any obftacle, need not fear

com-

competition *. In this, as in moſt other articles, the nature of things is entirely in favour of France, and ſuccefs depends wholly on the will of her government.

In the year 1785 the government of France invited, by an arret, foreign manufacturers of theſe linens to come and ſettle in France.

But this invitation is not made in terms fufficiently clear, or flattering, to induce ſtrangers to come and ſettle amongſt us ; eſpecially not ſuch as have a little energy and elevation in their characters, and it is of theſe alone that we are in need.

Among different favours granted them, there is one which entitles them to the *enjoyment of their ſtate or profeſſion, and of their uſages* ; in

---

* Lord Sheffield maintains in his work, that France has not even linen enough for her own confumption. A commercial dictionary, printed at Lyons in 1763, affures on the contrary, that France fends a great deal abroad. If the compiler of the dictionary fpoke truth, he might be anfwered according to the author of Les Etudes de la Nature—" Of " what uſe is it to a ſtate to clothe foreign nations, when " ones own people are quite naked ?"—Theſe two writers may be made to agree, by faying that France, reſtored to her energy, would eafily furnifh linens to foreigners and her own citizens, and that various interior caufes have hitherto prevented her from doing it.

that

that which fhall not be contrary to the laws of the kingdom, &c.

But what fignifies all the vague expreffions of enjoyment, of ftate and profeffion, liberty and ufages? What State is here fpoken of? Is it of the political, civil, religious, or domeftic ftate? Englifhmen, independent Americans, have a political ftate, a political liberty, that is, a right to take part in the adminiftration of public affairs; is this ftate underftood? Is the liberty of having a temple for communion, for marriage according to that communion, under-ftood by the liberty of ufages? Why are not thefe ufages fpecified?

And above all, what fignifies thefe words, *in that which fhall not be contrary to the laws of the kingdom.* If they convey a clear meaning, do not they completely deftroy the preceding fa-vours granted? or, at leaft, do not they leave a great uncertainty upon that which is or is not granted?

Why is not a language clear and without evafion made ufe of, efpecially in treating with ftrangers? Inftead of an equivocal jargon, dan-gerous in its nature, becaufe it produces mif-truft, and may give an opening for deceit, why not fay to them in clear terms, " If you come

within

within our ftates accompanied by your wives and children,—if you bring your manufactures, if you eftablifh yourfelves among us, you fhall enjoy all the rights of our fubjects ? Thefe rights are, to poffefs property in the fulleft fecurity, and not to be deprived of it but by the laws, tribunals, &c. If you fix your abode among us, your children will, without obftacle, be your heirs: you fhall alfo preferve your religious opinions. When there fhall be a certain number of you, you fhall have a temple wherein to worfhip, according to your own manner, the Everlafting Father; and you fhall have minifters, and hold affemblies; fhall intermarry according to your rules, &c. If France be not agreeable to you, nothing, abfolutely nothing, fhall hinder you from leaving it, and carrying with you your riches." It fhall be told that all this was meant to be faid by the arret: it was neceffary then to explain it clearly, and why were thefe obfcure words added,—*in that which fhall not be contrary to the laws of the kingdom?*

How fhould a German, an Italian, an Englifhman, who fhould be tempted to eftablifh themfelves in France, be acquainted with your ancient laws and ordinances? Will they turn over your innumerable folios? Certainly they will not,

not, they will ftay at home; you will therefore have failed in your intentions. On the other hand, do not they know that a century ago, and even fince that time, thoufands of ordinances were, and have been made againft the Calvinifts, and that thefe ordinances are not yet repealed? Ought not they to be afraid that thefe would be brought forth againft them if they gave the leaft offence? They will remain at home, and once more you have miffed your aim.

It is the more neceffary for monarchies not to difguife under a captious form the advantages by which they feek to entice ftrangers; as free ftates, fuch as Ireland and independent America, do not fubject emigrants to any capitulation or conftraint: they offer them all the rights of citizens the moment they fet their feet on free ground: and what rights! In Ireland that of voting at elections; in the United States, that of being elected themfelves; and confequently the moft feducing right, becaufe it is the moft proper one to maintain the dignity of a man who has dignity; the moft proper to give it to him who has it not.

When a nation perceives the neceffity of enticing ftrangers to fettle in it, nothing ought to be be fpared, efpecially in ftates far advanced in civilization.

It is a means of regenerating morals, if it be poffible to regenerate them, and efpecially to encourage induftry : for in order to exift in a ftrange land, and to gain in it confideration and confidence, emigrants are forced to have good morals, probity, and exactitude. Their example cannot but have a falutary influence upon the nation which receives them into its bofom.

Otherwife, having opinions, habitudes, and knowledge, different from thofe of that nation, they may help it to break its bad cuftoms, to give it a greater extent in its views, more cofmopolitifm, or of that character proper for approaching nations to each other, and for diminifhing national antipathies.

When the advantages which a country acquires by ftrangers who fix themfelves in it are confidered, it is aftonifhing to fee governments think fo little about them, and frequently not to refpect their rights.   They ought, on the contrary, to protect a ftranger fo much the more as he feems lefs fupported by the laws than a citizen ; that he is unacquainted with them ; that he may eafily be the victim of artifice and chicanery ; that it frequently happens

that

that he does not underſtand the language;
finally, that being alone, he has neither family,
friends, nor patrons.

In this ſituation, the ſtranger ought to be
environed by the ſafe-guard of a particular adminiſtration, which ſhould watch over his
ſafety; but it is the reverſe of this in many
ſtates *.

Thus whilſt we ſee in thoſe ſtates who underſtand their intereſts better, Frenchmen direct
the greateſt part of their manufactures, few
ſtrangers are ſeen to come and eſtabliſh themſelves amongſt us.

I could quote, as a proof of what I advance,
known facts, quite recent; but I will not write
a book upon every article of exportation; I will
confine myſelf to ſaying that *great liberty, and*

---

* If a ſtranger be ſuſpected, few examinations are made,
he is arreſted—liberty is left to a citizen, or at leaſt he is
treated mildly; the ſtranger is impriſoned: the ſubaltern, in-
ſolent by reaſon of the indifference of his ſuperiors, treats him
with ſeverity: for what is there to fear from him? Is the
word with them all,—ſet at liberty—will that ſtranger go and
make the temple of chicane ring with his complaints? He
fears, leſt it may be a new foreſt,—he flies, curſing that in-
hoſpitable country.

few

few regulations *, are the two beſt means of improving the linen manufactures in all countries, as well as in France.

SECTION VI.

ſilks, ribbons, ſilk-ſtockings, gold and ſilver lace, &c.

There are upwards of ſeventy thouſand looms and frames employed in theſe articles, and one half of the ſilk made uſe of is produced in the kingdom.

The other ſtates of Europe, except Spain and Italy, are obliged to procure from abroad the whole of the ſilk neceſſary for the manufactures

---

* I might quote, as a proof of what I have ſaid in the courſe of this work, that even the regulations which appear favourable to induſtry, are prejudicial to it; the new arret paſſed in favour of French linens, ſubjects them to a ſtamp duty, under the pretext of preventing fraud. The duty appears moderate, yet the manufacturers are ſenſibly injured by it; moreover it reſtrains them, in ſubjecting them to the caprices of revenue clerks; and this does not prevent fraud; therefore to prevent the manufacturer from being robbed, his money is taken from him, and the robbery ſtill takes place; he would prefer being left to defend himſelf againſt thieves.

which

which they have eftablifhed, in imitation of thofe of France.

If there be added to the advantage which thefe circumftances give to the French, their fingular aptitude for the manufacture of every article of luxury; their incredible fecundity in varying thefe articles; the abfolute and general empire allowed them over the tafte and mode which prefide in thefe manufactures; an empire fo particular, as to be every where copied; no doubt will remain, that French filks, ribbons, filk-ftockings, and lace, will be preferred to all others in the United States*.

It is not to be feared, that they will be manufactured there; from the cares, which the

---

* Yet Lord Sheffield gives for competition with France, England and Spain. It is to be obferved that England cannot undertake with advantage thofe manufactures wherein gold and filver are introduced, nor in general thofe which have for their bafis the ufe of brilliant metals. Fire is neceffary as an agent in fuch manufactures, and a coal fire is prejudicial to them. The atmofphere in England is perpetually charged with fulphureous vapours, where contact tarnifhes, in a very little time, gold or filver lace, &c. and this perhaps is the motive, which more than manners, has banifhed, and will for ever exclude this kind of luxury from England; and it is not a misfortune.

infect

infect that produces the filk, requires, to the arrival of the ftuff in the warehoufe where it is to be fold, almoft all is workmanfhip ; and the workmanfhip of Europe muft for a long time, if not for ever, be even cheaper than that of the United States.

The confumption * of thofe articles cannot be

* Our defign being to diffuade the free Americans from wifhing for manufactures, we ought not to lofe the prefent opportunity of defcribing to them the abufes and inconveniencies infeparable from thefe eftablifhments. There is none which has had more fuccefs in France than that of filk. Yet fee the frightful defcription given of it by M. Mayet, director of the manufactures of the King of Pruffia, in his Memoir on the manufactures of Lyons. (Paris, Moutard 1786.) He indicates as caufes of the decadency of thefe manufactures, the drunkennefs of workmen on Sundays, the infection of their difmal lodgings, bankruptcies which are the refult of ignorance and difhonefty, the ceffation of work during court mournings, which occafions fome workmen to emigrate, and others to fteal, the mifconduct of revenue officers, the monopoly of filk, &c. abufes fo much the more alarming, fays M. Mayet, as they are, for the moft part, the offsprings of luxury, and which are produced either by acquired riches, or the thirft of acquiring them ; it feems as if they could not but fpring up in manufactures.

Who can recommend the eftablifhment of manufactures, on reading the following reflections of the fame author ?

" The concurrence of manufactures neceffitates their
" cheapnefs :

be very confiderable there *, if America takes
advantage of that opening to which nature calls
her.   Ribbons excepted, the reft are proper for
great cities only ; where vanity being inceffantly
excited, makes drefs a defirable and almoft neceffary object.   But thefe great cities will,
without doubt, be very rare in the United
States.   It is ftill more certain that the confumption of filks does not, at prefent, form

" cheapnefs: to have a preference of fale, it is neceffary to
" fell at a lower price ; the wages of workmen muft there-
" fore be moderate, and they muft gain no more than will
" find them in neceffaries: the workman muft never be fuf-
" fered to enrich himfelf.   In becoming rich, he becomes
" difficult, exacting, enters into combinations, impofes laws,
" becomes diffipated and idle, he caufes the price of work-
" manfhip to increafe, and manufactures to fail."   *Thus rich
*ftuffs ought to be watered with the tears of the workman who
manufactures them.*

   Ought not this laft phrafe to difguft the free Americans for
ever with the mania of manufactures of luxury?—Let them
reflect, that to fupport the filk manufactures of Lyons, the
fame author propofes to the king of France, to facrifice his
tafte for fimplicity of drefs, and to wear brilliant clothes, &c.

   * Lord Sheffield fays, that it is not the fifth part of Indian
filks, &c. but what fignifies this calculation? The country
which confumes the greateft quantity of filk ftuffs, does not,
perhaps, confume the twentieth part of that which Lord Sheffield means by Indian filks.

there

there a confiderable article; that it will augment but very flowly, and in a manner almoft
infenfible. The Americans ought undoubtedly to be congratulated upon it. Their manners will be good and fimple as long as they do
not contract a want of thefe articles; but if
they do not want them for themfelves, they
will have occafion for them to form branches
of their fmuggling commerce with the Spani-
ards. Nature invites them to carry on this
commerce in an advantageous manner, both
by fea and land *.

It is known that wretched individuals, who
vegetate in South America, mafters and flaves,
all figh after nothing but luxury, pomp, and
drefs. Elegant and fhining ftuffs of France;
her filks and laces will therefore be fought after, demanded, and bought up with avidity.

However it may be with refpect to this commerce, which exifts but in futurity, and which
muft be preceded by other circumftances, there

* This commerce will be better eftablifhed by land—The
rifks there will be lef—The great rivers which water thofe
immenfe countries will favour it. A maritime commerce
muft be protected by a naval force, and the nature of things
will hinder the Americans from having one for a long time
to come.

is

is at prefent a certain confumption of filks, ribbons, &c. in the United States ; and the French
ought to be anxious to fupply them.

I will obferve upon this fubject, that if the
French government ordered that the regular
packet-boats going from France and America
fhould receive as much merchandize on board
as their deftination would permit, little ventures
of our filk, ftuffs, ribbons, gauzes, ftockings,
&c. would be frequently fent out, and thefe
articles would ferve better than any other to
eftablifh uninterrupted connexions, and which
by the infight they give, and the experiments
which they afford an opportunity of making,
conduct nature herfelf to thofe great commercial intercourfes to which we ought to afpire.

The facilities which packet-boats offer for
the fending out of merchandize of value and of
little incumbrance ought not to be neglected,
fince, in this clafs of merchandize, we have
things which have a decided preference.   I will
return to thofe packet-boats which it is important to keep up and to increafe, and it is to be
wifhed, that no monopoly of right or fact may
take poffeffion of them, in order to carry on
one branch of commerce in exclufion of others.

SECTION

SECTION VII.

HATS.

Although a fine hat be called a beaver, it does not follow that Canada and the United Northern States are more favourable to the fabrication of hats than France. Hats, purely of beaver, do not wear well, and are inconvenient on account of their weight. The fineſt, handſomeſt, and beſt hats, contain but little of the fur of that animal, which we eſteem at too high a price, when we think of the loſs of Canada. Wool, the furs of the hares and rabbits; the hair of goats, which is in fact wool, and camels hair, are more neceſſary for making of hats than the fur of beavers.

The few hats of beaver made in the United States, will be ſufficient for their conſumption. —The Americans muſt, however, be inceſſantly told this great truth, that manufactures are not proper for them except in thoſe articles which are immediately aſſociated with agriculture, and which facilitate its operations. That of hats is not of this kind.

Europe

Europe will therefore furnish hats to the Americans. And of what great importance is this object, when the rapid increase of their population is confidered? It may be affirmed, that every nation capable of fending them out merchandize, will fend them hats; but thofe of France will have the preference. This manufacture had there its origin. The French alone have carried it elfewhere, like many other things, but it has never ceafed to improve in France.

French hats are always the beft fulled and dyed, and the moft agreeable. When government fhall have refolved to do for wools that which it has done for mulberry trees, the manufacture of hats will be fo much the more advantageous, as we fhall be lefs tributary to foreigners for the articles employed therein.

SECTION VIII.

LEATHER.

SHOES, BOOTS, SADDLES, &c.

To what caufe ought the great fuperiority of Euglifh leather to be attributed over ours? Why is there in this leather-work of all kinds

that

that neatnefs, that feducing appearance, which
we have not yet approached? It muft be repeated, that in England men honour the profeffion of a tanner, and pride themfelves upon
it, whilft it is the contrary in France. An
Englifh tanner, fhoemaker, or faddler, does
not quit his trade when he is rich; but makes
his riches ferve, in proportion as they augment,
to give luftre to his profeffion, to multiply his
workfhops, to extend his affairs, to become important even in the article which has furnifhed
him the means of doing it. The leather which
comes from the tanneries whofe owner is in eafy
circumftances, is always well prepared, becaufe
he can advance fums of money, and give to
hides the time neceffary for their progrefs
through his tan-yard. A poor tanner is always
preffed by his wanting to take the leather out
of the tan-pit, where it is neceffary it fhould
remain a long time to acquire a good quality.
In general, it is impoffible with this penury,
unknown to the Englifh, that there fhould be
time to manufacture or fabricate good merchandize. Thofe who employ the leather, acquire
no reputation in their profeffions but in proportion to great provifions made before hand, which
puts it in their power to furnifh nothing but
leather

leather improved by being kept. It will be afked, how the wholefale dealers manage when they begin bufinefs ? They find credit, if in their apprenticefhips, which precede their eftablifhments, they have acquired a good reputation *

This

* We may readily perceive, that this hope of being fome day well eftablifhed with great fuccours, is worth all the books of morality. The engravings of Hogarth, which reprefent the fate of the idle apprentice, paint, to the life, Englifh manners. The intention of the workman is not to become *Secretaire du Roi* ‖. He marries the daughter of the good mafter who has brought him up, and fucceeds him in the fame bufinefs which he has contributed to extend.

It is not that the French tanner, who barters his profeffion againft a brevet of Secretaire du Roi, or commiffary of war, ought to be blamed. He reafons well. He fees that no confideration is attached to talents and induftry, and he delays not to buy himfelf a title. It is therefore wrong to joke merchants and artizans, who, for money, get themfelves enregiftered in a privileged clafs. It is an evil to the ftate, but it is not the fault of thofe who purchafe. The fault is due to the kind of difgrace from which government has not yet delivered the ignoble.

It ought to be obferved here, how fatal the fpeculation which eftablifhed this order of things has been to the nation. To procure money, offices were created ; which, by ennobling, induces the ignoble to purchafe them ; they are difgufted with

‖ A petty title of bought diftinction, which, in the language of ridiculous pride, is conftrued into nobility.

their

This credit is then fupported, not only by the certainty of fuccefs, but alfo by that of feeing them become a conftant means of confumption.

Such is the art of the Englifh to fupport and increafe their commerce in every thing, and every where. If we could put it in practice, all our commodities of leather would foon equal the perfection of theirs, fince we do not otherwife want materials. Their being beforehand with us, ought not to difcourage any body, but it is neceffary to the fuccefs of this rivality, that government fhould deliver the tanners from the fhackles with which they have fettered them*, and fupprefs or diminifh the

enormous

their fituation by being difhonoured, and for a few millions of livres, which this pitiful operation flowly procures, commerce is ruined by having its capital diminifhed: that commerce, which, by being fupported, would continually produce millions to the ftate.

* Two caufes have fingularly contributed to ruin the tanneries in France. The confiderable duties impofed fucceffively upon leather, (fuppreffed afterwards in part through prudence) and effentially the fevere infpection that the *commis* (in this cafe a kind of excifeman) may make every hour of the day and night at the tanners. Nothing difgufts a man, who has fome energy, more with his profeffion, than this difgraceful

enormous duties with which the tanneries are loaded *.

SECTION

graceful fervitude, than the fear, than the conftraint which arife from the idea of being difturbed at every moment, by his firefide, by contemptible fatellites who live on the mifchief only which they do, and whom the certainty of impunity, intereft, and habitude, render unmerciful, infolent, and frequently perjured.

Confiderable proceffes have been feen to arife from thefe vifits, and very rich tanners to quit a profeffion which promifed them nothing but torment, anguifh, lofs and law fuits. It will be a long time before the evil which the farm has done to the tanneries be repaired. Interefted men, who think to confole us for real evils, which we fuffer, by thofe which they fuppofe among our neighbours, fay, and repeat, that the fame vexation of *commis* and of cuftoms, produce in England the fame effects. This may fometimes happen, but there is a law to punifh them, without a hope of pardon, when they overleap the boundaries prefcribed to them. And thefe boundaries are much more contracted than ours, which the following fact will convince us.

Two officers of the excife, having taken it into their heads to follow a man carrying a hamper of wine to the houfe of a particular perfon, entered with him in contempt of the law; the mafter of the houfe called fome conftables and charged them with the officers: they were taken before Alderman Hamett, who read the act of Parliament to the culprits, and fent them to prifon, for having violated the rights of citizens.

Mercure politique 1786, p. 286.

* The following is a lift of duties paid on leather, whether it be French or foreign; and it muft be here obferved, that
the

SECTION IX.

GLASS HOUSES.

Englifh glafs ware is brought to great perfection, and England makes it a great object of
exportation.

the leather of France is far from fupplying our wants. We
get the greateft part of that which we confume from the
Spanifh and Portuguefe colonies, from the Levant, and from
the coaft of Barbary.

	livres	fols
Green leather, French or foreign, pays on entering the kingdom by the hundred weight	1	5
Leather worked up or tanned, pays afterwards the following duties		
Leather and fkins - 2 f. per pound		
Goat fkins - 4		
Ten fols per pound, which gives more upon leather - - 1		
Goat fkins - - 2		
General average - 4 6		
and by the hundred weight - -	22	10
Cuftom to the general farm - -	2	0
Total	25	15

Leather and fkins pay a duty of a third of their value.

When

exportation.   America ought to prefer Englifh glafs to ours, becaufe we ourfelves prefer it to

When in 1759 a duty was impofed, the king ordained that thefe two fols upon leather and fkins, and the four fols upon goat fkins, fhould be reimburfed to the manufacturer, when he fhould have fent his merchandize abroad.

But adminiftration demanded and obtained leave to reimburfe two-thirds only.

Since that time there has been a new impoft of ten fols per pound, which makes the duty one fol more upon leather, and two fols upon goat fkins.

This new duty has completed the ruin of the tanneries.

There is another abufe, which merits to be obferved. It is that the adminiftration receives its duties undiminifhed upon leather half rotten, fcraped or tanned.

After thefe facts, it may be comprehended, that the tanners in France are reduced to a fmall number, and are in general miferable.

An important note relative to the article of leather.

The note on the duties paid on leather, is true with refpect to the reality of the duties ; but we have been convinced, fince the note was printed, that a middle price cannot be fettled between hides, and calf and goat fkins.   There are at leaft two hundred of the two firft for one of the laft.   We have been equally convinced, that the hundred weight of fkins bought at thirty-feven livres, and fold after the tanning at fixty-four livres, fixteen fols, produces to the tanner a profit of no more than five livres five fols.

This eafily explains how the tanners have been ruined.

TRANSLATOR.

that

that of our own manufactory, common bottles
excepted, which we make better, and which are
of a finer glafs than that of the Englifh.　But
although this opinion may hurt the intereft of
thofe who have fuch eftablifhments, it is neceffary to fay, that France, far from encouraging
them, ought to wifh for their deftruction.
This kind of manufacture deftroys combuftibles, of which the rapid progrefs is alarming,
when it is compared to the flownefs with which
they are produced.

The Englifh, feated upon their coal mines,
are little uneafy about the voracity of furnaces
wherein glafs is melted; but although it be faid
that we have the fame advantage, it is ftill
permitted to doubt of it.　And moreover it is
not fufficient to have immenfe coal mines under foot, it is neceffary to be able to work them
at a little expence.　Glafs manufactories, placed
within the reach of mines, fhould not be too
far diftant from the fea, for the tranfports becoming expenfive, would give to the Englifh
an advantage over us, who from every part of
their ifland can eafily get to the fea.　Finally,
our own confumption of glafs-ware, much
greater than that of the Englifh, may already
be too confiderable, if it be compared with the
means

means to which the ever growing fcarcity of combuftibles reduces us *.

To be fully convinced that we ought not to put glafs-ware into the lift of articles of exportation to America, it is only neceffary to reflect upon the fituation of the United States. They have immenfe forefts to clear, confequently it is highly proper that they fhould eftablifh glafs manufactories, and increafe them as much as poffible. The labour employed to deftroy the woods for the clearing of lands, at the fame time that it difpofes the land to culture, will ferve for the production of a very extenfive object of manufacture, therefore the utility of this deftruction is double to the Americans †. It cannot be doubted, that this confideration

* The fcarcity of wood, which begins to be manifeft, becomes fo much the more alarming, as combuftibles which have been attempted to be fubftituted for it have not fucceeded, and that luxury and population naturally inclined to increafe, efpecially with commerce, the confumption of combuftibles will be doubled.

† This is what is done in New Jerfey for the forges. It is impoffible, fays the author of the *Cultivateur Americain*, to travel acrofs this province without meeting with fome little iron forges. If a proprietor has a great marfh full of wood, and that he wifhes to clear it, he begins by making a dyke at one extremity to ftop the water of the rivulets which run

acrofs

fideration will ftrike them, that they will one day conceive the project of furnifhing Europe with glafs-ware, of adding this article to thofe which they can exchange for fuch European productions as are improper for little States to cultivate or manufacture within themfelves.   It can be no more doubted, that France will gain greatly by feeing her glafs manufactories deftroyed by thofe of the Americans, who will fell us glafs-ware in exchange for our wines, cloths, printed linens, filks, &c.   In the mean time, it would undoubtedly be a falutary meafure, to open the kingdom to the importation of foreign glafs.

SECTION X.

IRON AND STEEL.

The confumption of thefe two articles is immenfe in the United States; the fingle article

acrofs it.   He fixes in this water the wheels neceffary for the manufacture of iron, &c.   And in a fmall number of years the traveller, who had feen in paffing by nothing but a vaft pond full of trees thrown down, and had heard the noife of hammers and anvils, fees well enclofed fields, vaft meadows, &c.

of

of nails amounts to confiderable fums. This will not appear extraordinary, when it is remembered, that all the houfes, all the enclofures of the Americans, are of wood, that they build a great number of fhips, which require frequent reparations.

It is the fame with refpect to faws, fhovels, hoes, and in general all the inftruments neceffary to agriculture and navigation.

The Americans are fingularly curious in the choice of the firft neceffity. They have therein the general tafte of the Englifh ; they will have that only which is good. On comparing thofe which they make themfelves with the tools made in France, it muft be acknowledged that we are far from that perfection at which they are arrived in them : this perfection is owing to the eafe of the labourer, and to the confideration attached to agriculture. Imperfection is a neceffary confequence of reftraint and difhonour.

The Americans have attempted to make iron and fteel. Many manufactories have been fet up at New York, in New Jerfey, and in Penfylvania ; it is true that thefe manufactures are few in number, but they will neceffarily increafe for the reafons which I fhall hereafter give.

England

England heretofore exported a confiderable quantity of iron and fteel * : her mines not having yet furnifhed iron proper for certain inftruments, fhe had recourfe to thofe of Ruffia, and efpecially to thofe of Sweden, whofe iron and fteel are moft efteemed. She did no more with regard to America than ftand between her and others, and this circuit augmented the expences of the colonift, without procuring him any benefit. This will exift no longer, becaufe the Americans are about to trade directly with the Swedes and Ruffians.

Lord Sheffield calculates, that one year with another England imported 50,000 tons of foreign iron, of which from 15 to 20,000 was

---

* To favour the exportation of thefe articles, the parliament had forbidden all the eftablifhment of mills and other machines in the United States for making of fteel. See 25 Geo. II. ch. 29, fect. 10.

It may be judged by this circumftance to what a point the mother country, or rather the monopolizers, can carry avaricioufnefs; fince the Americans were forbidden to enjoy thofe advantages which nature had thrown before them. Monopoly refpects nothing. When thefe attempts are confidered, ought we to be furprifed at the eternal mifunderftanding between colonies and the mother country, a mifunderftanding which finifhes either by the ruin of the former, or their feparation from the latter.

afterwards

afterwards exported to the colonies either in its natural ftate or worked up.

The profit to the mother country was, according to his Lordfhip, 12,000,000 livres, or thereabouts.

During the war, and fince the peace, fome exports of this kind have been made from France to the United States ; but they did not fucceed. Accuftomed, according to the principles of monopolifers, who have hitherto directed our foreign commerce, to furnifh our colonies with brittle utenfils, and otherwife very imperfect, our merchants were willing to treat the independent Americans like their flaves in their iflands * ; and the Americans refufed

our

* The Chamber of Commerce of Marfeilles, in an inftruction very well drawn up, addreffed in 1784 to the merchants, had recommended them to act contrarily—" Recollect," faid it, " that you have not ignorant or enflaved colonifts to treat " with, but a free people ; and, confequently, rapidly tending " to perfection. If you wifh to fucceed, act with fidelity, " upon extended and liberal views," &c. &c.

I have not read this inftruction. A man of letters, who has refided a long time in the country, has given me the ideas of it, which I have related. We muft not be furprifed to find in the merchants of Marfeilles intelligence *on commerce fo rare any where elfe*. Lefs fhackled, commerce muft offer more folid ideas.

The

our merchandife.   They faid, that we did not
even know how to make nails; and, in ftrict
truth, they were right in their affertion.   They
preferred the iron and fteel of England, although the duties on exportation increafed their
dearnefs.

It is probable enough that the Englifh legiflature will fupprefs them, according to the advice of Lord Sheffield; and this, joined to the
benefit of the œconomy procured by the difcovery of Lord Dundonald, and of Meffrs. Watts
and Boulton, for heating furnaces at half the
common expence, will undoubtedly produce a
reduction in the price of iron.

This diminution is one of the caufes which
muft neceffarily hinder us from attempting a
rivality in this particular with the Englifh;
but there is another, which is ftill more decifive.

In fact, the obfervations made heretofore upon the neceffity of deftroying our glafs manufactories, apply naturally to that confiderable
branch of iron-work, of which the workmanfhip
is the leaft expence, and which requires a great

The fame energy is found in an excellent Memorial on the
Franchifes of this city, lately publifhed againft the general
farm, and of which we fhall have occafion to fpeak.

quantity

quantity of combuftible materials. The United States are obliged to deftroy their immenfe forefts : France ought, on the contrary, to think of re-producing hers ; therefore, the founderies and forges will offer in America the advantage of turning to profit woods, which, without thefe manufactures, it would be equally neceffary to burn : whilft in France, wood and charcoal, becoming every day more fcarce and dear, renders thefe eftablifhments more expenfive. Now, as the abundance in which iron mines are every where found *, makes the price of iron depend almoft entirely on that of combuftibles neceffary to melt it, it is evident that the United States have over us, and even over the Englifh, a confiderable advantage.

Moreover, forges are a part of the equipage neceffary to country labour ; for, if it were neceffary to feek at a diftance the utenfils of agriculture, the progrefs of clearing of lands would foon be ftopped—the productions would not pay the expences. Thefe would ftill be increafed by the repeated neceffity of fubftituting new utenfils to thofe which there would be no means

* It is now proved, that there are many of them in America. Mines of tin, and of very good copper, have alfo been difcovered there.

of

of repairing. As soon as a people have mines of iron; as soon as they are led by the nature of things, and by neceffity, to eftablifh founderies and forges, it is not a long time before they renounce all foreign aid in the articles of iron * ; therefore, the Americans are, as I have obferved, already provided with thefe eftablifhments: and as Englifh induftry has eftablifhed and directed them, they are all at that degree of perfection which we have not yet attained.

Let it be remarked, that thefe manufactures being joined to a life of agriculture, and carried on in the midft of it for its ufes, can have none of the pernicious influences which ought to be feared in thofe complicated manufactures which are obliged to be concentrated in the inclofures of cities, whofe deftructive employ exhaufts the natural ftrength of men, by corrupting their morals.

* Perhaps nails muft be excepted. Their price will be a long time in Europe lower than in America. If, as Mr. Smith afferts in his Treatife on the Wealth of Nations, a young man of twenty years of age can make 2,400 nails a day, let it be judged to what a degree of cheapnefs low-priced workmanfhip ought to reduce them; therefore, wherever workmanfhip is dear, nails cannot be made. Yet we read in the American Gazettes, that there has been eftablifhed in one of the States a manufacture of nails. Will this fucceed?—Futurity will fhew us.

Therefore,

Therefore, to refume this article—far from encouraging the exportation of iron manufactured in France, we ought, for our own intereft, to encourage the importation of foreign iron, becaufe manufactures of this kind take away combuftibles from things more preffingly wanted, and from lefs deftructive manufactures, where workmanfhip produces a greater profit.

This, however, is not the cafe with every article of curiofity of iron, fteel, or copper work, wherein the workmanfhip exceeds the other expences. They belong to that weak organifation which the Americans ought not to envy. But it muft not be diffimulated, that a competition with the Englifh will, on this head, be difficult to maintain : their great ability and addrefs in the diftribution of work and different proceffes, the invention of which has not been conftrained by any error * or falfe view

of

* Thofe falfe views cannot be too much deplored—thofe narrow ideas—thofe fears of ignorance, which fnatch from the hands of induftry the happy inventions which are proper to enrich a whole nation! Who can calculate the riches that England owes to the fole application of the coining-mill, or engine and dye, whofe free ufe has been left to all the manufactures which it was capable of improving in accelerating

their

of the adminiſtration of England, gives them
over us a confiderable advantage; yet it is not
impoſſible

their effects? How many proceedings more ingenious and
expeditious has this machine produced? Happily for England,
there have not been found in her bofom thofe able miniſters,
who, feeing that this machine is of ufe in making money, have
drawn from it the profound confequence that every one would
make falfe money if the free ufe of it were permitted: as if
it was poſſible to make falfe money for a long time; as if the
more general ufe of the machine did not awaken the public,
and even private intereſt, and render them more attentive to
abufes which might be committed; as if its ufe would not
produce much more benefit to the revenue, than it could deprive it of by the falfe coinage of money, which can never be
either extenfive or dangerous.—When therefore will thofe
who hold the reins of empire calculate like ſtatefmen?

It is true that at prefent artiſts are permitted to have mills,
&c. by conforming themfelves to certain formalities,—always
formalities! No other are required in England than thofe of
being able to pay the expence of the machine,—and has England perceived from it any pernicious effects? Has falfe money overturned public order, impoveriſhed the nation, or diminiſhed her revenues?

With what difficulty has the invention of the coining mill
made its way into France? It is due to an induſtrious Frenchman of the fifteenth century, named Briois. Perfecuted for
this difcovery, he was obliged to take refuge in England; the
Engliſh received him favourably, and put his invention into
execution. Another Frenchman of the name of Warin, of
the laſt century, wiſhed to procure the advantages of it to his
countrymen, he experienced a like abfurd perfecution; and
without

impoffible for us to balance it, for this diftribution of work and proceedings are neither fecrets
nor fuperior to French induftry. Let government adopt and follow the trivial maxim—
‘ Who will have the end will find the means.’
Let it in confequence not interdict any of the
means, and this induftry will not have to envy
the fuccefs of our rivals.

without the fupport of the Chancellor Sequier, he would have
failed in his attempt.—I do not allow myfelf to fpeak of the
perfection to which M. Droz pretends to have brought the
coining mill at prefent; but by the vexations he fuffers, it
may be judged that he has in fact fimplified that machine, that
he has rendered fewer hands neceffary, and the coinage of money more perfect and expeditious; two advantages very precious in this art, as the expences of it cannot be too much
reduced, and the exactitude and perfection of the ftamp of
money are the fureft means of difconcerting coiners. What
fatal genius is it therefore which purfues induftry in France?
That of companies, of corporations, of privileges. As foon
as a happy difcovery attacks their profits, they employ even
the bafeft means to defend them; intrigue, falfehood, feduc-
tion, are all legitimate with the people which compofe thofe
affociations, whilft the man of genius, ftanding alone for the
moft part, and who attaches too great a value to his time to
proftitute it to thefe manœuvres, generally experiences the
moft humiliating difgufts.

SECTION

SECTION XI.

JEWELLERY, GOLD AND SILVERSMITHS' ARTICLES, CLOCK-WORK, &c.

If the inhabitants of the United States concentrate their labours and pleafure in a life of hufbandry; if they continue to feek happinefs, not in pomp, but in nature herfelf, and in a fimplicity of manners; in that fimplicity which naturally produces eafe, and the population and profperity of ftates; they will not feek after, but difdain plate and jewels, to which we attach fo great a price. They will referve precious metals for mints and commerce.

It is not however to be prefumed, that this order of things fhould long fubfift in great cities, and efpecially in frequented ports: European tafte and wants prevail in America *, and French induftry ought to be anxious to fupply

---

* Plate is ufed in the Southern States—magnificence is feen there; on which account, travellers having but little philofophy, fpeak highly of them:—but obferve what is attached to this luxury,—flavery reigns in the South, and there are many poor.—There are none in the Northern States,—no plate is there ufed.

their

their confumption, feeing that the French can underfell the Englifh in thefe articles.

But it is probable that the plated ware (copper plated with filver) invented in England, will take place in the United States of that of filver plate, as painted paper has replaced there much more expenfive hanging : this new fort of plate has for ufe all the advantages of the other, and cofts a great deal lefs.

How comes it that the Englifh are already fo advanced in this branch of induftry, whilft there exifts in France but one or two manufactures where copper is plated on one fide only and filvered over on the other ? How have the Englifh already carried this invention to fo high a degree of perfection ? How have they made of it a matter of extenfive commerce, whilft we are reduced to the two manufactures wherein no progrefs is feen, and where the inferiority of the workmanfhip difgufts thofe who would otherwife find it to their advantage to make ufe of this kind of plate ?

Thefe manufactures have an exclufive privilege : there is the word—Government fearing left falfe money might be made in them, has forbidden even the plating on both fides.

Reafoning would here be fuperfluous : it is
                                                fufficient

fufficient to open the eyes to fee which of the
two adminiftrations has beft ferved its country;
whether it be that of England, by not cramp-
ing induftry, and in not giving way to fears,
whofe illufion is fhewn by the moft trifling
obfervation, or ours, in following a contrary
plan. Again, was it apprehended, that coun-
terfeit crowns would be made my millions; as
a facrifice is made to this fear of an induftry
which would certainly produce many millions
of them ?

Thus when we confider all thefe articles,
wherein trifling confiderations fhall be our induftry, and condemn to mediocrity our means
of profperity; when we thence turn our attention towards the different fpirit which governs England, it is aftonifhing that induftry
ftill exifts in France, and that the nation does
not fall into floth, and remain there. Let us
give thanks unto nature, who has richly gifted
us, and her guardian ftrength has hitherto demonftrated itfelf fuperior to the malignant influence of the falfe fcience of our adminiftrators *.

Shall

* A curious and more ufeful work would be, a faithful and
more rational hiftory of all the errors into which the rage of
regulating

Shall we remain behind the Englifh and Swifs in clock-work? The Americans muſt have watches; this admirable invention carries with it ſuch a degree of utility for even the poor claſſes of ſociety, that it ought not to be conſidered as a ſimple acquiſition of luxury, eſpecially in the United States, where the diſtance of habitations one from another make the neceſſity of it more fully perceived.

But watches muſt be made good and at a cheap rate; theſe two conditions will aſſure them a prodigious ſale wherever civilization exiſts; time is there a precious property, and its price renders the inſtrument neceſſary which divides it: they will be made good and at

---

regulating and prohibiting has thrown adminiſtration. It is very probable that the reſult would be, that French commerce has always proſpered, in proportion to the inexecution of regulations; that in cauſing them to be rigorouſly executed, foreign commerce has been favoured and enriched. The ſpirit of invention and induſtry which our prohibitory regimen has developed on foreign nations, was never perhaps ſuſpected; neither the innumerable quantity of workſhops which are there conſtructed, in proportion to the multiplication of exclufive privileges in France. Thus, that of the India Company has made Switzerland like the Eaſt Indies, for the manufacture of muſlins, and plain and painted linens.

a cheap

a cheap rate, when able artifts are confulted *.

This fpecies of manufacture will always belong to great cities, where the excefs of population keeps workmanfhip at a low price, where
the difficulty of fubfifting enflaves that crowd
of weak and indolent beings which are under
the law of the rich undertaker. The United
States are far from fuffering this difficulty of
fubfiftence, this excefs of population ; they are
therefore far from thefe manufactures.

---

* Paris has produced fome very diftinguifhed ones ; they
honoured their art becaufe they had great fenfe and ingenuity,
and had been well inftructed ; but their pupils, for the moft
part ftrangers, and not having the fame means of gaining confideration, were afraid of our injudicious manner of defpifing
the hands which work at mechanical employments, and quitted the country. We have at prefent a Swifs, M. Brequet,
whofe talents are equal, if not fuperior,· to thofe of the moft
celebrated Englifh watch-makers. Happily for us, his character, his elevated views, his obliging zeal, command refpect
in fome meafure, and place him above prejudices. Let government confult him, and he will foon indicate certain means
whereby France may have a national manufacture of clock
and watch-work.

We are informed that he has prefented to the Miniftry a
profound memorial upon this fubject.

SECTION

SECTION XII.

DIFFERENT SORTS OF PAPER, STAINED
PAPER, &c.

This uſeful production from old rags, thrown off by people at eaſe, and gathered with care by the indigent, is daily improved in France *.

The

* The manufacture of M. M. Johannot d'Aunonay, produces finer paper than any other manufacture in Europe, and the proof is ſimple.—There is more demand from Ruſſia, England, and Holland, for this paper than the manufacturer can furniſh ; this ſcarceneſs of paper d'Aunonay explains, for why, our ſhopkeepers ſtill get paper from Holland. To diminiſh this ſcarcity, theſe good citizens have generouſly offered to communicate their proceſs to all the manufacturers of paper in the nation, and even to form ſchools, wherein the art of paper-making may be taught. Many perſons have profited by theſe offers ; the States of Burgundy have lately ſent three pupils—Theſe manufacturers have proved that it was not more expenſive to make good and excellent paper than that of a middling quality. M. Le Clerc, who has a great paper manufactory at Eſſone, found with concern, that his manufactory coſt him a great deal, and produced bad paper only: he communicated his regret to M. Johannot; the latter went to Eſſone and produced good paper with common paſte. This was certainly a great ſervice done to France, and a good example given to the ſordid avarice of monopolizers, who,

The Englifh themfelves buy our paper for printing, and our writing paper will not be long unequal to theirs, if it does not furpafs it *.

But if there be an object of commerce for which Europeans need not fear a reciprocal competition ; if there be an article which offers to all European manufactures a certain and lucrative employ, it is that of paper : the confumption will always be equal at leaft to the production, and its numerous ufes infure a ftill greater confumption, in proportion as population, commerce, and knowledge, fhall increafe.

who, not being able to do and embrace every thing, hinder others from d ing it. May thefe generous patriots receive that honour which they deferve : may their example be followed every where and by all. This will be to them a more flattering eulogium, a more brilliant and lafting recompenfe than cordons and ribbons, unworthy of true merit, becaufe they are frequently the price of intrigue, and the ornament of mediocrity. The pleafure of well-doing, and the fuffrages of honeft men, are pure and unchangeable recompenfes.—The artift who does not know how to confine himfelf to thefe, will never do any thing which is great.

* Rags are more fcarce, and confequently dearer, in England than in France, and they are articles of illicit commerce between the two cou tries. There are very fevere laws againft this commerce, but it is, and ever will be, carried on, as long as there fhall be any thing to be gained by it.

Every

Every nation ought therefore to obferve with-out jealoufy, that each country ftrives to have within itfelf manufactures of this kind.

The Americans cannot however enjoy this advantage for a long time to come: befides the dearnefs of workmanfhip, their population cannot furnifh them old rags in quantities fufficient to eftablifh paper mills whofe productions would be equal to the confumption of the inhabitants.

Will their population ever furnifh them with this fufficiency? This is a queftion difficult to refolve. In fact, in proportion to the knowledge which nations may acquire, and to the liberty of the prefs, which may be enjoyed in America, a prodigious quantity of paper muft be confumed there; but can the population of this country produce rags in the fame proportion? It cannot reafonably be hoped that it will. It is therefore probable that the American markets will not for a long time be provided with any other than European paper, and that this will find a place there*.

* Rags are exceffively dear in America: but the time is arriving when, by an increafe of population, they will become plenty. In Pennfylvania they already make very good paper.

But

But fince the ufe of paper is fo advantageous to men, fince it is fo varied, it behoves every nation to look upon foreign confumption as a fupplement only, as an open port in the cafe of a fufpenfion of interior commerce. It behoves every nation to keep paper at a moderate price within itfelf, and to attain this end, means muft be thought of to increafe materials which ferve to compofe this article, and to purfue the happy attempts already made to do it*. Thefe refearches

---

* In the moment of writing this note, I have before me very interefting effays on vegetables, and on the bark of feveral trees, to transform them into paper; thefe effays are due to the refearches of M. Delille, to whofe care the manufacture of Montargis is indebted for a great part of its reputation. He has far furpaffed that Scheffer, whom our men of erudition have quoted with fo much emphafis.—On feeing the books which M. Delille has printed, on paper made from a fpecies of mallows, and the bark of the linden tree; and on perceiving the advantages which might be reaped from this invention, at leaft in packing and ftained paper, of which fo great a confumption is made; we wifh that this invention may be more and more known, received and adopted, as a means of remedying the want of rags and the dearnefs of paper, which ought to have more influence than is commonly believed on the progrefs of knowledge.

It is almoft impoffible that this invention fhould not foon become general, and it is greatly the intereft of the free Americans to naturalize it among them.

Strong

fearches are fo much the more effential, fo much the more urgent, as the happy invention of coloured paper for hanging is of a nature always to caufe a greater confumption of paper; and this manner of hanging with paper will fubfift for a long time, becaufe it gives a neat and agreeable appearance to apartments.

No other is known in the United States; it is there univerfal; almoft all the houfes are neat and decent.

S E C T I O N XIII.

PRINTING.

The liberty of the prefs being a fundamental principle of the American conftitution, there can be no doubt that printing will increafe there.

Strong lies of lime and pot-afh, and the intelligent ufe of vitrolic acid, are great means of reducing hemp and flax to that kind of fubflance extremely attenuated, foft and brittle, which is proper for making of paper. It might be contrived by thefe means to fupply the want of rags by old cordage. Thefe would even ferve to make good paper, fince being reduced to tow, it may eafily be bleached. The attenuation to be feared for linen is not fo for the material of which paper is made.

                                                    But

But it muſt be obſerved, that extenſive printing requires workmen at a little expence; that is to ſay, men without property, talents, or con-duct; whom great cities produce and employ in work which requires neither intelligence nor emulation; and it has already been obſerved, that the United States, unleſs the rage of great cities takes poſſeſſion of them, will contain but few of theſe wretched beings.

Printing will not therefore, it may be pre-ſumed, be extended among the free Americans, at leaſt beyond that which is neceſſary for the public prints*. Their conſtant and conſider-able ſale, permitting a greater expence in work-manſhip, conſequently draws about the preſs many individuals, becauſe they have, in a good ſalary, a view of the means of becoming pro-prietors or traders †.

The

* Gazettes are ſingularly multiplied in the United States. They will become ſtill more ſo with an increaſe of population, and this is an advantage, for they are what that excellent pa-triot Dr. Jebb called them, " Sentinels which watch over " public liberty and the preſervation of truth."

† However, conſiderable works are ſometimes printed in the United States, and of which the edition is carefully enough corrected.—I have ſeen, for inſtance, the Memoirs in Quarto of the Academies of Boſton and Philadelphia, of the laſt year, which

The furnifhing of books of fcience and amufement muft therefore make a confiderable object of importation into the United States. It is for France to appropriate to herfelf this commerce, and to encourage the impreffion of Englifh books. Our workmanfhip being cheaper than that of England, and the Englifh making ufe of our paper, our binding being lefs expenfive, why fhould not all the books in which the Americans ftand in need of be printed in France ?

It will be faid that we do not enjoy the liberty of the prefs,—be it fo :—But it is only with refpect to our books* ; for undoubtedly the

which proves at the fame time that free America is not fo totally without typographical eftablifhments, and that the inhabitants are not all fuch idiots as a prejudiced German dreamed they were.

* Under the reign of Louis XIV. whofe ambition extended to every thing, it was ferioufly attempted to make the French language univerfal. This abfurd pretenfion was ridiculoufly fupported by the tyranny exercifed upon books and authors. This tyranny could not but produce bad ones, and confequently difguft ftrangers. Happily fome judicious men had the courage to make facrifices, and to get their works printed abroad. It is thefe prohibited books which have enriched the French language and increafed the reputation of French literature. What authors are heard quoted in every country ? Roufſeau, Voltaire, Helvetius, Montefquieu, &c.

that

the adminiftration does not pretend to extend
its coercive principles to books written in foreign languages; it would not attain its end,
feeing that it does not do it with refpect to
French books*; and by this impolitical rigour
France would be deprived of a lucrative article of commerce, certain, and of continual increafe.

The Dutch, fo active and vigilant in feizing
the rifing branches of commerce, have for a
long time fpeculated on books in the United
States: many bibles and books of prayer, for
the ufe of the Americans, are printed in Holland. Lord Sheffield is obliged to acknow-

that is to fay, men who have been patriotic enough to violate
the tyrant's laws of the prefs.

* So that even more than half of the libraries in France
are compofed of French books, printed abroad, for which there
are two caufes—the cheapnefs and goodnefs of the books; the
octavo leaf printed, is commonly fold in Switzerland to the
public at nine deniers or a fol, and it cofts three or four fols
in France. Prohibited books are fold at Paris at the fame
price as books permitted, which proves the dearnefs of French
printing —For to the original price of prohibited books, there
muft be added the expences of carriage, rifks of entry, the
commiffions of different agents, &c.; with refpect to the goodnefs of the works, the beft, as I have already obferved, are
printed abroad: Helvetius has faid with reafon, " *On ne dit la
verite, que dans les livres, prohibes, on ment dans les autres.*"

ledge,

ledge, that printing in Holland is by far more cheap than that of England, and of courſe muſt have the preference. They will ſome day extend this commerce to claſſical books*.

SECTION XIV.

SALT.

This article, ſo neceſſary to the Americans, and ſo abundant in France, muſt not be forgotten in the enumeration of commodities to be imported into America. The Americans will for a long time be obliged to get it from Europe; not that they have no ſalt marſhes upon the coaſts, and ſalt pits in the interior parts of the country; but theſe marſhes, theſe ſalt pits, muſt have hands to work them ; and hands are

---

* A man of letters, who had remarked the dearneſs of Engliſh books in France, and how difficult it was to get them from England, thought of getting the beſt Engliſh works reprinted in Paris;—this was a ſpeculation really patriotic— he abandoned it after having got a few volumes reprinted, probably becauſe the conſumption in France was not great enough, and that of England was not open to him. He might at preſent revive it, independent America preſents a great opening to him.

better

better employed in the United States*. The falt exported from Europe will for this reafon be a long time cheaper than that of America: —moreover, its freight will coft but little, as veffels coming from Europe may be ballafted with it. The Americans ought to give the preference to French falt; it is lefs fharp, lefs corrofive, and poffeffes a better quality for falting, than any other European falt.

The three millions of inhabitants which the United States contain at prefent, are fuppofed to confume fixty million pound weight of falt, without reckoning that which is given to cattle, and that employed in falting provifions; of which great quantity is confumed in the United States, and with which they will carry on a commerce more and more confiderable: I will not at prefent go into a calculation of the immenfe riches which the furnifhing of made falt to foreign population, continually increafing, would produce to France. I ought to guard againft exaggerations: but it may not be im-

* Salt, during the late war, was very dear in America, it was worth twenty times its ordinary price.—The deprivation of this article was very fenfibly felt by the Americans, who confume much falted provifion, and give a great quantity of falt to their cattle.

proper

proper to obferve that a confiderable part of the
States of the North will never make any falt.
It is therefore poffible that French falt may
have a preference among them, as being cheaper
and more within their reach : the population of
thefe States will be more rapid than that of the
others, and the commerce more varied and extenfive.

SECTION XV.

GENERAL CONSIDERATIONS ON THE CATA-LOGUE OF FRENCH IMPORTATIONS INTO THE UNITED STATES.

I will extend no further the lift of articles,
which French commerce may furnifh to the
United States : there are many others which I
omit, becaufe the bounds of my work will not
permit me to examine any more than the principal ones.

If faith be given to the calculations of Lord
Sheffield, and of other political writers, it appears that the amount of the exportations of
Great Britain into free America was, upon an
average, calculated upon three years, taken
before 1773, near three millions fterling, upwards of feventy-two millions of livres tournois.

nois. How much will it increafe in following the progreffion of population, and clearing of lands ? It is efpecially for this future ftate of things that France ought to prepare her means.

Let it be alfo obferved, that this commerce employed feven or eight hundred veffels, and about ten thoufand failors.

Ought France to let flip fo important a commerce, and a means fo natural of fupporting her marine ? For without commerce there can be no marine. Has not fhe, in the richnefs of her foil, in a variety of her manufactures, in the low price of her workmanfhip, in the induftry and tafte of her inhabitants, in her population, and in the fituation of her ports, an infinity of means, fufficient to eftablifh in America a folid and extenfive commerce ? It muft be continually repeated, that if it be wifhed that peace fhould reign upon the earth, the words *preference and competition*, which are frequently fignals of difcord, muft be ufed with circumfpection. Why fhould there be any jealoufy with refpect to this commerce ? In the courfe of time, independent America will offer a field wide enough for all the European manufactures.

CHAP.

C H A P. VI.

OF THE ARTICLES WHICH INDEPENDENT
AMERICA MAY FURNISH IN RETURN FOR
IMPORTATIONS FROM FRANCE.

ARRIVED at this part of my work, I cannot do better than confign to it the letter addreffed by M. de Calonne to Mr. Jef-ferfon, Minifter Plenipotentiary from the Unit-ed States of America.

L E T T E R

ADDRESSED TO M. JEFFERSON, MINISTER PLENIPOTENTI-
ARY FROM THE UNITED STATES OF AMERICA TO THE
COURT OF FRANCE.

Fontainbleau, 22d October, 1786.

SIR,

The King's intention being to favour as much as poffible the commerce of the United States, I have the honour to communicate to you fome difpofitions made for that purpofe.

By

By a letter of the 9th of January, 1784, to the Marquis de la Fayette, I informed him, that inſtead of two free ports, promiſed by the treaty to the United States, the king had determined to grant them four, which has been effected; and I promiſed him to conſider the cuſtoms and duties on importation and exportation which ſhackle commerce; obſerving to him, that theſe objects required conſiderable application; they have not yet been completed. By another letter, I informed the Marquis, that his Majeſty had ſuppreſſed the duties on the exportation of brandy, a meaſure which he hoped would be uſeful to American commerce; I aſſured him alſo, that the duties of the king and admiralty, payable by an American veſſel on its arrival in a port of France, ſhould be diminiſhed; and afterwards that ſuch of them as remained, ſhould be reduced to a ſingle duty, to be regulated according to the number of maſts or draught of water, and not according to the too uncertain eſtimation of gauging. This reduction requires an exact knowledge of all the duties received in the ports, and as they are of various ſpecies, the ſtate which I ordered to be drawn up of them has not yet been given in.

You know, Sir, the king has charged a particular

ticular committee, to examine our commercial
connexions with the United States, and that
the Marquis de la Fayette has laid before it a
project analogous to the ideas contained in your
letter to the Count de Vergennes: but you
muſt perceive, how imprudent it would be to
hazard, by a change of ſyſtem, the produce of
a branch of revenue, which amounts to twenty-eight millions of livres, without falling upon
any object of the firſt neceſſity.   After an ample diſcuſſion of every thing which might at
preſent favour the importation of tobacco from
America to France, it has been decreed, not
that the agreement made with Mr. Morris
ſhould be departed from, but that, after the ex-
piration of it, no other of the ſame import
ſhould be made; and that in the mean time
the Farmers General ſhould be obliged to pur-
chaſe annually about fifteen thouſand hogſheads
of American tobacco, coming directly from the
United States in French or American ſhips, at
the ſame prices as ſtipulated in the contract
made with Mr. Morris.

You will recollect, Sir, that whilſt the demands which had been made for whale oil were
under conſideration, the Marquis de la Fayette
made a private arrangement with M. Sangrain,

permitting

permitting him to receive as much of that article as fhould amount to eight hundred thoufand livres tournois, and that I had granted paffports to exempt this firft quantity from all duties whatfoever. M. Sangrain made afterwards an agreement with the merchants of Bofton for whale oil, to the amount of four hundred thoufand livres a year, for fix years, for which his Majefty has promifed the fame favours as enjoyed by the Hanfe towns.

This manner having lately been examined under a more general point of view, the adminiftration, to which the committee has made its report conformable to the requeft of the Marquis de la Fayette, and to your opinion, relative to the entire abolition of all duties on oils, has difcovered that it cannot confent to it for the prefent, on account of engagements entered into with other powers. All that could be done was to infure, for ten years, whale oil, fpermaceti, and every thing comprehended under thefe denominations, coming from the United States in French or American fhips, the fame favours and moderation of duties as are enjoyed by the Hanfe towns.

His Majefty hopes commercial connexions between the United States and France will
become

become extenfive enough to engage him to continue the effect of this provifionary decifion;
and as it has been obferved in the committee,
that a confiderable duty was paid upon the
making of the moft favoured whale oils, and
even upon national ones, his Majefty confents
to abolifh this duty with refpect to the former,
and upon fpermaceti coming immediately from
the United States in French and American
fhips; fo that fpermaceti and thefe oils will
have to pay, for ten years to come, no more than
feven livres ten fols, and the ten fols per pound,
for all manner of duty; the laft augmentation
of ten fols per pound to ceafe in 1790.

It has been determined to gain particular information upon the confumption in France
of rice from Carolina, and that encouragement
fhould be given to the exportation of that article.

Upon the reprefentations which have been
made, touching the confiderable duties paid on
the entry of pot afh and pearl afh, as well as
relative to thofe of beaver fkins and fur, and raw
hides, his Majefty has fuppreffed all the duties
on pot afh,—on the fur and fkins of beavers,—
and on hides, coming raw from the United
States, on board American or French veffels.

He

He will alfo confider of proper encouragements
to be given to every article of the fkin and fur
trade.

His Majefty has equally confented to free
from all duties mafts and yards of every fpecies, red cedar, green oak, in fhort, all timber proper for the conftruction of veffels, coming from the United States in French or American fhips.

The committee having alfo reprefented, that
there was a duty of five per cent. upon the purchafe of veffels built abroad, and that this duty
was prejudicial to the fale of American veffels,
his Majefty has taken this into his confideration, and exempted the purchafe of all fhips,
which fhall be proved to have been conftructed
in the United States, from every duty of the
kind.

Trees, fmall fhrubs, and feeds of trees alfo,
pay high duties, which his Majefty has agreed
to abolifh upon fuch as fhall be fent from the
United States to France, on board French or
American fhips.

It having been reprefented, that the State of
Virginia had ordered arms for its militia to be
made in France, it has been determined, that
the prohibitions which have hitherto hindered
the

the exportation of arms and gunpowder, as well as the duties required in cafes of particular per-miffions, fhould be abolifhed, and that when-ever the United States fhall wifh to have from France arms, fufils, and gunpowder, they fhall have full liberty to do it, provided it be in French or American fhips, and that thofe arti-cles fhall be fubject to a very moderate duty only, folely for the purpofe of calculating the exportations.

Finally, his Majefty has received in the fame favourable manner the demand made to the committee to fupprefs the confiderable duties hitherto paid on books and paper of every kind. His Majefty fupprefles all duties on articles of this kind, deftined to the United States, and put into French or American veffels.

It is with pleafure, Sir, I announce to you thefe difpofitions of his Majefty, which are a new proof to you of his defire to unite clofely the commerce of the two nations, and of the favourable attention he will always give to pro-pofitions which fhall be made to him in the name of the United States of America.

I have the honour to be, with a fincere at-tachment,   Sir,

Your very humble and very obedient Servant,

(Signed)   DE CALONNE.

Your nation, Sir, will undoubtedly fee, with pleafure, the facilities the king has juft given to the exportation of the wines of Bourdeaux, Guienne, and Touraine, and the fuppreffions of duties granted to that effect, by different Arrets of Council, with which the Marquis de la Fayette will be able to acquaint you.

EXPORTS

EXPORTS of AMERICA.

———————

I will treat but of a few of the articles which America furnifhes, on account of the attention which they all merit.

SECTION I.

TOBACCO.

Of all the articles which France may procure from the United States, tobacco is the moft important one to the inhabitants of the two countries. If it cannot be claffed with our moft urgent neceffities, it follows them fo clofe, that excepting cafes wherein the ufe of it excites difguft, the deprivation of it ordinarily difcovers the laft degree of mifery.

We muft not be furprifed at its general ufe. The man greedy of fenfations, has found one
lively

lively enough in tobacco: it is perhaps the only one which he can enjoy at pleafure without injuring his health, diminifhing his ftrength, or fufpending his work or meditations. Tobacco awakens the mind agreeably, and obfervers who have remarked the innocent pleafure, the fpecies of inftantaneous comfort, which a little tobacco procures to a poor man, borne down by the weight of afflicion, have always wifhed that fo fimple an enjoyment fhould be improved and become lefs and lefs expenfive; and they cannot reflect without horror on the crime of that fifcal induftry, which, hardened by monopoly to increafe its profits, adulterates fnuff fo much, as to make it pernicious to health.

The confumption of tobacco muft therefore become more and more confiderable, and the commerce of this leaf, already very important, cannot be decreafed but by the diminution of its cultivation; which the policy of America will never permit.

The cultivation of tobacco is by no means proper for the European States, which have acquired population enough to apply another kind of cultivation to all their good lands.

It is true the Alfaciens cultivate a little tobacco, and they boaft of it; but they would
make

make a greater profit if they cultivated their
lands for provifions. This experience is decifive for France, where none of thofe rich lands
exift which are fo well known in America.
It is therefore the intereft of France to get tobacco from abroad, but it muft be paid for by
her manufactures: fhe may enjoy this advantage more fully with free America than with
any other country. I will not repeat the reafons of it; I will obferve only, that the free
Americans, having an immenfe extent of lands
which cannot be cleared but in the courfe of
feveral centuries, muft have, for a long time
to come, tobacco to fend to Europe, fince this
production pays with ufury the expences of
clearing.

It is true, that the cultivation of tobacco in
America muft be farther and farther from the
fea, and that the expences of carriage may become confiderable.

But different confiderations place this epocha
at a diftance; firft, in cultivating tobacco in
none but abfolute new lands, the cultivation is
much lefs expenfive, and the produce confiderably more abundant; confequently it will coft
much lefs in a new foil than when the foil requires more labour and manure.   Secondly,
America,

America, interfected in every direction by rivers
and lakes, has infinite refources for rendering
water carriage every where eafy, and confequently never expenfive. It is eafy to multiply canals, and confequently communications :
no part of the world is fo much favoured in this
refpect as America. Thirdly, The banks of
the Ohio and the Mifliffippi offer immenfe
lands to be cleared ; the Ohio falls into the
Mifliffippi, which falls in its turn into the fea :
thefe two rivers are almoft every where navigable, and the lands near them produce already
excellent tobacco, and will continue to do fo
for a long time*. Fourthly, If the price of

---

* It is impoffible to view, without indignation, that narrow
policy of Spain, which would fhut out the Americans from all
communication with the fea by the Mifliffippi. How is it,
that fhe cannot perceive, that her mercantile interefts invite
her, on the contrary, to favour this navigation, by erecting
ftore houfes upon the banks of this river near to its mouth?
Is fhe ignorant of the advantages of depofitories? And with
refpect to her political intereft, is there a greater one for her
in thefe countries, than to make herfelf immediately neceffary
to American eftablifhments, within the reach of the Ohio?
Muft fhe wait till they adopt other means? What will be
gained by creating difcontent among a free people? If it be
wifhed that thefe people fhould not become powerful, they
muft be deftroyed; and if this barbarity belongs not to the
eighteenth century, it is neceffary to make friends of them.
Expedients in politics are childifh and vain.

tobacco

tobacco fhould be increafed, France would not feel the difference, if the free Americans, preferring the culture, continued to want European manufactures, and gave the preference to thofe of France. According to this fyftem, the exchange of merchandize, manufactured in France for the productions of the foil of America, may be ftill made with advantage, if even thefe productions were fold in France below the firft coft in America. We have long feen the French commerce of the Levant produce great profits, although the merchandize brought in return was fold at a lefs price in France than it coft at the place where it was produced. This circumftance ftill exifts.

Therefore the fpeculation, moft to the intereft of France, is to take as much tobacco as fhe can confume from the Americans, and pay for it with her manufactures *.

---

* The tobacco leaf, of which the farmers general had the entire monopoly, or exclufive fale, produced to the king a clear nett revenue, annually, of between twenty-eight and twenty-nine millions of livres.

SECTION II.

FISHERIES, WHALE OIL, &c. SPERMACETI CANDLES.

Among the articles of fubfiftence which nature has liberally given to men, fifh is one of
the moft abundant, the moft eafy to be procured, and the moft proper to preferve their health
and ftrength *. By what fatal privilege is this
food confined in France almoft to the rich?
Why does not fifh abound in all places, where
this tribute of the fea can be received in its original ftate, and without being charged with the
expences of too long a carriage? Since it is fo
well known, that it is advantageous to a ftate,
and to every clafs of citizens, to procure an
abundance and a variety of eatables, let them
come from where they will, or of whatever

---

* Such is the powerful influence on population, of the
abundance of articles of fubfiftence, and efpecially that of fifh,
that it is principally to this article of life that the empire of
China owes the incredible number of its inhabitants.

nature

nature they be, provided they be cheap and wholefome; why is this political rule departed from, with refpect to fifh, to that aliment which nature produces every where with fuch fecundity ? Whatever may be the motives which may repel it, by an overcharge of duties, they can proceed from nothing but a culpable ignorance.

Fully convinced of the benefit which muft refult to mankind from an abundance of provifions, and from the facility of producing this abundance, in receiving from each nation the fuperfluity which nature has given it, I fhall take great care not to copy the narrow fyftem of Lord Sheffield with refpect to fifheries.— His Lordfhip agrees, that the independent Americans have, for the great fifhery, natural advantages, with which it is impoffible for the Europeans to contend.

In fact, the Americans are near that part of the Atlantic where great fifh abound; therefore their fifhery muft be lefs expenfive to them. If accidents happen, they are foon repaired; all their operations are more prompt and fure; having a better knowledge of thefe feas, they are expofed to lefs rifks than Europeans : finally, their proximity to the fifheries, affures them

provifions

provifions more frefh*, and puts it in their power to renew them more frequently; confequently their fifhermen enjoy more conftant health, and have older officers and failors among them: thefe are ineftimable advantages to America.

The Englifh have very few of thefe advantages; the French fcarcely any.—But ought we to conclude with Lord Sheffield, from this order of things, that American fifh fhould be charged with duties, in order to fupport the national fifhery, againft this competition; the nature of things dictates to France more wife and advantageous means.—Fifh is nourifhing, —whatever is nourifhing is prolific: if the Americans fifh at lefs expence than the French, fo much the better for the laft; fifh will be more abundant, and at a lower price in France. Let France open her ports; the Americans will bring fifh into them, and will pay themfelves with either the productions of the foil of France,

* Such is the advantage of the Americans, that they furnifh provifions to the fedentary fifheries of the Englifh. According to Colonel Champion, the provifions of Europe are more dear, and not fo good; the difference in favour of the Americans is in the proportion of four to feven; and it cannot be otherwife.

or

or of her induſtry ; and the population to which
this abundance and cheapneſs are favourable
will increaſe the productions of French induſtry.

Moreover, it is neceſſary, either to renounce
exterior commerce, or to conſent that there
ſhall be ſomething to exchange on both ſides.
To wiſh to eſtabliſh and encourage a commerce with a foreign nation, and not to leave
it to the care of furniſhing that which it col-
lects with the greateſt facility, is a manifeſt
contradiction. The enlightened policy of commerce is not to invade all the branches of it,
but to do nothing but that which can be done
better and cheaper than any other. Therefore,
ſince the Americans have fiſh on their coaſts,
ſince they are in the neighbourhood of Newfoundland, leave to their induſtry that branch
which nature has given to them in preference ;
let us not diſpute it with them ; firſt, becauſe
it would be in vain to do it, and in the next
place, becauſe France may reap, without fiſh-
ing, more advantageouſly the fruit of the American fiſheries.

" But," ſays Lord Sheffield, " ſailors muſt
" be found for the navy ; and the fiſheries are
" the nurſeries for them ; therefore, the fiſh-
" eries

" eries muft be fupported; and no fifh con-
" fumed but that which we take ourfelves; on
" which account premiums are neceffary."

There is no doubt but failors are formed in
the fifheries, but it is not in throwing nets or
hooks, in curing or preparing fifh, that this is
done; it is by a frequent and long exercife on board
veffels in laborious manœuvres, in living, fo to
fpeak, among rocks, and in feas, which the vicinity or nearnefs of oppofite coafts makes continually dangerous : now this exercife of vigi-
lance, agility, and intelligence, is performed by
the failor in coafting and fifhing on the coafts
of his own country. Let coafting be frequent,
and let not this fifhery be difcouraged in France,
and it will not be neceffary, in order to form
failors, to fend them fo far to take fifh, which
they cannot bring to Europe without great expence : by which the confumption is confequently limited, and which deprives us of the
ineftimable advantage of receiving in abundance,
that which the independent Americans can take
at much lefs expence.

Without doubt the exercife of the fifheries
of the North forms intrepid failors; and this
painful life muft be confented to. But when
nature has placed men in a climate where they

have

have but a few fteps to make to the interior of
the country*, to find an occupation exempt
from dangers and lefs fatiguing; when they can
get their bread upon land, under a clear and
calm fky, if he reafons, how will he be engaged to truft his life to boards, and to brave icy
feas, to expofe himfelf during the fineft months
in the year to perpetual ftorms, which affail
thefe fifhing banks, fo frequently ftained, by
means of the moft fatal errors, with European
blood?

It will be anfwered, by premiums †, by privileges,

* The French fifh but a part of the year; moft of the
fifhermen are day labourers, employed on land, which they
leave in the month of February, and return to it in July.

† England gives confiderable premiums to her fifhermen.
—But the inconveniences and abufes of the firft premiums,
render them of no effect. Thefe abufes are chiefly as follows:
The fifhing veffel muft go to a certain port; the equipage
muft pafs in review before the Officers of the Cuftoms; the
fhip muft complete her cargo, or remain three months at fea
to do it:—fo that if in the firft week fhe procured nine-tenths
of it, fhe would be obliged to keep the fea for the other tenth.
The fhip can take no inftruments but thofe proper for the
fifhery, to which the premium is applied; the cargo cannot be
difcharged but in a certain port; there are general formalities
to be obferved with refpect to the falt which fhe carries out
and brings home; the owners are expofed to vexations from
Cuftom-houfe Officers, to law fuits which they are obliged to
carry

vileges, and by prohibitions or overcharges of duties, which are equivalent to prohibitions on foreign induftry.

But it muſt not be forgotten, that articles of fubfiſtence are here in queſtion, that thofe forced means make them dearer, that their confumption is then limited, and their effect reſtrained; that in forcing nature in this manner, is doing it at the expence of population, for by this barbarous regimen, men are deſtroyed inſtead of being produced, whilſt permiſſion to bring into fea-ports the fiſh of thofe who have nothing better to do than to take it would infallibly increafe population.

Moreover, to whom are thefe premiums and all other favours, with which it is wiſhed to combat the nature of things, diſtributed? Does the individual of whom it is intended to make a failor enjoy any advantage from them? Let not men be deceived in this, they are the prey

carry on in courts of juſtice, far from their refidence.—Judge if a poor fiſherman can expofe himfelf to thefe inconveniencies; this is what has caufed fiſheries to decline, efpecially thofe of Scotland.—It is what has given fo much afcendancy to the Dutch, who have no premiums. It is that which has rendered premiums ufelefs. Other Governments adopt this method of giving premiums: the fame difficulties are attached to them, and yet people are aſtoniſhed that things go not on better.

of

of the navigator, who goes not out of his clo-
fet but to walk about, and who directs his steps
sometimes toward the sea side. He begins by
taking his own share, and be persuaded that
the wages which he offers to those whom he
employs to conduct his perilous enterprize are
parsimoniously calculated: therefore the end is
not attained.

If there be an absolute want of sailors who
have passed their noviciate about the Banks of
Newfoundland, and in the North seas, there is
a more simple and sure means, less expensive,
and what is more important, one which is exempt from destructive consequences, to form
them. Choose from honest families young,
robust, and intelligent men ; insure to them a
personal recompense if, after a certain number
of voyages on board fishing vessels, they bring
certificates of good behaviour, and of experience
acquired by practice. Oblige them to go on
board vessels belonging to nations or cities, to
which these difficult fisheries are a necessary re-
source. It is there they will acquire real
knowledge. These, added afterwards to sailors
exercised in the coasting and in the fisheries on
their own coasts, will form for the navy experienced sailors.

Whale oil belongs to the fisheries: it is another

ther great article of commerce with the United States.   All oil of this denomination is not produced by whales only; great quantities of it is drawn from feals, and other fpecies of fifh.

The ufe of this oil is much reftrained in France*: that of the white of the whale, and of which fuch fine candles are made, is little known there.   The ufe of oil will become more general.

Lord Sheffield is of opinion, that found policy makes it neceffary that the Englifh fhould prohibit, or at leaft difcourage by duties, American oil.   It was with this idea that the government of England impofed a duty of four hundred and fifty livres tournois per ton on oils imported by the independent Americans, to favour the oils of Canada and Nova Scotia.

This rigour fhould make this production, which has been hitherto profcribed, received in France.   The introduction of it is fo much the more neceffary, as the French whale fifhery is ruined.   Bayon, formerly celebrated for this fifhery, has abandoned it; Dunkirk, which con-

---

* By ftatements which deferve fome faith it appears, that in 1784 the importation into France of whale oil, and that of other fifh taken by the French, was 1,610,6~9 lb.—Foreign oil 2,748,099 lb. Portugal furnifhed almoft half of the laft.

tinues

tinues to fit out veſſels, furniſhes but little of this oil, and at a very high price.

Whether the French go to the North, or towards Braſil, they will labour under a diſad-vantage :—Without aſylum in caſe of misfor-tune, their navigation is always longer and more expenſive than that of other nations which carry on a whale fiſhery. It is therefore more to the advantage of France to receive American oil, and to pay for it with her wines and ma-nufactures.

The French government ſoon perceived the neceſſity of receiving the oils of America. Had not this been done, an emigration of American fiſhermen into Canada and Nova Scotia would have been the conſequence. This was near happening, ſome time after the peace, in the iſland of Nantucket. In deſpair on ſeeing the ports of England ſhut, and not knowing where to ſell their oils, which alone ſupplied all their wants, the inhabitants had reſolved to emigrate to Nova Scotia, when, on the moment of de-parture, they received a letter from the Marquis de la Fayette, whom they juſtly looked upon as their patron and father. He perſuaded them to be patient until the French government ſhould ſuppreſs or reduce the duties on oils, which

have

have been reduced for a limited time; but during this time the independent Americans are to enjoy, with refpect to their oils, all the advantages given to the moft favoured nation*; and this favour, joined to all their other advantages, cannot fail to give them a great fuperiority in this branch of commerce, as beneficial to France as to them,

The white of the whale muft be added, and the candles made with this fubftance; they are known by the name of fpermaceti candles, and ferve inftead of very fine bougies or wax candles. The American Colonies exported of them, according to Lord Sheffield, to the amount of five hundred thoufand livres tournois, in the years 1768, 1769, and 1770, calculating thefe candles at thirty-two fols a pound. It is probable, that thefe would be better made in France.

* Such are the duties on whale oil, &c. paid in France, according to the tarifs of 1664, and 1667; whale bone, cut and prepared by the French, thirty fols per cwt. fins three livres per cwt. a barrel of oil of five hundred pounds weight, three livres.—Whale bone from foreign fifheries, pays in the firft inftance, nineteen livres, in the fecond, thirty livres, and twelve livres in the third. The Hanfe Towns pay nine livres in the firft inftance, and feven livres ten fols in the third.—It is this laft duty which the American oils now pay.

SECTION

SECTION III.

CORN, FLOUR, &c.

Foreign corn and flour enter France on paying a duty too inconfiderable to make any fenfible increafe in their price. The principles laid down in the preceding article, with refpect to articles of fubfiftence, muft be adopted for the commodities of corn and flour.

The corn merchant, the moft ufeful of all merchants (whatever the vulgar, who, from a want of information, confounds a dealer in corn with a monopolifer, may think of him), fears arbitrary exceptions, fudden prohibitions, and unexpected ftrokes of authority. This ftate of uncertainty prevents the folid eftablifhment of the true fyftem of liberty, whence refult innumerable inconveniencies, which no other fyftem would bring on provided it were fixed, and that it afforded a certain bafis of calculation.

But how could a legiflation for corn be formed which fhould not be one of liberty, and which fhould neverthelefs afford a like bafis?

This

This is impoſſible : ſeeking, firſt of all, the particular rules for every caſe, when theſe are of
a nature not to be foreſeen, is ſeeking for a
chimera.

Not to fall into contradiction it is neceſſary
to chooſe between arbitrary power and liberty.
—But that which is arbitrary preſents nothing
but a perſpective which is naturally diſcourag-
ing. No property is ſafe under this ſyſtem :
when it exiſts, the merchant and the cultivator
are obliged to hazard their property in a lottery,
of which the chicaneries cannot be calculated ;
for it is neceſſary to foreſee the falſe informa-
tions, errors, and manœuvres, of an intereſt different from their own, and even from that of
the public, the attempts of power, &c. ; and if
all theſe conſiderations ought to enter into the
elements of their calculations, how can they
found hopes on ſuch a variable baſis ?

Liberty conſiſting, on the contrary, in the
choice which every one may make of that
which is moſt agreeable to him, according to
the circumſtances of the moment. This is a
general rule; it is applicable to every caſe, and
the hope of gain is always accompanied by the
deciſive certainty that an individual will be
maſter of all his induſtry, and of combining his

ſpeculations

fpeculations according to circumftances, which human power cannot govern.

From this demonftrated truth, that in every ftate of circumftances, the firft thing needful to the commerce of grain is a fixed rule, refults the neceffity of embracing the fyftem of liberty, and of protecting it in its fulleft extent, without oppofing any reftrictive condition *.

Governments fhould be determined by the neceffity alone of this fixed rule, if the fyftem of liberty was not even demonftrated to be the beft in every refpect.   But this fyftem is moreover the moft certain prefervative againft the alternatives of ruinous abundance, and fcarcity ftill more ruinous, which are both calamities, wherever impofts are confiderable.

Lord Sheffield obferves, that Europe, not being conftantly under the neceffity of recurring to American corn, the United States cannot put corn and flour into the clafs of productions, which found an effential and durable com-

---

* The Englifh fometimes prohibit importation or exportation.—But it muft be obferved, that the Englifh previoufly fix the price of corn, which determines prohibitions.   This is therefore a fixed law, and which, confequently, deranges not fpeculators like an arbitrary law.

merce.

merce *. Lord Sheffield is miftaken. It is a truth, which every man of obfervation is acquainted with, that not a year comes forward without fhewing that fome one or more nations in Europe are in want of corn. This want of grain therefore being occafionally extended to all Europe, France ought to be anxious to become the magazine of it, fince England was fo formerly. Therefore it would be advantageous to conftruct in the free ports opened to the United States commodious depofitories to receive and preferve American corn. By this means

---

* We have no fimple expreffion in France for *ftaple commodities*; words by which the Englifh term thofe forts of productions of foil or induftry, fo naturalized as to form an effential part of national riches, and of which the commerce is favoured by great eftablifhments, fuch as public buildings, depofitories, and places or markets, deftined to thefe productions. Thefe are called the *ftaple*, whence the expreffion *ftaple commodities* was naturally formed.

We have not, like the Englifh, the happy liberty of making words: their language becomes more rich, their elocution rapid, and we lofe ourfelves in long circumlocutions, to defcribe a thing of which we want the name; an inconvenience more pernicious to inftruction than is believed. This remark is not at prefent ill timed: it is to thofe who conduct affairs, who live among them, whofe vocation it is to treat thereon, to create words which explain them clearly and properly.

corn

corn would be always ready to be tranfported to the place where the beft price was to be had for it. Thefe free ports being depofitories where articles neceffary to the United States would be collected, the commerce of corn would thereby acquire a continuation advantageous to the two nations:—advantageous to America, becaufe the certainty of a place of depofit, fafe and little expenfive, would caufe grain to be fent more frequently; advantageous to France, becaufe, befides the continual poffeffion of an important commodity, and which would guarantee it from every manœuvre of interior monopoly, thefe depofitories would furnifh the means of a coafting trade, almoft continual, from the north of France to the fartheft part of the Mediterranean.

France does not grow all the corn fhe confumes*; fhe is obliged to get it from the north, from Sicily, and the coafts of Africa;

* This is a fact, though contrary to the common opinion. Another fact, which proves the neceffity of admitting corn at a low rate, fuch as the corn of America is, that three-fourths of the inhabitants of the province of Beauce, which produces fuch fine corn, eat black bread and no other, and of which they have not even enough. What muft this fcarcity be in other provinces where no corn is grown?

that

that of the United States ought to be more proper for her, for two reasons: First, it must be cheaper, being the produce of a cultivating people. Secondly, the people have more various and general wants of fresh provisions than the southern countries of Europe. The American may receive wines, fine oils, and fruits of France, in exchange for his corn. The Neopolitan, the Sicilian, and the African, cannot be paid in the same manner.

Finally, there is another consideration favourable to the importation of American corn: it may easily arrive at Honfleur *; there it may be stored up, and undergo all the processes necessary to its preservation; processes which are become very simple and little expensive †.

Thefe

---

* I quote Honfleur, because this port, from various circumstances, useless to mention here, is destined by nature to become the depository of a great commerce, and that especially of the United States with France. The project of making it a free port has been under consideration; and it is to the greatest interest of France that this project should be carried into execution.

† These consist in nothing but placing magazines in the open air, opened to dry winds, and constructed in such a manner as to be entirely removed. This operation, performed once a fortnight, in proper weather, needs only to be repeated a certain number of times; after which the corn

may

Thefe eftablifhments would keep up a confider-able quantity of foreign corn within the reach of the capital, a greater advantage than may be imagined.

There are ftill other motives which ought to engage the French to encourage the importa-tion of American corn. They have need of it for the vaft magazines which the land and fea forces, and frequently fcarcity, oblige them to keep ftored.

What fhould hinder Government from form-ing magazines of American corn in the French fugar iflands, which tempefts, conflagrations, and other unforefeen accidents, expofe fo fre-quently to famine, becaufe contracted victual-ling is carried on by monopolifers, who fend but little in order to fell dear?

may be left in a heap, without fear of its heating. Experi-ments of this kind have been carefully made. The method of preferving corn ufed at Geneva may be quoted: The go-vernment has eftablifhed one of its greateft revenues in the fale of corn to the people, and its intereft has, confequently, led it to improve the art of preferving this commodity. Be-fides, in depofitories deftined wholly to the corn dealers, the fame corn never remains long enough to render its preferva-tion difficult. There is fome reafon to believe that the falt air of the fea is favourable for it.

SECTION

SECTION IV.

MASTS, YARDS, AND OTHER TIMBER FOR THE NAVY.

France, like other European ftates which have a royal navy and fleets of merchant fhips to keep in repair, imports timber from Livonia and Ruffia. This general magazine begins to be exhaufted; the quality of its mafts is not fo good as formerly. This commerce is, moreover, attended with the difadvantage to France of requiring confiderable remittances of money, without reckoning the inconveniences of a dangerous navigation, frequently interrupted by ice; alfo the competition of feveral nations, which their proximity and many other circumftances naturalize, fo to fpeak, in the ports and feas of the North; advantages which the French cannot have.

Thefe confiderations ought to determine France to turn her attention to the United States, to procure from them the timber neceffary for her navy, and maft timber efpecially. There is but one objection to this, and it arifes from prejudice. It is pretended in France, that

the

the quality of American timber is very much inferior to that of the Baltic. Some people go fo far as to maintain that it is improper for the conftruction of veffels. I have reafon to believe that this judgment is not only hafty, but dictated either by ignorance, or the partiality of perfons interefted in the Baltic timber.

It is not in the laws of nature, that immenfe countries, whofe afpects are as varied as thofe of Europe can be, and in whofe foil there are the fame diverfities, fhould produce no timber but of a quality inferior to that of the timber of Europe.

Better directed inquiries, and a more attentive examination, will foon deftroy this prejudice againft the quality of American timber; a prejudice fo much the more difagreeable, as it would deprive the commerce between France and the United States of an article important to the two nations.

If France will inform herfelf ferioufly of this matter, let her confult even the enemies of America; let her confult Lord Sheffield, fo moderate in his eulogiums, when it is neceffary to give them to the independent Americans. His Lordfhip fays exprefsly, " that the nego- " ciators of the treaty of peace, who have ceded " the

" the territory of Penobſcot, to the eaſt of
" Caſco bay, belonging to Great Britain, de-
" ſerve the ſevereſt cenſure; as this country
" produces, without contradiction, the beſt
" timber. The coaſt," adds his Lordſhip,
" is covered with timber proper for navigation
" and other uſes, and in quantities ſufficient to
" the wants of Great Britain for centuries to
" come. The white pine, known in England
" by the name of the Weymouth Pine, or
" the Pine of New England, abounds in this
" territory; it is inconteſtably the beſt for
" maſts, and grows there to a prodigious
" height."

This is confirmed to us by men who have
travelled and reſided in the United States.
Theſe men aſſure us, that the States produce
all kinds of timber of which we are in need,
and that the white pine of the Connecticut,
Penobſcot, and Kennebeck rivers is, at leaſt,
equal in quality to that of the north of Europe.
The ſhip-builders of Philadelphia eſteem it ſo
much, that they begin to make uſe of it for
ſide planks above the ſurface of the water.

Green oak, of which there are ſuch fine foreſts in Georgia, unites the moſt precious qualities; it may be procured from St. Mary's,

of

of a more confiderable fcantling than that
which comes from the Levant and the ifland
of Corfica; it is compact, the worms never attack it, and its duration is unequalled. The
green oak of Carolina is the hardeft timber
known ;—the veffels built with it are of a very
long duration.

SECTION V.

SKINS AND FURS.

In this trade Lord Sheffield looks upon the
United States as dangerous rivals to Canada;
and it is not without reafon that his lordfhip is
of this opinion.

The proximity of the great eftablifhments
which the independent Americans form at prefent at *Pitfburgh*, and in many other places of
their poffeffions beyond the mountains, muft
infenfibly give them great advantages in this
commerce, and make them partake with Canada a large fhare of the profits.

In fact, the regions fituated between the waters of the lake *Ontario*, and thofe of the Miffiffippi, interfected by the numerous rivers
which fall into the South and North-Weft of

Lake

Lake Erie, of the *Michigan*, and of the *Superior*, as far as the *Ouifconfing* *, and even to the *lac des bois*; the great undertakings in which the Virginians are at prefent employed, to improve the navigation of the *Potowmack*, to the foot of the Alle-Gheny; the probability of another communication with the ultramontane waters, by means of the weftern branches of the *Suf-quehannah*; without omitting the facility with which the inhabitants of the ftate of New York went to *Niagara* before the war, in going up the Hudfon's river from their capital to Albany, beyond that of the Mohawks, croffing the little lake of Oneida, and by means of an eafy carriage going down the river of *Ofwego*, in the mouth of which the Ontario forms an excellent harbour; all thefe reafons, and many others which relate not only to geography, but to climate, proximity, &c. muft in a few years put the Americans in poffeffion of the greateft part of the fur trade.

Thefe advantages will be ftill more certain, when the Englifh fhall have evacuated the forts

---

* A great river which falls into the Miffiffippi, at feven hundred leagues from the fea.

of

of Niagara*, the great eftablifhment of the ftreight †, and that of the Michillimakinack ‡.

The annual fales in London of furs from Canada, produced, in 1782, four millions feven hundred thoufand livres tournois, fomething more in 1783, and in 1784 they amounted to upwards of five millions. All thefe furs are paid for with Englifh manufactures, and the fourth part is prepared in England, by which their value is doubled. Now this rich commerce, carried on by way of Quebec, will certainly fall as foon as the forts and the countries which they command fhall be reftored to the Americans. It is from this confideration that the reftitution of thefe forts is withheld; to the period of which the Englifh look forward with pain.

---

* A very important one, which commands the fpace of the thirteen leagues which feparates the lakes Erie and Ontario.

† A city founded by the French, on the height of St. Claire, which carries the waters of the lakes Michigan and Huron into the Erie.

‡ A fort and eftablifhment at the point, in the ifland of this name, which commands the paffage of the falls of St. Mary, through which the waters of the upper lake fall into thofe of the Huron.

SECTION

SECTION VI.

RICE, INDIGO, FLAX-SEED.

It is not poffible to fpeak of American rice without thinking of the pernicious inconveniences which its cultivation produces. The wretched flaves who cultivate it, obliged to be half the year in water, are expofed to fcrophulous diforders and a premature death. It is faid, that this confideration prevents the ftates, wherein rice is produced, from abolifhing flavery. Free men would not devote themfelves willingly to this deftructive labour*.

Were this even true, and that in the fyftem of liberty means could not be found to reconcile this culture to the health of the labourers, a fufficient motive could not be drawn from it to condemn to death, or to cruel difeafes, a part

---

* Rice is cultivated in Piedmont and in Italy, by people who have no habitations, and are known by the name of Banditti, the fruit of the bad political conftitutions of that part of Europe. When thefe Banditti have finifhed their work, the Sbirres conduct them to the frontiers, for fear of the diforders to which their inaction and mifery might incline them.

of

of our fellow creatures, born free, equal us*, and with an equal right to live. Were the culture of this commodity even abfolutely ne-ceffary, this neceffity would give us no right over the lives of negroes, or it would be the effect of a ftate of war; for fervitude was never a right.

* They are of a different colour from that of the Euro-peans; but does the quality of man depend on colour? Are not the negroes organized as we are? Have not they like us every thing which belongs to the production of the fpecies, to the formation of ideas, and to their development? If their black colour ought to have any moral effect, to have any in-fluence over their fate, or to determine our conduct towards them, it fhould be that of inducing us to leave them where they are, and not to force them away from their country; not to punifh them by the moft barbarous treatment on account of their colour; not to drag them into a foreign land, to con-demn them there to the vile and painful life of animals. Do they come and offer themfelves voluntarily as flaves? Do they afk to leave thofe torrid zones, wherein nature feems to have circumfcribed them by their colour, as fhe has done by us in more temperate ones by our white complexions? Their wants being few, keep them in ignorance; we add every thing capable of changing it into imbecility, and we argue upon this degradation, of which we are the culpable authors, to tranquillize ourfelves on the juft reproaches which nature makes us! Can we boaft therefore of our knowledge, as long as it remains an accomplice in thefe horrors? See on this fubject, *l'examen critique des Voyages*, de M. de Chaftelux.

There

There is a fpecies of dry rice no way dangerous to cultivate. Moreover the example of the
Chinefe and the Indians, among whom the
culture of rice makes not fuch ravages, ought
to make us hope, that in imitating them life
and health would be reftored to men, of which
we have never had a right to deprive them.

After having confidered this production as a
man fhould confider it, I muft now confider it
as a merchant ought to do.

The French government has not yet taken a
determined refolution relative to the introduction of American rice. It is a wholefome and
fimple article of fubfiftence, proper to fupply
the place of principal commodities. It cannot be
too often repeated, that the multiplication of
articles of fubfiftence ought to be encouraged;
it would render life lefs painful to the people,
increafe population, and confequently natural
riches.

If France wifhes to have a great and folid
commerce with the United States, fhe ought
to admit all the productions of the United
States.

The Americans exported annually, during
the years 1768, 1769, and 1770, to Great Britain and the fouth of Europe, a hundred and
fifteen

fifteen thoufand barrels of rice, worth fix millions and a half of livres tournois*. It is the
moft confiderable article of exportation after tobacco, wheat, and flour. It deferves therefore that France fhould think of it for her
commerce, and endeavour to bring it into her
ports, to be diftributed there to other European
markets.

INDIGO.

The fame thing may be faid of the indigo
of the Carolinas and Georgia; it makes a part
of the important productions of the United
States, and is confumed in Europe;—it is therefore neceffary to open for its reception all the
French ports, and afterwards to give it eafy
communications. The Englifh received of it
annually, during the years 1768, 1769, and
1770, to the amount of three millions of livres
tournois †. It was principally confumed in
England, Ireland, and the north of Europe, by
reafon of its low price. The indigo of St. Domingo is much dearer.

---

* The exportation from Charleftown, from December
1784, to December 1785, amounted to 67,713 barrels.

† The exportation of dye-ftuff, made in 1785, from Charleftown, amounted to 500,920 pound weight.

The

The Indigo of Carolina and Georgia has acquired a much better quality fince the firft
quantities of it arrived in England; but I have
not learnt that it is to be compared with the
indigo of Domingo. Travellers fay, that Carolina produces indigo almoft as good as that of
the French iflands.

There are kinds of dying to which low
priced indigo is proper; and, for this reafon,
certain dyers ufe that of the Carolinas and Georgia. In thefe cafes, it will always have the
preference. Therefore American indigo fhould
be admitted as long as there is a confumption
for it, for the Americans will continue to cultivate it; and fince this cultivation cannot be
prevented, the moft advantageous thing is to
ftrive to become agents in the general commerce of America.

FLAX-SEED.

North America fent to England and Ireland,
during the years 1768, 1769, and 1770, flax-
feed to the amount of two millions and a half
of livres tournois;—it was all confumed in
Great Britain. The advantage of paying for
this feed with Irifh linens, gave it the preference to that of Flanders and the Baltic. Flax-
feed

feed from thefe countries is, moreover, very dear.

It is the bufinefs of thofe French merchants, who may be interefted in the commerce with the United States, to confider what advantages they may derive from this commerce. If the culture of flax becomes extenfive in France, foreign feed ought to be preferred for two reafons: —the quality of the production is improved by it, and there is more advantage in fpinning flax in peopled and induftrious countries, than in letting it ripen to gather feed. It appears, that flax-feed comes not in abundance, but from countries where there are not hands fufficient to fpin, or give the firft preparation, even to the flax they produce; it is then proper to cultivate it for its feed, which becomes a confiderable article of commerce: as long as this ftate of things fubfifts, it muft alfo be proper for peopled countries to get flax-feed from abroad.

Flanders feems to be an exception; but the exportation of flax is there prohibited, for the purpofe of encouraging fpinning, &c.; in this cafe Flanders, being a country very proper for the cultivation of flax, may leave to many cultivators of this plant no other refource than the commerce of the feed. It is probable, that if the

the flax could be fent from Flanders, after the
firft preparation for fpinning, nobody would
think of gathering the feed.

SECTION VII.

NAVAL STORES, SUCH AS PITCH, TAR, AND TURPENTINE.

Before the emancipation of America, England
received confiderable fupplies of thefe articles
from America, particularly from Carolina and
the fouth. The quantities of thefe articles
amounted annually, during the years 1768,
1769, and 1770, to twenty-feven thoufand
feven hundred barrels of pitch; eighty-two
thoufand four hundred barrels of tar; and
twenty-eight thoufand one hundred of turpentine: the whole amounting, in the port of
exportation, to one million two hundred and
twenty-eight thoufand livres tournois.

Thefe ftores were very valuable to the Englifh, as well for their commerce as for their
proper confumption. Two confiderable manufactures, eftablifhed at Hull, were fupported
by them; tar was there converted into pitch,
confiderable quantities of it were exported to
the

the fouth, where it was received in competition with that from the north of Europe.
Turpentine, converted in thefe manufactures
into oil or fpirit, furnifhed a confiderable object
of commerce. England confumes a great deal
of it in the preparation of colours, varnifhes,
&c.

The American revolution has not made the
Englifh lofe fight of thefe ftores: the want
they have of them makes it imprudent to truft
wholly to the exportation of thefe articles from
Ruffia and Sweden, where the Englifh have
the Dutch for competitors. Moreover, the
navigation of America, lefs dangerous than
that of the Baltic, is not, like the laft, limited
to a certain time of the year, it is confequently
more frequent and lefs expenfive; fo that thefe
ftores will come for a long time from America
at a lower price than from the north. American tar is as good as that of Europe, thicker and
more proper for making pitch; it is preferred
for fheep, even at a higher price. American
turpentine is inferior to none but that of
France.

An Englifh merchant has taught the Ruffians
how to furnifh as good turpentine as that from
any other nation: this production will be in
great

great abundance there, by the numerous and immenfe forefts of firs in the neighbourhood of Archangel, where their corps are depofited.

This ftate of things fhews to France what value fhe ought to attach to the naval ftores which may be furnifhed from America. The quantities of them exported from Charleftown becomes more and more confiderable*. The fandy foil near the fea, in North Carolina and the fouth of Virginia, produces a great quantity of firs, from which tar and turpentine are extracted; this is done without much trouble, and the facility of felling and preparing the trees is a great encouragement.

---

* In 1782,—2041 barrels of pitch, tar, and turpentine, were exported from Charleftown. In 1783,—14697 barrels. I know not how many barrels the exportation of 1784 amounted to; but that of 1785 confifted of 17,000. The fame increafe is obferved in other articles. The moft confiderable is rice, afterwards indigo;—the other articles are, tobacco, deer-fkins, timber, wheat, butter, wax, and leather. This exportation amounts to near four hundred thoufand pounds fterling.

SECTION VIII.

TIMBER AND WOOD, FOR CARPENTERS AND COOPERS WOOK; SUCH AS STAVES, CASK-HEADS, PLANKS, BOARDS, &c.

France as well as England ought to be, for their own interefts, engaged to favour the importation of thefe articles, of which the United States can furnifh fuch great quantities.

Timber fails in France, and will become more and more fcarce; population deftroys it:—yet timber muft be found for houfes, mills, &c.—hogfheads muft be made for fugars; cafks and barrels for wine, brandy, &c. Thefe articles of timber are principally furnifhed from the North to the ports of France—but they become dear, their quality diminifhes, and the Americans have the advantage in the carriage *.

The

* It is neceffary to give our readers an idea of the price of fome of thefe articles: an American very converfant in them has furnifhed us with the neceffary particulars.

White oak planks, of two inches and a half thick, fawed by the hand, were fold, in 1785, at fifteen piaftres, or two hundred and fixty livres ten fols tournois, the thoufand feet.

Ordinary

The value of thefe articles, exported from America to Great Britain only, amounted to two millions of livres tournois in the year 1770, according to a ftatement drawn up in the Cuf-tom-Houfe of Bofton. The general exporta-tions to the Englifh, French, American, and Spanifh iflands, and to the different parts of Europe, are immenfe, and become daily more confiderable. Were not this timber of a good quality, the increafe of this commerce would not be fo rapid. The French have in this re-fpect fome prejudices, which it is of importance to deftroy. If the American ftaves are efteem-ed in making rum cafks, &c. they will un-doubtedly preferve our brandies.

Ordinary planks of fine white pine an inch thick, fourteen or fifteen feet long, and from a foot to fourteen inches wide, were fold at the fame time at feven piaftres, or thirty-feven livres tournois, the thoufand feet.—Thofe of a double thick-nefs, double the price.

Planks, from two to five inches thick, and from fifteen to fixty feet long, at twenty-one pounds New York money, or two hundred and feventy-three livres tournois, the thoufand feet.—The fame perfon faid he had feen curbs or bent tim-ber at ten fhillings, New York money, a ton, the expence of cutting, &c. not included.

SECTION

SECTION IX.

VESSELS CONSTRUCTED IN AMERICA, TO BE SOLD OR FREIGHTED.

It has been obferved that the bulk of the commodities which might be exchanged by the commerce between France and the United States, was, at an equal value, much more confiderable on the fide of America than that of France. There refults from this, that in thefe exchanges a great number of American veffels muft be fubject to return to America in ballaft. —This ftate of things would certainly be prejudicial to the commerce between the two nations, if fome compenfation could not be eftablifhed which fhould remove the inequality.

This compenfation may be made in a very advantageous manner to both. The independent Americans conftruct veffels for fale: if it be agreeable to a nation to purchafe of another the articles which this manufactures at a lefs expence, and with more means, it follows, that the French ought to buy American veffels ;
and,

and, in fact, this commerce begins to be eftablifhed.

Lord Sheffield reprobates this commerce
with refpect to his own country.—" Its exift-
" ence," fays his Lordfhip, " depends on its
" navy ; this depends as much on Englifh fhip-
" builders as on Englifh failors ; therefore, of
" all trades, that of fhip-building is the moft
" important to be preferved in Great Britain."
The advances, according to his Lordfhip, are
of little confequence, and thefe veffels not being deftined to be fold to foreigners, what they
coft ought to be confidered fo much the lefs, as
the expence is incurred in the country.

Lord Sheffield prefumes alfo, that fhip-building will be encouraged in New Scotland, Canada, the Ifland of St. John, &c. Finally, his
Lordfhip declares, " that the encouragement
" of fhip-building in the United States is ruin-
" ous to Great Britain ; that it is the fame to
" thofe who may purchafe American built vef-
" fels ; becaufe, notwithftanding their cheap-
" nefs, thefe veffels are little durable, from the
" nature of their materials." This obfervation
relates particularly to veffels built for fale,
which, his Lordfhip fays, " are very inferior to
thofe which are befpoken."

It

It cannot be denied, that it is of confequence to a nation which attaches a great importance to its navy, to have fhip-builders. The repairs &c. of which veffels are conftantly in want, would be badly directed, if there were not, in the clafs of workmen to whom this induftry belongs, men capable of conftructing a veffel, and habituated to this conftruction. What is ftill more, as foon as a nation has a navy, it is greatly to its intereft to poffefs every means of improving it; and the poffeffion of thefe means is fo much more fecure when there are eftablifhments in the country which, in this cafe, fupport emulation, by the conftant exercife of the art.

But it does not follow, that to preferve fuch an advantage, a nation ought to have no other veffels than thofe which are home built: it is here neceffary to diftinguifh fhips belonging to the royal navy from merchant fhips. The firft are alone fufficient to employ a requifite number of able builders, and to fupply every thing which the conftruction and repairs of veffels require. But merchant fhips, of which a confiderable number is wanted, may be procured from abroad, if thofe of an equal quality can be had at a price confiderably lefs.

Will it be faid, that a nation becomes fo much

much the more powerful at fea, as the conftruction of veffels is encouraged in her ports?
that under this point of view it is neceffary to
be cautious not to furnifh the independent
Americans the means of forming a navy, which
would render them formidable? that it is at
leaft unneceffary to haften thefe means?

If this confideration were true, it would in
fome meafure impofe on France a law to encourage the United States to form their navy:
for, however formidable her own may be, fhe
has too many natural obftacles to remove for
her navy to be the effect of any thing but painful
efforts, and confequently that it fhould be an
eftablifhment very difficult to maintain,—very
expenfive, and fubject to long intermiffions.
And fince it is neceffary to fpeak conftantly of
a threatening rivality,—of an armed rivality,—
France has the greateft intereft, to balance
more furely the force of her rivals, by calling
to her aid the naval force of a friendly people,
—of a people to whom nature has been prodi-
gal in the means fhe has given them of having
a confiderable one.

But the policy which refufed to purchafe
American veffels, for fear the Americans fhould
become formidable at fea, would be badly
founded.

founded. A fure manner of retarding the eftablifhment of a navy, by a nation which poffeffes the means and materials; the power and
activity which fuch a great eftablifhment requires, is to employ it continually in the conftruction of veffels for fale, and to habituate it
to this kind of commerce. If this nation, and
fuch is the pofition of the United States, has
nothing to fear interiorly from any other power,
it will certainly defpife all fuch military preparations, whofe profit and utility will not be fo
immediately perceived, as the frequent gains of
peaceful commerce. Therefore, let the independent Americans be perfuaded to build veffels
for fale: let them not be provoked to build
fhips for defenfive and offenfive operations, and
they will neglect the great means with which
nature has furnifhed them, of having a refpectable navy: they will even neglect them, when
greater riches, and a more confiderable population, fhall facilitate to them the ufe of their
natural means.

Far from fuffering by this new arrangement
of things, France would gain thereby. This
idea will undoubtedly appear extraordinary, becaufe, in abandoning workmanfhip to American
fhip-builders, France is deprived of it: but how
easily

eafily may fhe compenfate this apparent lofs! In fact, when nothing is to be had without labour, it is then confidered as real riches : therefore, it ought to be employed with a prudent economy, efpecially in the fyftem of national rivalities. The workmen who will not build veffels, will make cloth, with which veffels may be paid for. The expence of manufacturing thefe cloths will be paid at home, as that for the conftruction of veffels would have been ; by which means, thefe will be had at a cheaper rate. This labour and expence will therefore produce greater advantages, and place the nation in a more defirable relation with its rivals.

Finally, Lord Sheffield, whofe narrow policy is here refuted, propofes that fhip-building fhould be encouraged in Canada, New Scotland, &c. But do phyfical circumftances favour thefe countries as much as the United States ? Can England reap real advantages from this encouragement? It is a queftion with which feveral writers have combated Lord Sheffield, and on which I cannot decide.

But if England had this refource, France would be without it. Veffels built in America will always coft her lefs than her own, or thofe
conftructed

conftructed elfewhere: fhe ought therefore to favour the introduction of the firft.

A celebrated minifter, whom France has reafon to regret, thought as follows: his defign was to get a part of the veffels of the French navy conftructed in Sweden; he thereby expected to make great favings: they will be greater and more real, in getting the veffels conftructed in the United States.

The Englifh themfelves will not be able to refift the force of things; they will fooner or later return to the ufe of American veffels; for thefe coft but a third * of what Englifh veffels are built for; and cheapnefs is the firft law of commerce.

The bad quality attributed to American veffels is a fable, arifing from the following circumftances: in the contention for independence, the Americans built veffels in hafte, to arm them as cruifers: they were forced to make ufe of wood which was green, and unprepared; other things were either wanting to thefe veffels, or precipitately prepared. Confequently

* In New England the conftructors of veffels make their bargains at the rate of three pounds fterling per ton, carpenter's work included. On the Thames, the price is nine pounds fterling for the work alone of the carpenter.

the

the veffels were imperfect; but this imperfection was but accidental. A cruife is a lottery,
wherein no notice is taken of the goodnefs and
durability of the veffel. It is fufficient that it
be a good failer, this is the effential quality.

Peace has re-eftablifhed the conftruction of
veffels in the manner it ought to be ; and there
are American veffels built before the war, and
fome thirty years ago, which for goodnefs and
duration are not inferior to any Englifh veffel.

More progrefs has been made in America than
any where elfe in the art of fhip-building; this
is eafily explained :—it muft not be forgotten,
when the independent Americans are fpoken of,
that they are not recovering from a ftate of
barbarity. They are men efcaped from European civilifation, employed, fo to fpeak, in
creating their country and refources : no fhackles reftrain their efforts, every thing in Europe
is looked upon as perfect, and made ufe of,
without thinking of improving it. Thefe two
effential differences caufe a very confiderable
one in the intenfity of induftry.

Bofton has produced a man aftonifhing in the
art of fhip-building. Long and clofely employed in the fearch of means to unite fwiftnefs
of failing in veffels to their folidity, Mr. Peck
has

has had the greateſt ſuccefs. It was his hand which produced the Beliſarius, the Hazard, and the Rattleſnake, which were ſo particularly diſtinguiſhed during the late war by their ſwiftnefs of failing. Veſſels conſtructed by this able builder have qualities which others have not; they carry a fourth more, and fail faſter. Theſe facts are authenticated by a number of experiments.

The Engliſh themſelves acknowledge the ſuperiority of American ſhip-building: " The " fineſt veſſels," ſays Colonel Champion, " are " built at Philadelphia; the art of ſhip-build- " ing has attained in that city the higheſt de- " gree of perfection. Great veſſels are built in " New York, alſo in the Cheſapeak, and in " South Carolina: theſe laſt, made of green " oak, are of an unequalled ſolidity and dura- " bility."

The American proverb ſays: *That to have a perfect veſſel, it muſt have a Boſton bottom and Philadelphia ſides.*

The French, if connoiſſeurs be believed, are very inferior to the Americans in the minutiæ of ſhip-building. This ſuperiority of America ought not to ſurpriſe us: it will ſtill increaſe. The independent Americans who inhabit the coaſts,

coasts, live by the sea, and pride themselves in navigation. As they have competitors, their genius will never sleep, nor will its efforts be shackled in any manner whatever. In France, the people are, and ought to be cultivators; the marine is but a subordinate part, and by the nature of things, it must enjoy but a very precarious consideration. Honour, which affects the head of every Frenchman, is distributed but at Paris and at Court; and there men are, and must still be, far from perceiving the importance of attaching merit to the improvement of ship-building: it must therefore languish, or yield to that of the Americans. Hence it results, that the French, in preserving every thing which can maintain amongst them an able class of ship-builders, must buy vessels of the Americans; because every convenience is united to that of facilitating their reciprocal importations and exportations, of which the bulks are so different in one nation from those of the other.

This circumstance is attended with the advantage of procuring the French merchant an American vessel at a less price than if he had ordered it to be built, or if he bought it in America, because it will always be more to

the

the intereſt of the American to ſell his veſſel, than to take it back in ballaſt.

Such is the fitneſs of American veſſels for the French marine, and eſpecially for merchant ſervice; ſuch is that fitneſs for all the European powers who have harbours and ſeaport towns, that I think a ſure and commodious road in Europe would ſoon be aſſorted with American veſſels for ſale, if every thing which can encourage a like depoſitory were granted to the port wherein this road might be. This market for veſſels will be eſtabliſhed;—the Engliſh rejeƈt it. France will, in a ſhort time, encourage it.

SECTION X.

GENERAL CONSIDERATIONS ON THE PRECEDING CATALOGUE OF IMPORTATIONS FROM THE UNITED STATES INTO FRANCE.

The liſt which I have gone through of the articles with which the independent Americans may furniſh Europe in exchange for her merchandize is not very long; but theſe articles are conſiderable, and important enough in themſelves, to merit the attention of European merchants:

merchants: they are fufficient to deftroy the prejudices of thofe who, under the falfe pretext of the inability of the Americans to furnifh articles of exchange, difdain a reciprocal commerce with the United States. Thefe articles are not, however, the only ones which France may receive from them. Independently of pot-afh, fo precious to manufactures, and of which the fcarcity becomes daily more fenfible; iron, vegetable-wax, wool, flax, hemp, &c. may increafe the number. The Englifh received of pot-afh to the amount of four hundred thoufand livres per annum, during the years 1768, 1769, and 1770; pot-afh being the produce of the wood burnt by the Americans, and as the burning of wood muft increafe with the number of people, the quantities of pot-afh muft have increafed with population.

I ought to hope that this work, once known in the United States, will excite the independent Americans to co-operate with me, in what I have propofed to myfelf, which is to fpread inftruction on every thing which relates to their country. They will make known to Europe, in a more extenfive and complete manner, every thing which can maintain that reciprocal commerce in favour of which I write:

they

they will affemble in a work correfpondent to this, all that I have been able to expofe but imperfectly : they will rectify my errors. I invite them to apply to this interefting fubject : I pray them to give it for a bafis, more philofophical, and philanthropical principles, than thofe which have hitherto directed the jealous induftry of each fociety. For each, led on by a blind ambition, has wifhed to embrace every thing, to do every thing at home, and furnifh every thing to others; each has taken for principle to receive nothing from others, except it be gold; each has accuftomed itfelf to look upon every production, manufactured or unmanufactured, which it fent abroad as a profit, and all thofe which it received as fo many loffes. Such is the falfe principle, according to which all the European nations have directed their exterior commerce.

What would be the confequence of a like fyftem, if it continued to prevail? All nations would be ftrangers to each other, and exterior commerce abfolutely annihilated; becaufe it tends to take from this commerce that which fupports it. For the gold which is wifhed for in payment for exportations is refufed to thofe who would obtain it : all nations look upon the

neceffity

neceffity of giving it alike; that it is difadvantageous—and ftrive to avoid it. If, therefore,
on one fide, none will take returns in kind,
and on the other, nobody will difpoffefs himfelf
of his gold, what will become of exchanges?
what will become of commerce?

Nature, which intended to make men fo
many brothers, and nations fo many families;
—nature, which, to unite all men by the fame
tie, has given them wants, which place them
in a ftate of dependence one on the other;—
this wife nature has, by the diftribution of her
gifts, anticipated and condemned this exclufive
fyftem. She has faid to the inhabitants of
Nantucket, The rock which thou inhabit is
rude and ftormy; renounce, therefore, the defire of drawing from it the delicious wines and
fruits which more calm and temperate climates
produce. Look at the fea which furrounds
thee,—that is thy property and thy treafure: I
have made it inexhauftible; and if thou knoweft
how to make ufe of it, if thou wilt confine
thyfelf thereto, all the enjoyments of the other
continent are thine: a fingle ftroke of a har-
poon, dexteroufly thrown, will produce a thoufand times more wine in thy cellar, than if by
a painful

a painful cultivation thou continueft obftinate,
in acting contrary to my intentions.

Nature holds the fame language to the other
inhabitants of the earth: fhe tells the French
to ufe all their efforts in the fruitful foil which
fhe has given them, and to ceafe traverfing foreign feas to obtain, at an immenfe expence and
much rifk, the fifh and oil which the inhabitants of Nantucket procure with greater facility
and more fuccefs and economy.

Why fhould not all nations underftand a language fo fimple, fo wife, and fo proper to produce univerfal harmony ? But how are they to
be made to underftand it ? By what means are
they to be prevailed upon to adopt it ? What
means are proper to engage nations which
might have a direct commerce between them,
to fign a treaty of commerce, which fhould
leave each at liberty to furnifh that which it
could export better and cheaper than others;
and thus eftablifh exchanges on the immutable
laws of nature ?

As foon as nations fhall be enlightened
enough to perceive the advantage of fuch a
treaty, from that moment it will ceafe to be
neceffary, and every other treaty will be ftill
lefs fo. It will then be feen, that they all center

ter in the fingle word *liberty*.   It will be difcovered that liberty can put every thing in its
place; that liberty alone, without negociation
or parchment, can every where give birth to
an advantageous induftry.   Finally, that every
where, and at all times, fhe has fported with
thofe commercial conventions, of which politicians have fo ridiculoufly boafted; of thofe
conventions wherein the contracting parties are
inceffantly on the defenfive with refpect to
each other, inceffantly difpofed to deceive, and
frequently multiply the feeds of war in a work
of peace.

Under fuch a fyftem of liberty, there would
be no longer occafion for craftinefs in national
policy with refpect to commerce:—of what ufe
would it be? No more ftrife; for it would
have no object: no more jealoufy or rivality;
no more fear of making others profper and become rich; becaufe the riches of each ftate
would be advantageous to the whole. In a
word, according to this fyftem, each nation
would wifh the other more means, in order to
have more to give and more to receive.   Commerce would become what it ought to be, the
exchange of induftry againft induftry; of enjoyments againft enjoyments, and not againft
                                    deprivations:

deprivations : finally, a ftate of riches, without poverty on any fide.

What people have more right and title than the Americans, to be the firft in adopting fo philanthropical a fyftem, and which is fo conformable to the laws of nature; at leaft to do nothing which fhall retard it among them? Let their Congrefs,—that refpectable affembly, which may become the light of nations, and from whofe deliberations univerfal happinefs may refult,—remain faithful to the indications of this nature; let it interrogate her conftantly, and give every nation the fame falutary habitude.

If Europe refufes to admit the productions of the United States, let Congrefs,—rejecting the poor policy of reprifals,—open, by a great and republican refolution, their ports to all European productions. What evil can refult from this to the independent Americans? If European prohibitions rendered their means of exchange ufelefs, European merchandize muft of courfe be without a market in America; or, falling to a mean price in the United States, it would become profitable to the Americans, in paying for it even with gold.

The law may be given to an idle and degraded

graded nation, but never to one which is active and induftrious. This always punifhes, in fome manner or other, the tyrannical proceedings of other nations. The force of things is alone fufficient to revenge it.

It is a misfortune to the United States, in not having been able to eftablifh at firft the noble fyftem of which I have fpoken, and to be obliged to have recourfe to the miferable means of other governments,—that of impofing duties on foreign merchandize to pay their debts. Every impofition but a quit-rent upon lands is a fource of errors. The *pretended protecting duties* impofed in Europe are one confequence of thefe errors, and of which the effect leads government aftray, fo far as to perfuade them, that they poffefs a creative force equal to that of the Divinity himfelf. And what are thefe enterprifes by which men would force nature? Miferable hot-houfes,—wherein every thing is haftened to finifh the fooner; wherein induftry vainly exhaufts itfelf to fupport an unnatural exiftence; and wherein a vigorous whole is frequently facrificed to a corrupted part.

Let the Americans carefully avoid thefe erroneous enterprifes;—to infure themfelves therefrom,

therefrom, let them confider the ftate of Europe. The Europeans have no longer any
judgment in matters of impoft; fimple ideas are
loft, and become impoffible to be realized by the
metaphyfician which it is neceffary to employ
to combat ignorance, prejudices, and habitudes:
all ideas of juftice and propriety are confounded.
A truth cannot be advanced without meeting,
at every moment, falfe notions to combat.
The man of information is fatigued, difgufted,
and frequently at a lofs what to anfwer to objections preceeding from habits of error. He
perceives with concern, that the laws of happinefs cannot be written, but upon tables from
which there is nothing to be effaced: and fuch,
I flatter myfelf, is the fituation of the United
States. They are yet virgin ftates, they are
unacquainted with the inftitutions which end
in chaos, wherein the love of public good lofes
all its force.

Montefquieu obferves, that the enterprifes of
merchants are always neceffarily mixed with
public affairs; but that in monarchies, public
affairs are for the moft part fufpicious in the
eyes of the merchants. But profperity and national glory depend on commerce, as much in
monarchies as in other conftitutions. It is
therefore

therefore the intereſt of monarchies to give to merchants that hope of proſperity which they have in republics, and which inclines them with ardour to every kind of commercial enter-priſe.

Provincial adminiſtrations are the ſureſt means of producing this happy effect. If they were already eſtabliſhed, the French would compre-hend, how abſurd it is to imagine that the United States will not diſcharge their public debt ; how impoſſible it is that Republicans ſhould make uſe of the diſhonourable reſource of bankruptcy and deception; and that their public ſpirit, their morals, and intereſt, require them to diſcharge this debt, contracted for the moſt legitimate and honourable cauſe that ever exiſted ; and which is otherways but an atom when compared with their immenſe reſources. French merchants would then give themſelves leſs concern about the manner in which their merchandize was to be paid for in America. For in the improbable caſe of a want of Ame-rican productions, or of precious metals, they have, as a laſt reſource, the paper of Congreſs and the States; which paper it is an advantage to acquire, by the price at which it is obtained, by the intereſt it bears, the certainty of its be-

ing

ing paid, and by the confequent tranfmiffion which may be made of it in commerce to the Dutch merchant, to whom the paper of the whole world becomes neceffary the moment it merits confidence.

I have mentioned precious metals. The Americans are in the neighbourhood of the countries which produce them. Thefe countries are the abodes of indolence, which difpenfes not with neceffaries. Skins, &c. of animals, and fome metals, are every thing that can be given there in exchange for articles of fubfiftence, which the inhabitants have not the courage to make their lands produce; and for the neceffaries, for which they find it more convenient to pay with gold than with their induftry. The independent Americans will become factors, advantageoufly placed between European manufactures, and the inhabitants of regions condemned by nature to the fterile productions of metals. All the powers of Spain cannot prevent this, nor ought even to undertake it. This new confideration promifing to the French payment, fo foolifhly defired in gold, ought to encourage them to prepare for a commercial connexion with the United States.

CONCLUSION

CONCLUSION

AND REFLECTIONS ON THE SITUATION OF THE UNITED STATES.

It will be proper to finifh this volume by fome explanations of the pretended troubles which agitate the United States. Thefe explanations are neceffary to deftroy the unfavourable impreffions which muft be made by the unfaithful recitals of gazette writers, who, from fervile prejudices or mean intereft, affect to fpread doubts of the happy confequences of the revolution. If we believe thefe people, the independent Americans are plunged into inextricable embarraffments, forced to become bankrupts, given up to the moft violent anarchy, expofed to the tomahawk of the implacable Indians, &c. How is it poffible to refolve to carry on a commerce with people whofe fituation is fo deplorable? Ought not their ruin to be feared rather than their fortune hoped for, in the connexions which it is wifhed to form with them?

It is neceffary to refute thefe falfehoods. It

is

is fo much the more fo, as ignorance eafily
leads people, little acquainted with republican
conftitutions, into error; and that, led aftray
by the prejudices of their educations, a great
number of Frenchmen look upon this form of
government as a ftate perpetually in a ferment,
wherein life and property are continually expofed to the greateft dangers.

Thefe prejudices lead to the belief of the
moft puerile and abfurd fables. The leaft attention is not paid to circumftances. Would
the United States have a Congrefs of magiftrates
if it were true that the people were at war with
them? For how could Congrefs and the magiftrates defend themfelves? They have no other
defence but the refpect which each individual
has for the law, this is their only force. It is
the obligation that the conftitution impofes on
them in common, with the meaneft citizens, of
being obedient to the law, as the laft means which
conftitute their only fafety, and which maintains,
in all cafes and every where, the authority which
the people have confided in them. They cannot employ a phyfical force farther than the
people are willing to lend them, becaufe they
have neither an army nor foldiers in pay.

A diverfity of opinion exifts wherever there
are

are men. It belongs not to one conſtitution more than to another; but the eſſence of a republican government is to leave to each individual the liberty of expreſſing his ſentiments on every ſubject.

In the United States, legiſlation is more and more formed in proportion as things relative to each other are verified, extended, and multiplied. Is it aſtoniſhing that debates ſhould ariſe on account of the different laws which are propoſed, diſcuſſed, and adopted? Theſe debates become public, animate converſation, and make it highly intereſting. But is this an archy?

The word *anarchy* is one of thoſe words which has been moſt abuſed and miſapplied. It is therefore neceſſary to explain it.

Where anarchy reigns, there is neither chief, government, laws, nor ſafety. Each individual becomes the defender of his own perſon, the ſocial contract is broken, and there is no longer any confidence or tranſactions, becauſe there can be no more contracts. Authority, changing at every inſtant, its rules, principles, and aim, becomes cruel or contemptible; it deſtroys, or is deſtroyed. Such a ſtate exiſts not long; or if it does exiſt, it ſoon divides ſociety into armed herds, enemies to each other, and which

ſubſiſt

subsist but in proportion as they fear and counterbalance each other's power.

Is any thing like this seen in the United States? Are there disputes even about the principles of the constitution, the fundamental laws, or the proposed end? Has not every thing relative to this been long since agreed upon? The present debates relate wholly to some rules of administration: it is upon the best manner of serving the public cause, and of supporting it, that minds are still in a salutary agitation; and this agitation hinders not more the regular course of public affairs and transactions, than the debates in the English Parliament hinder the monarch from naming to offices and conferring rank—than they stop the course of justice, or are impediments to the affairs of every class of citizens.

The word *anarchy* is proper to states which, like Egypt, have twenty-four sovereigns, and neither laws nor government. It is applicable to the degenerated constitutions of Asia, where the administration is divided into several departments, independent of each other, traversing one another in their views and pretensions, the operations of one part interfering with those of the other, all having the power of making particular

ticular laws, or of fufpending the effect of thofe
which exift.   There a real anarchy reigns, becaufe it is not known where the government is,
nor in whom the legiflative power is vefted.
This incertitude brings on diforder, renders
property unftable, and endangers perfonal fafety.

None of thefe evils exift in the United States.
America is not yet gnawed by the vermin
which devour Europe, by indeftructible mendicity : thieves render not her forefts dangerous ; her public roads are not ftained with blood
fhed by affaffins.   How fhould there be affaffins
and robbers ?   There are no beggars, no indigent
perfons, no fubjects forced to fteal the fubfiftence of others to procure one to themfelves.
Every man finds there lands to produce him articles of fubfiftence : it is not loaded with taxes,
but renders to each, with ufury, a recompenfe
for his labour.   A man who can live eafy and honourably, never confents to difhonour himfelf by
ufelefs crimes, which deliver him to the torments of remorfe, difhonour, and the vengeance
of fociety.

The ravages of the feven years war were
undoubtedly terrible; but as foon as the faul-
chion could be converted into a plough-fhare,
the

the land became fertile, and mifery difappear-
ed. The American foldiers were citizens; and
they were alfo proprietors before they became
foldiers; they remained citizens in uniform,
and returned to their profeffions on quitting it;
they did not fight for money, nor by profeffion,
but for their liberty, their wives, children, and
property; and fuch foldiers never refembled
the banditti of the old continent, who are paid
for killing their fellow-creatures, and who kill
on the highways for their own account, when
peace obliges their mafters to difband them.
There has been feen in America (what the an-
nals of the world prefent not in any ftate, except that of Rome) a General, adored by his
foldiers, diveft himfelf of his power as foon as
his fervices became no longer neceffary, and retire into the bofom of peace and obfcurity; a
numerous army, which was not paid, was feen
generoufly to confent to difband without payment; the foldiers to retire, each to his home,
without committing the leaft diforder, and
where each tranquilly retook either his plough,
or his firft trade or profeffion; thofe trades
which we in Europe look upon as vile.

The following advertifement is taken from
the

the American papers, in which there are a thoufand others of a like nature.

Two brothers, Captains who diftinguifhed themfelves during the war, returned at the peace to their trade of hat-making;—they inferted in the gazette an advertifement as follows :

" The Brothers *Bickers* inform the public,
" that they are returned to their old profeffion
" of hatters, which they had abandoned to de-
" fend the liberty of their country. They
" hope that their fellow-citizens will be pleafed,
" in confideration of their courage and fervices,
" to favour them in their bufinefs, and prefer
" them to others." What European captain would put his name to a like advertifement?

This is what refults from liberty ; but what is inconceivable in moft European ftates, a military fpirit reigns there, and its prejudices are predominant. War is the road to glory, ambition, and fortune; and to preferve to this profeffion its luftre and preponderance, it is an eftablifhed principle, that a *ftanding army* is neceffary to maintain order in fociety ; that it ought always to threaten the citizens, although peaceful, to keep them in fubmiffion to authority. This ufelefs burden, this pernicious fpirit, is unknown

known to the United States;—public fpirit, much more favourable to good order, takes its place, and peace and fafety reign without mare-chauffée, or fpies, or that police which difparages the morals and characters of citizens. Public fpirit fupplies the place of all thefe means, whilft they will never fupply the want of public fpirit; nor, like it, produce the happinefs of fociety.

In vain will prejudiced men exclaim, that this is declamation—I offer them facts. It is neceffary to read the American gazettes, not thofe altered by the Englifh gazette-writers, but thofe which are printed in America; thefe only can give a juft idea of the fituation of the United States.

The American fhould rather defpife Europe, in remarking to us the continual flaughter we make of thieves and affaffins; in comparing the immenfe number of dungeons, prifons, hofpitals, and eftablifhments of every kind, inftituted to cure or palliate the incurable ulcers of the old inftitutions. In comparing this difgufting lift with the very few murders and thefts committed in the United States, with the hofpitals, truly *domeftic* and humane, which are eftablifhed there, with the happinefs of each

American

American family and their fimple manners, and
in proving to us, by their example, that a wife
liberty regulates the focial man, and renders
ufelefs thofe ruinous machines with which he
is crufhed, left he fhould do any harm.

Thefe are the men, the laws, and the government, which Europeans have calumniated.
Thefe men who are deftined to regenerate
the dignity of the human fpecies!—Thefe laws
which fcourge nothing but crimes,—which
punifh them every where, and are never filent
in the face of power!—This government,
which is the firft that ever prefented the image
of a numerous family, well united, and completely happy; wherein power is juft, becaufe
it circulates through every hand, and refts in
none; wherein obedience, becaufe it is voluntary, anticipates command; wherein adminiftration is fimple and eafy, becaufe it leaves induftry to itfelf; wherein the magiftrate has little to do, becaufe the citizen is free, and that a
citizen always refpects the law and his fellow
creatures! Thefe are the prodigies which we
calumniate; we, Europeans, enflaved by anti-
quated conftitutions, and by the habitudes given
to us by prejudices, of which we know not
either the barbarity or the frivoloufnefs! We
fpeak well, but act badly; why, therefore, do
we

we calumniate men, who not only ſpeak but act well? If it be not permitted us to have their virtues, nor to enjoy their happineſs, let us not decry them ; let us reſpect that ſuperiority to which we cannot attain.

It will, perhaps, be objected, that the government of England has deferred the concluſion of a treaty of commerce with the United States, under the pretext that their conſtitutions were not yet ſufficiently eſtabliſhed. But can it be imagined that the Engliſh, who trade in Turky, with the Algerines, and at Grand Cairo, were ſerious when they decried and rejected commercial connections with the United States, under the pretence that their legiſlation was not yet well enough eſtabliſhed?

It cannot be doubted that the difference of poſition between the French and Engliſh merchants, reſpecting their governments, has a great influence upon their reciprocal proſperity; and for this reaſon, it ſhould be inceſſantly repeated to the French government, that if it wiſhes to inſure proſperity to its commerce, it ought to adopt the means, which are, *liberty of acting,—the right of proteſting againſt the attempts made on that liberty,—and the certainty of juſtice,—without reſpect to perſons:*—theſe are

the

the bafis of the genius, induftry, and greatnefs
of a ftate; and without which, a great commerce cannot exift : this bafis may be eafily
conciliated with the French conftitution.

Paris, February,
    1789.

APPENDIX;

APPENDIX;

CONSISTING OF

AUTHENTIC PAPERS,

AND

ILLUSTRATIONS.

Added by the Editor.

APPENDIX.

Return of the whole Number of Perfons within the feveral Diftricts of the United States, according to " an Act providing for the Enumeration of the Inhabitants of the United States;" paffed March the Firft, One Thoufand Seven Hundred and Ninety-one.

The Return for SOUTH CAROLINA having been made fince the foregoing Schedule was originally printed, the whole Enumeration is here given complete, except for the N. Weftern Territory, of which no Return has yet been publifhed.

DISTRICTS	Free white Males of 16 years and upwards, including heads of families	Free white Males under fixteen years.	Free white Females, including heads of families.	All other free perfons.	Slaves.	Total.
Vermont	22435	22328	40505	255	16	85539
N. Hampfhire	36086	34851	70160	630	158	141885
Maine	24384	24748	46870	538	NONE	96540
Maffachufetts	95453	87289	190582	5463	NONE	378787
Rhode Ifland	16019	15799	32652	3407	948	68825
Connecticut	60523	54403	117448	2808	2764	237946
New York	83700	78122	152320	4654	21324	340120
New Jerfey	45251	41416	83287	2762	11423	184139
Pennfylvania	110788	106948	206363	6537	3737	434373
Delaware	11783	12143	22384	3899	8887	59094
Maryland	55915	51339	101395	8043	103036	319728
Virginia	110936	116135	215046	12866	292627	747610
Kentucky	15154	17057	28922	114	12430	73677
N. Carolina	69988	77506	140710	4975	100572	393751
S. Carolina	35576	37722	66880	1801	107094	249073
Georgia	13103	14044	25739	398	29264	82548
	807094	791850	1541263	59150	694280	3893635

Total number of Inhabitants of the United States exclufive of S. Weftern and N. Territory.	Free white Males of 21 years and upwards.	Free Males under 21 years of age.	Free white Females.	All other perfons.	Slaves.	Total.
S. W. territory N. Ditto	6271	10277	15365	361	3417	35691

Schedule of the whole number of Persons in the Territory of the United States of America, South of the River Ohio, as taken on the last Saturday of July 1791, by the Captains of the Militia within the limits of their respective Districts.

	Free white Males of 21 years and upwards, including heads of families.	Free white Males under 21 years	Free white Females, including heads of families.	All other free Persons.	Slaves.	Total of each county.	Total of each district.
WASHINGTON DISTRICT.							
Washington -	1009	1792	2524	12	535	5872	
Sullivan -	806	1242	1995	107	297	4447	
Greene -	1293	2374	3580	40	454	7741	
Hawkins -	1204	1970	2921	68	807	6970	
South of French Broad	681	1082	1627	66	163	3619	
							28649
MERO DISTRICT							
Davidson -	639	855	1288	18	659	3459	
Sumner - -	404	582	854	8	348	2196	
Tennessee - -	235	380	576	42	154	1387	7042
	6271	10277	15365	361	3417		35691

Note.—There are several Captains who have not as yet returned the Schedules of the numbers of their Districts, namely;—in Greene County, three—in Davidson, one—and South of French-Board, one District.

September 19*th,* 1791.

W. BLOUNT.

By the Governor,
DANIEL SMITH, *Secretary.*

Truly stated from the original Returns deposited in the Office of the Secretary of State.

T. JEFFERSON.

October 24, 1791.

In point of size the towns in the United States may be ranked in this order; Philadelphia, New York, Boston, Baltimore, Charlestown, &c. In point of trade, New York, Philadelphia, Boston, Charlestown, Baltimore, &c.

From the preceding tables it is indubitable, that the number of inhabitants in the United States confiderably exceeded Four Millions in the year 1791; exclufive of thofe in the Northern territory, and fome other diftricts. If to this we add, Dr. Franklin's calculation, " That the number of the inhabitants of America is double every twenty years," this number muft be increafed to confiderably above Eight Millions in the year 1811; exclufive of emigrants from the Old World.

The Englifh reader, we hope, will not be offended, if, in this place, we fay a word or two on the population of Great Britain. It is a current opinion, that the population of our ifland is yearly increafing. The fact is quite the reverfe: but the affertion would fignify nothing, if there were not inconteftable proofs of it. The proofs are thefe.

Number of houfes in England and Wales, taken from the return of the furveyors of the Houfe and Window Duties; wherein they are ftated diftinctly, *charged*, *chargeable*, and *excufed*.

Total of Houfes in 1759	- - -	986,482
———————— in 1761	- - -	980,692
———————— in 1777	- - -	952,734
		Total

Total of houfes according to the hearth-books in 1690, as ftated by Dr. Davenant (fee his works, vol. i. page 38) - - - - 1,319,215

In Scotland the number of houfes paying the houfe and window duties was, in 1777, only 16,206.

If the diftinct returns of the parifhes are examined, it will be manifeft, that a calculation of five perfons to every houfe is a large allowance. From all which this refult is obvious ——That the number of inhabitants in England and Wales is confiderably fhort of FIVE MILLIONS!——That, perhaps, including Scotland, the *whole* Ifland of Great Britain does not exceed that number.

The curofity of the prefent moment may allow us to caft our eye upon France, concerning this fubject. The intendants of the provinces of France were ordered in the year 1771 and 1772 to make a return of the number of inhabitants in their refpective diftricts. The return of 1772 ftates the number to be 25,741,320. *See Recherches fur la population de la France, par M. Moheau.*

It would be a right meafure in every government to caufe a furvey to be made annually of the

the number of inhabitants. It is done at Naples by order of the King, and is publifhed annually in the Court Calendars. America will probably follow the example.

Obfervations on the Population of America. Written by Dr. Benjamin Franklin. Printed at Philadelphia in the year 1755.

Tables of the proportion of marriages to births, of deaths to births, of marriages to the numbers of inhabitants, &c. formed on obfervations made on the bills of mortality, chriftenings, &c. of populous cities, will not fuit countries; nor will tables formed on obfervations made on full fettled old countries, as Europe, fuit new countries, as America.

For people increafe in proportion to the number of marriages, and that is greater in proportion to the eafe and convenience of fupporting a family. When families can be eafily fupported, more perfons marry, and earlier in life.

In cities where all trades, occupations, and offices, are full, many delay until they can fee how to bear the charges of a family; which charges are greater in cities, as luxury is more common; many live fingle during life, and continue fervants to families, journeymen to

trades,

trades, &c. hence cities do not by natural generation fupply themfelves with inhabitants; the
deaths are more than the births.

In countries full fettled, the cafe muft be
nearly the fame; all lands being occupied and
improved to the height; thofe who cannot
get land, muft labour for thofe who have it;
when labourers are plenty, their wages will be
low; by low wages a family is fupported with
difficulty; this difficulty deters many from
marriage, who therefore long continue fervants
and fingle.——Only as cities take fupplies of
people from the country, and thereby make a
little more room in the country, marriage is a
little more encouraged there, and the births exceed the deaths.

Great part of Europe is full fettled with hufbandmen, manufacturers, &c. and therefore cannot now much increafe in people.   Land being
plenty in America, and fo cheap as that a labouring man, who underftands hufbandry, can
in a fhort time fave money enough to purchafe
a piece of new land fufficient for a plantation,
whereon he may fubfift a family, fuch are not
afraid to marry; for even if they look far enough
forward to confider how their children when
grown are to be provided for, they fee that

more

more land is to be had at rates equally eafy, all circumftances confidered.

Hence marriages in America are more general, and more generally early, than in Europe. And if it is reckoned there, that there is but one marriage per annum among one hundred perfons, perhaps we may here reckon two; and if in Europe they have but four births to a marriage (many of their marriages being late), we may here reckon eight; of which, if one half grow up, and our marriages are made, *reckoning one with another, at twenty years of age, our people muft at leaft be doubled every twenty years.*

But notwithftanding this increafe, fo vaft is the territory of North America, that it will require many ages to fettle it fully; and until it is fully fettled, labour will never be cheap here, where no man continues long a labourer for others, but gets a plantation of his own; no man continues long a journeyman to a trade, but goes among thefe new fettlers, and fets up for himfelf, &c. Hence labour is no cheaper now, in Pennfylvania, than it was thirty years ago, though fo many thoufand labouring people have been imported from Germany and Ireland.

In proportion to the increafe of the Colonies,

a vaft

a vaft demand is growing for Britifh manufactures; a glorious market wholly in the power
of Britain, in which foreigners cannot interfere,
which will increafe.in a fhort time even beyond
her power of fupplying, though her whole
trade fhould be to her colonies.

Of the Weftern Territory.

It is a miftake in thofe who imagine that the
new State of Kentucky compri*es the Weftern
territory of North America.   That new ftate
includes but a fmall part of this great domain.
The State of Kentucky is defcribed to be
bounded on the fouth by North Carolina, on the
north by Sandy creek, on the weft by Cumber-
land river, making about 250 miles in length
and 200 miles in breadth; whereas the whole
Weftern territory is infinitely more extenfive.
The limits are unknown; but that part of it,
which was furveyed by Captain Hutchins, geo-
grapher to the Congrefs, he has given us a fhort
account of.   From his account, becaufe it is
known to be authentic, we have extracted the
following.

The part he furveyed lies between the 33d
and 45th degrees of latitude and the 78th and
94th

94th degrees of longitude, containing an extent
of territory which, for healthfulness, fertility of
foil, and variety of productions, is not perhaps
furpaffed by any on the habitable globe.

" The lands comprehended between the river
Ohio, at Fort Pitt, and the Laurel mountain,
and thence continuing the fame breadth from
Fort Pitt to the Great Kanhawa river, may, according to my own obfervations, and thofe of
the late Mr. Gift, of Virginia, be generally, and
juftly defcribed as follows.

" The vallies adjoining to the branches or
fprings of the middle forks of Youghiogeny, are
narrow towards its fource,—but there is a confiderable quantity of good farming grounds on
the hills, near the largeft branch of that river.
—The lands within a fmall diftance of the
Laurel mountain (through which the Youghiogeny runs) are in many places broken and
ftony, but rich and well timbered; and in fome
places, and particularly on Laurel creek, they
are rocky and mountainous.

" From the Laurel mountain, to Monongahela, the firft feven miles are good, level farming grounds, with fine meadows; the timber,
white Oak, Chefnut, Hickory, &c.—The fame
kind of land continues foutherly (12 miles) to
the

the upper branches or forks of this river, and about 15 miles northerly to the place where the Youghiogeny falls into the Monongahela.—The lands, for about 18 miles in the same course of the last-mentioned river, on each side of it, though hilly, are rich and well timbered.—The trees are Walnut, Locust, Chesnut, Poplar, and Sugar or sweet Maple. The low lands, near the river, are about a mile, and in several places two miles wide. For a considerable way down the river, on the eastern side of it, the intervals are extremely rich, and about a mile wide. The upland for about 12 miles eastwardly, are uncommonly fertile, and well timbered; the low lands, on the western side, are narrow; but the uplands, on the eastern side of the river, both up and down, are excellent, and covered with Sugar trees, &c.

" Such parts of the country which lie on some of the branches of the Monongahela, and acrofs the heads of several rivers, that run into the Ohio, though in general hilly, are exceedingly fruitful and well watered. The timber is Walnut, Chesnut, Afh, Oak, Sugar trees, &c. and the interval or meadow lands are from 250 yards to a quarter of a mile wide.

" The lands lying nearly in a north-westerly direction

direction from the Great Kanhawa river to the Ohio, and thence north-easterly, and also upon Le Tort's creek, Little Kanhawa river, Buffaloe, Fishing, Weeling, and the two upper, and two lower, and several other very considerable creeks (or what, in Europe, would be called large rivers), and thence east, and south-east to the river Monongahela, are, in point of quality, as follows.

" The borders or meadow lands, are a mile, and in some places near two miles wide; and the uplands are in common of a most fertile soil, capable of abundantly producing Wheat, Hemp, Flax, &c.

" The lands which lie upon the Ohio, at the mouths of, and between the above creeks, also consist of rich intervals and very fine farming grounds. The whole country abounds in Bears, Elks, Buffaloe, Deer, Turkies, &c.— An unquestionable proof of the extraordinary goodness of its soil! Indiana lies within the territory here described. It contains about three millions and an half of acres, and was granted to Samuel Wharton, William Trent, and George Morgan, Esquires, and a few other persons, in the year 1768.

" Fort Pitt stands at the confluence of the
Allegheny

Allegheny and Monongahela rivers; in latitude
40° 31' 44"; and about five degrees weftward
of Philadelphia. In the year 1760, a fmall
town, called Pittfburgh, was built near Fort Pitt,
and about 200 families refided in it ; but upon
the Indian war breaking out (in the month of
May 1763) they abandoned their houfes, and
retired into the fort.

" In the year 1765 the prefent town of
Pittfburgh was laid out. It is built on the
Eaftern bank of the river Monongahela, about
200 yards from Fort Pitt.

" The junction of the Allegheny and Monongahela rivers, forms the river Ohio, and
this difcharges itfelf into the Miffiffippi, (in
latitude 36° 43') about 1188 computed miles
from Fort Pitt. The Ohio in its paffage to the
Miffiffippi, glides through a pleafant, fruitful,
and healthy country ;   and carries a great uniformity of breadth, from 400 to 600 yards, except at its confluence with the Miffiffippi, and
for 100 miles above it, where it is 1000 yards
wide. The Ohio, for the greater part of the
way to the Miffiffippi, has many meanders, or
windings, and rifing grounds upon both fides
of it.

" The reaches in the Ohio are in fome parts
from

from two to four miles in length, and one of
them, above the Mufkingum river, called the
Long Reach, is fixteen miles and an half long.
The Ohio, about 100 miles abóve, or northerly
of the Rapids, (formerly called the Falls) is in
many places 700 yards wide; and as it ap-
proaches them, the high grounds on its borders
gradually diminifh, and the country becomes
more level. Some of the banks, or heights of
this river, are at times overflowed by great
frefhes, yet there is fcarce a place between Fort
Pitt and the Rapids (a diftance of 705 computed miles) where a good road may not be made;
and horfes employed in drawing up large barges
(as is done on the margin of the river Thames
in England, and the Seine in France) againft a
ftream remarkably gentle, except in high
frefhes. The heights of the banks of the Ohio
admit them évery where to be fettled, as they
are not liable to crumble away.

" To thefe remarks, it may be proper to add
the following obfervations of the ingenious Mr.
Lewis Evans. He fays that ' the Ohio river,
as the winter fnows are thawed by the warmth
or rains in the fpring, rifes in vaft floods, in
fome places exceeding 20 feet in height, but
fcarce any where overflowing its high and up-
                                              right

right banks. 'Thefe floods,' Mr. Evans adds, ' continue of fome height for at leaft a month or two, according to the late or early breaking up of the winter. Veffels from 100 to 200 tons burthen, by taking the advantage of thefe floods, may go from Pittfburgh to the fea with fafety, as then the Falls, Rifts, and Shoals, are covered to an equality with the reft of the rivers;'— and though the diftance is upwards of 2000 miles from Fort Pitt to the fea, yet as there are no obftructions to prevent veffels from proceeding both day and night, I am perfuaded that this extraordinary inland voyage may be performed, during the feafon of the floods, by rowing, in fixteen or feventeen days.

" The navigation of the Ohio in a dry feafon, is rather troublefome from Fort Pitt to the Mingo town (about feventy-five miles), but from thence to the Miffiffippi, there is always a fufficient depth of water for barges, carrying from 100 to 200 tons burthen, built in the manner as thofe are which are ufed on the river Thames, between London and Oxford;—to wit, from 100 to 120 feet in the keel, fixteen to eighteen feet in breadth and four feet in depth, and when loaded, drawing about three feet water.

" The

" The Rapids, in a dry feafon, are difficult to defcend with loaded boats or barges.

[But inftead of the carrying place now ufed, it is intended to fubftitute a canal on the contrary fide of the river.]

" Moft of the hills on both fides of the Ohio are filled with excellent coal, and a coal mine was in the year 1760 opened oppofite to Fort Pitt on the river Monongahela, for the ufe of that garrifon. Salt fprings, as well as iron ore, and rich lead mines, are found bordering upon the river Ohio. One of the latter is opened on a branch of the Sioto river, and there the Indian natives fupply themfelves with a confiderable part of the lead which they ufe in their wars and hunting.

" About 584 miles below Fort Pitt, and on the eaftern fide of the Ohio river, about three miles from it, at the head of a fmall creek or run, where are feveral large and miry falt fprings, are found numbers of large bones, teeth and tufks, commonly fuppofed to be thofe of elephants :—but the celebrated Doctor Hunter of London, in his ingenious and curious obfervations on thefe bones, &c. has fuppofed them to belong to fome carnivorous animal, larger than an ordinary elephant.

" On

" On the north-western fide of Ohio, about
11 miles below the Cherokee river, on a high
bank, are the remains of fort Maffac, built by
the French, and intended as a check to the
fouthern Indians. It was deftroyed by them in
the year 1763. This is a high, healthy, and
delightful fituation. A great variety of game;
——Buffaloe, Bear, Deer, &c. as well as
Ducks, Geefe, Swans, Turkies, Pheafants,
Partridges, &c. abounds in every part of this
country.

" The Ohio, and the rivers emptying into
it, afford green, and other Turtle, and fifh of
various forts; particularly Carp, Sturgeon, Perch,
and Cats; the two latter of an uncommon fize,
viz. Perch, from 8 to 12 pounds weight, and
Cats from 50 to 100 pounds weight.

" The lands upon the Ohio, and its branches,
are differently timbered according to their quality and fituation. The high and dry lands are
covered with red, white, and black Oak, Hickory, Walnut, red and white Mulberry and Afh
trees, Grape vines, &c.; the low and meadow
lands are filled with Sycamore, Poplar, red and
white Mulberry, Cherry, Beech, Elm, Afpen,
Maple, or Sugar trees, Grape vines, &c.; and
below, or fouthwardly of the Rapids, are feveral
large

large Cedar and Cyprefs fwamps, where the Cedar and Cyprefs trees grow to a remarkable fize, and where alfo is a great abundance of Canes, fuch as grow in South Carolina. The country on both fides of the Ohio, extending fouth-eafterly, and fouth-wefterly from Fort Pitt to the Miffiffippi, and watered by the Ohio river, and its branches, contains at leaft a million of fquare miles, and it may, with truth, be affirmed, that no part of the globe is bleffed with a more healthful air, or climate; watered with more navigable rivers and branches communicating with the Atlantic Ocean, by the rivers Potowmack, James, Rappahannock, Miffiffippi, and St. Lawrence, or capable of producing, with lefs labour and expence, Wheat, Indian Corn, Buck-wheat, Rye, Oats, Barley, Flax, Hemp, Tobacco, Rice, Silk, Pot-afh, &c. than the country under confideration. And although there are confiderable quantities of high lands for about 250 miles (on both fides of the river Ohio) fouthwardly from Fort Pitt, yet even the fummits of moft of the Hills are covered with a deep rich foil, fit for the culture of Flax and Hemp; and it may alfo be added, that no foil can poffibly yield larger crops of

red

red and white Clover, and other ufeful grafs, than this does.

" On the north-weft and fouth-eaft fides of the Ohio, below the great Kanhawa river, at a little diftance from it, are extenfive natural meadows, or favannahs. Thefe meadows are from 20 to 50 miles in circuit. They have many beautiful groves of trees interfperfed, as if by art, in them, and which ferve as a fhelter for the innumerable herds of Buffaloe, Deer, &c. with which they abound.

" I am obliged to a worthy friend, and countryman, for the following juft and judicious obfervations. They were addreffed to the Earl of Hillfborough, in the year 1770, when Secretary of State for the North American department; and were written by Mr. Samuel Wharton of Philadelphia, who at time refided in London, having fome bufinefs there. with Mr. Strahan, Mr. Almon, &c.

" No part of North-America," he fays, " will " require lefs encouragement for the produc- " tion of naval ftores, and raw materials for " manufactories in Europe; and for fupplying " the Weft-India iflands with Lumber, Provi- " fions, &c. than the country of the Ohio;— " and for the following reafons:

" Firft,

" First, The lands are excellent, the climate
" temperate, the native Grapes, Silk-worms, and
" Mulberry-trees, abound every where: Hemp,
" Hops, and Rye, grow spontaneously in the
" valleys and low lands, lead, and iron ore are
" plenty in the hills, salt springs are innumer-
" able; and no soil is better adapted to the cul-
" ture of Tobacco, Flax, and Cotton, than that
" of the Ohio.

" Second, The country is well watered by
" several navigable rivers, communicating with
" each other; by which, and a short land car-
" riage, the produce of the lands of the Ohio
" can, even now (in the year 1772) be sent
" cheaper to the sea-port town of Alexandria,
" on the river Potomack in Virginia (where
" General Braddock's transports landed his
" troops), than any kind of merchandise is sent
" from Northampton to London.

" Third, The river Ohio is, at all seasons of
" the year, navigable with large boats, like the
" west country barges, rowed only by four
" or five men; and from the month of Febru-
" ary to April large ships may be built on the
" Ohio, and sent to sea laden with Hemp, Iron,
" Flax, Silk, Tobacco, Cotton, Pot-ash, &c.

" Fourth, Flour, Corn, Beef, Ship-Plank,
" and

" and other useful articles, can be sent down
" the stream of the Ohio to West-Florida, and
" from thence to the West-India islands, much
" cheaper, and in better order, than from New
" York or Philadelphia to these islands.

" Fifth, Hemp, Tobacco, Iron, and such
" bulky articles, may also be sent down the
" stream of the Ohio to the sea, and at least 50
" per cent. cheaper than these articles were
" ever carried by a land carriage, of only 60
" miles, in Pennsylvania; where waggonage
" is cheaper than in any other part of North
" America.

" Sixth, The expence of transporting Euro-
" pean manufactories from the sea to the Ohio,
" will not be so much as is now paid, and
" must ever be paid, to a great part of the
" counties of Pennsylvania, Virginia, and Ma-
" ryland. Whenever the farmers, or mer-
" chants of Ohio, shall properly understand
" the business of transportation, they will build
" schooners, sloops, &c. on the Ohio, suitable
" for the West-India, or European markets;
" or, by having Black-Walnut, Cherry-tree,
" Oak, &c. properly sawed for foreign markets,
" and formed into rafts, in the manner that
" is now done by the settlers near the upper
" parts

" parts of Delaware river in Pennfylvania, and
" thereon ftow their Hemp, Iron, Tobacco,
" &c. and proceed with them to New Or-
" leans.

" It may not, perhaps, be amifs, to obferve,
" that large quantities of Flour are made in the
" diftant (weftern) counties of Pennfylvania,
" and fent by an expenfive land carriage to the
" city of Philadelphia, and from thence fhipped
" to South Carolina, and to Eaft and Weft
" Florida, there being little or no Wheat raifed
" in thefe provinces. The river Ohio feems
" kindly defigned by nature as the channel
" through which the two Floridas may be fup-
" plied with Flour, not only for their own
" confumption, but alfo for the carrying on an
" extenfive commerce with Jamaica and the
" Spanifh fettlements in the Bay of Mexico.
" Millftones in abundance are to be obtained in
" the hills near the Ohio, and the country is
" every where well watered with large and
" conftant fprings and ftreams, for grift, and
" other mills.

" The paffage from Philadelphia to Pennfa-
" cola, is feldom made in lefs than a month,
" and fixty fhillings fterling per ton freight
" (confifting of fixteen barrels) is ufually paid
" for

" for Flour, &c. thither. Boats carrying 800
" or 1000 barrels of Flour, may go in about
" the fame time from the Ohio (even from
" Pittfburgh) as from Philadelphia to Pennfa-
" cola, and for half the above freight, the Ohio
" merchants would be able to deliver Flour,
" &c. there in much better order than from
" Philadelphia, and without incurring the da-
" mage and delay of the fea, and charges of
" infurance, &c. as from thence to Pennfa-
" cola.

" This is not mere fpeculation; for it is a
" fact, that about the year 1746 there was a
" great fcarcity of provifions at New Orleans,
" and the French fettlements, at the Illinois,
" fmall as they then were, fent thither in one
" winter upwards of eight hundred thoufand
" weight of Flour."

" I fhall now proceed to give a brief account
of the feveral rivers and creeks which fall into
the river Ohio.

" Canawagy, when raifed by frefhes, is paffable with fmall battoes, to a little lake at its
head;—from thence there is a portage of 20
miles to lake Erie, at the mouth of Jadághque.
This portage is feldom ufed, becaufe Canawagy
has fcarcely any water in it in a dry feafon.

" Bughaloons,

" Bughaloons is not navigable, but is re-markable for extenfive meadows bordering up-on it.

" French Creek affords the neareſt paſſage to lake Erie. It is navigable with ſmall boats to Le Beuf, by a very crooked channel; the portage thence to Preſquile, from an adjoining peninſula, is 15 miles. This is the uſual route from Quebec to Ohio.

" Licking and Lacomic Creeks do not afford any navigation; but there is plenty of coals and ſtones for building in the hills which ad-join them.

" Toby's Creek is deep enough for batteaus for a conſiderable way up, thence by a ſhort portage to the weſt branch of Suſquehannah, a good communication is carried on between Ohio and the eaſtern parts of Pennſylvania.

" Moghulbughkitum is paſſable alſo by flat bottom boats in the ſame manner as Toby's Creek is to Suſquehannah, and from thence to all the ſettlements in Northumberland county, &c. in Pennſylvania.

" Kiſhkeminetas is navigable in like man-ner as the preceding creeks, for between 40 and 50 miles, and good portages are found be-tween Kiſhkeminetas, Juniatta, and Potomac rivers.

rivers.—Coal and Salt are difcovered in the neighbourhood of thefe rivers.

"Monongahela is a large river, and at its junction with the Allegheny river ftands Fort Pitt. It is deep, and gentle, and navigable with battoes and barges, beyond Red Stone creek, and ftill farther with lighter craft. At fixteen miles from its mouth is Youghiogeny; this river is navigable with batteaux or barges to the foot of Laurel hill.

"Beaver Creek has water fufficient for flat bottom boats. At Kifhkufkes (about 16 miles up) are two branches of this creek, which fpread oppofite ways; one interlocks with French Creek and Cherâge,—the other with Mufhingum and Cayahoga; on this branch, about thirty-five miles above the forks, are many Salt-fprings.—Cayahoga is practicable with canoes about twenty miles farther.

"Mufkingum is a fine gentle river, confined by high banks, which prevent its floods from overflowing the furrounding land. It is 250 yards wide at its confluence with the Ohio, and navigable, without any obftructions, by large battoes or barges, to the three Legs's, and by fmall ones to a little lake at its head.

"From thence to Cayahoga (the creek that leads

leads to lake Erie) thé Muſkingum is muddy, and not very ſwift, but no where obſtructed with falls or rifts. Here are fine uplands, extenſive meadows, Oak and Mulberry-trees fit for ſhip building, and Walnut, Cheſnut, and Poplar trees, ſuitable for domeſtic ſervices.—Cayahoga furniſhes the beſt portage between Ohio and lake Erie; at its mouth it is wide and deep enough to receive large ſloops from the lake. It will hereafter be a place of great importance.

" Muſkingum, in all its wide-extended branches, is ſurrounded by moſt excellent land, and abounds in ſprings, and conveniencies particularly adapted to ſettlements remote from ſea navigations;—ſuch as ſalt ſprings, coal, clay, and free ſtone. In 1748 a coal mine oppoſite to Lamenſhicola mouth took fire, and continued burning about twelve months, but great quantities of coal ſtill remain in it. Near the ſame place are excellent whetſtones, and about eight miles higher up the river, is plenty of white and blue clay for glaſs works and pottery.

" Hockhocking is navigable with large flat bottom boats between ſeventy and eighty miles; it has fine meadows with high banks, which ſeldom overflow, and rich uplands on its borders.

ders. Coal and quarries of freestone are found about 15 miles up this creek.

" Big Kanhawa falls into the Ohio upon its south-eastern side, and is so considerable a branch of this river, that it may be mistaken for the Ohio itself by persons ascending it. It is slow for ten miles, to little broken hills,— the low land is very rich, and of about the same breadth (from the pipe hills to the falls) as upon the Ohio. After going 10 miles up Kanhawa the land is hilly, and the water a little rapid for 50 or 60 miles further to the falls, yet batteaus or barges may be easily rowed thither. These falls were formerly thought impassable ; but late discoveries have proved, that a waggon road may be made through the mountain, which occasions the falls, and that by a portage of a few miles only a communication may be had between the waters of great Kanhawa and Ohio, and those of James river in Virginia.

" Tottery lies upon the south-eastern side of the Ohio, and is navigable with batteaux to the Ouasioto mountains. It is a long river, has few branches, and interlocks with Red Creek, or Clinche's River (a branch of the Cuttawa) and has below the mountains, especially
ally

ally for 15 miles from its mouth, very good land. Here is a perceptible difference of climate between the upper and this part of Ohio. Here the large Reed, or Carolina Cane, grows in plenty, even upon the upland, and the winter is fo moderate as not to deftroy it. The fame moderation of climate continues down Ohio, efpecially on the fouth-eaft fide, to the Rapids, and thence on both fides of that river to the Miffiffippi.

"Great Salt Lick Creek is remarkable for fine land, plenty of buffaloes, falt fprings, white clay, and lime ftone. Small boats may go to the croffing of the war path without any impediment. The falt fprings render the waters unfit for drinking, but the plenty of frefh fprings in their vicinity, makes fufficient amends for this inconvenience.

"Kentucke is larger than the preceding creek; it is furrounded with high clay banks, fertile lands, and large falt fprings. Its navigation is interrupted by fhoals, but paffable with fmall boats to the gap, where the war path goes through the Ouafioto mountains.

"Sioto, is a large gentle river, bordered with rich flats, or meadows. It overflows in the fpring, and then fpreads about half a mile, though

though when confined within its banks it is scarce a furlong wide.

" If it floods early, it feldom retires within its banks in lefs than a month, and is not fordable frequently in lefs than two months.

" The Sioto, befides having a great extent of moft excellent land on both fides of the river, is furnifhed with falt, on an eaftern branch, and red bole on Necunfia Skeintat. The ftream of Sioto is gentle and paffable with large battoes or barges for a confiderable way, and with fmaller boats, near 200 miles, to a portage of only four miles to Sandufky.

" Sandufky is a confiderable river abounding in level land, its ftream gentle all the way to the mouth, where it is large enough to receive floops. The northern Indians crofs lake Erie here from ifland to ifland, land at Sandufky, and go by a direct path to the lower Shawanoe town, and thence to the gap of the Ouafioto mountain, in their way to the Cuttawa country.

" Little Mineami river is too fmall to navigate with batteaux. It has much fine land and feveral falt fprings; its high banks and gentle current prevent its much overflowing the furrounding lands in frefhes.

" Great

" Great Mineami, Affereniet or Rocky river, has a very ftony channel; a fwift ftream, but no falls. It has feveral large branches, paffable with boats a great way ; one extending weft-ward towards the Quiaghtena river, another to-wards a branch of Mineami river (which runs into Lake Erie), to which there is a portage, and a third has a portage to the weft branch of Sandufky, befides Mad Creek, where the French formerly eftablifhed themfelves. Rifing ground, here and there a little ftony, which begins in the northern part of the peninfula, between the lakes Erie, Huron, and Michigan, and extends acrofs little Mineami river below the Forks, and fouthwardly along the Rocky river, to Ohio.

" Buffaloe river falls into the Ohio on the eaftern fide of it, at the diftance of 925 com-puted miles from Fort Pitt. It is a very confi-derable branch of the Ohio; is 200 yards wide, navigable upwards of 150 miles for battoes or barges, of 30 feet long, 5 feet broad, and 3 feet deep, carrying about 7 tons, and can be navi-gated much farther with large canoes. The ftream is moderate. The lands on both fides of the river are of a moft luxuriant quality, for the production of Hemp, Flax, Wheat, Tobacco, &c. They are covered with a great variety of
lofty,

lofty, and useful timber; as Oak, Hickory, Mulberry, Elm, &c. Several persons who have ascended this river say, that salt springs, coal, lime and free stone, &c. are to be found in a variety of places.

" The Wabash is a beautiful river, with high and upright banks, less subject to overflow than any other river (the Ohio excepted) in this part of America. It discharges itself into the Ohio, one thousand and twenty-two miles below Fort Pitt, in latitude 37° 41'.—At its mouth it is 270 yards wide; is navigable to Ouiatanon (412 miles) in the spring, summer, and autumn, with battoes or barges, drawing about three feet water. From thence, on account of a rocky bottom, and shoal water, large canoes are chiefly employed, except when the river is swelled with rains, at which time it may be ascended with boats, such as I have just described (197 miles further) to the Miami carrying place, which is nine miles from the Miami village, and this is situated on a river of the same name, that runs into the south-southwest part of lake Erie.—The stream of the Wabash is generally gentle to fort Ouiatanon, and no where obstructed with falls, but is by several rapids, both above and below that fort,

some

fome of which are pretty confiderable. There is alfo a part of the river, for about three miles, and 30 miles from the carrying place, where the channel is fo narrow, that it is neceffary to make ufe of fetting poles, inftead of oars. The land on this river is remarkably fertile, and feveral parts of it are natural meadows, of great extent, covered with fine long grafs.—The timber is large, and high, and in fuch variety, that almoft all the different kinds growing upon the Ohio and its branches (but with a greater proportion of black and white mulberry-trees) may be found here—A filver mine has been difcovered about 28 miles above Ouiatanon, on the northern fide of the Wabafh, and probably others may be found hereafter. The Wabafh abounds with falt fprings, and any quantity of falt may be made from them, in the manner now done at the Saline in the Illinois country: —the hills are replenifhed with the beft coal, and there is plenty of lime and free ftone, blue, yellow, and white clay, for glafs works and pottery. Two French fettlements are eftablifhed on the Wabafh, called Poft Vincient and Ouiatanon; the firft is 150 miles, and the other 262 miles from its mouth. The former is on the eaftern fide of the river, and confifts

of

of 60 fettlers and their families. They raife Indian corn, wheat, and tobacco of an extraordinary good quality; fuperior, it is faid, to that produced in Virginia. They have a fine breed of horfes (brought originally by the Indians from the Spanifh fettlements on the weftern fide of the river Miffiffippi), and large ftocks of fwine and black cattle. The fettlers deal with the natives for furs and deer fkins, to the amount of about 5000 l. annually. Hemp of a good texture grows fpontaneoufly in the low lands of the Wabafh, as do grapes in the greateft abundance, having a black, thin fkin, and of which the inhabitants in the autumn make a fufficient quantity (for their own confumption) of well-tafted red-wine. Hops large and good are found in many places, and the lands are particularly adapted to the culture of rice. All European fruits;—apples, peaches, pears, cherries, currants, goofberries, melons, &c. thrive well, both here, and in the country bordering on the river Ohio.

" Ouiatanon is a fmall ftockaded fort on the weftern fide of the Wabafh, in which about a dozen families refide. The neighbouring Indians are the Kickapoos, Mufquitons, Pyankifhaws, and a principal part of the Ouiatanons.

The

The whole of thefe tribes confift, it is fuppofed, of about one thoufand warriors. The fertility of foil, and diverfity of timber in this country, are the fame as in the vicinity of Poft Vincient. The annual amount of fkins and furs obtained at Ouiatanon is about 8000 l. By the river Wabafh, the inhabitants of Detroit move to the fouthern parts of Ohio, and the Illinois country. Their rout is by the Miami river to a carrying-place, which, as before ftated, is nine miles to the Wabafh, when this river is raifed with frefhes; but at other feafons, the diftance is from 18 to 30 miles, including the portage. The whole of the latter is through a level coun-try. Carts are ufually employed in tranfport-ing boats and merchandife from the Miami to the Wabafh river.

" The Shawanoe river empties itfelf on the eaftern fide of Ohio, about 95 miles fouth-wardly of the Wabafh river. It is 250 yards wide at its mouth, has been navigated 180 miles in battoes of the conftruction of thofe mentioned in the preceding article, and from the depth of water, at that diftance from its mouth, it is prefumed, it may be navigated much fur-ther. The foil and timber of the lands, upon
this

this river, are exactly the same as those upon
Buffaloe river.

" The Cherokee river difcharges itfelf into
the Ohio on the fame fide that the Shawanoe
river does, that is, 13 miles below or foutherly
of it, and 11 miles above, or northerly of the
place where Fort Maffac formerly ftood, and 57
miles from the confluence of the Ohio with
the river Miffiffippi. The Cherokee river has
been navigated 900 miles from its mouth.
At the diftance of 220 miles from thence, it
widens from 400 yards (its general width) to
between two and three miles, and continues
this breadth for near thirty miles farther. The
whole of this diftance is called the Mufcle
Shoals. Here the channel is obftructed with a
number of iflands, formed by trees and drifted
wood, brought hither, at different feafons of the
year, in frefhes and floods. In paffing thefe
iflnads, the middle of the wideft intermediate
water is to be navigated, as there it is deepeft.
From the mouth of the Cherokee river to
Mufcle Shoals the current is moderate, and
both the high and low lands are rich, and abundantly covered with oaks, walnut, fugar-trees,
hickory, &c. About 200 miles above thefe
fhoals is, what is called, the Whirl, or Suck,
occafioned,

occafioned, I imagine, by the high mountain, which there confines the river (fuppofed to be the Laurel mountain). The Whirl, or Suck, continues rapid for about three miles. Its width about 50 yards. Afcending the Cherokee river, and at about 100 miles from the Suck, and upon the fouth-eaftern fide of that river, is Highwafee river. Vaft tracts of level and rich land border on this river; but at a fmall diftance from it, the country is much broken, and fome parts of it produce only pine trees. Forty miles higher up the Cherokee river, on the north weftern fide, is Clinche's river. It is 150 yards wide, and about 50 miles up it feveral families are fettled. From Clinche's to Tenefee river is 100 miles. It comes in on the eaftern fide, and is 250 yards wide. About 10 miles up this river, is a Cherokee town, called Chota, and further up this branch are feveral other Indian towns, poffeffed by Indians, called, the Over-hill Cherokees. The navigation of this branch is much interrupted by rocks, as is alfo the river called French Broad, which comes into the Cherokee river 50 miles above the Tenefee, and on the fame fide. 150 miles above French Broad is Long Ifland (three miles in length) and from thence to the fource of the Cherokee river is

6o

60 miles, and the whole diſtance is ſo rocky, as to be ſcarcely navigable with a canoe.

" By the Cherokee river, the emigrants from the frontier counties of Virginia, and North Carolina, paſs to the ſettlements in Weſt Florida, upon the river Miſſiſſippi. They embark at Long Iſland.

" I will now proceed to give a deſcription of that part called the Illinois country, lying between the Miſſiſſippi weſterly, the Illinois river northerly, the Wabaſh eaſterly, and the Ohio ſoutherly.

" The land at the confluence, or fork of the rivers Miſſiſſippi and Ohio, is above 20 feet higher than the common ſurface of theſe rivers; yet ſo conſiderable are the ſpring floods, that it is generally overflowed for about a week, as are the lands for ſeveral miles back in the country. —The ſoil at the fork is compoſed of mud, earth, and ſand, accumulated from the Ohio and Miſſiſſippi rivers. It is exceedingly fertile, and in its natural ſtate yields hemp, pea-vines, graſs, &c. and a great variety of trees, and in particular the aſpen tree, of an unuſual height and thickneſs.

" For 25 miles up the Miſſiſſippi (from the Ohio)

Ohio) the country is rich, level, and well timbered ; and then feveral gentle rifing grounds appear, which gradually diminifh at the diftance of between four and five miles eaftward from the river. From thence to the Kafkafkias river is 65 miles. The country is a mixture of hills and vallies; fome of the former are rocky and fteep ; but they, as well as the vallies, are fhaded with fine oaks, hickory, walnut, afh, and mulberry-trees, &c. Some of the high grounds afford moft pleafant fituations for fettlements. Their elevated, and airy pofitions, together with the great luxuriance of the foil, every where yielding plenty of grafs, and ufeful plants, promife health, and ample returns to induftrious fettlers.

" Many quarries of lime, free-ftone, and marble, have been difcovered in this part of the country.

" Several creeks and rivers fall into the Miffiffippi, in the above diftance (of 65 miles), but no remarkable ones, except the rivers à Vafe and Kafkafkias; the former is navigable for battoes about 60, and the latter for about 130 miles ;—both thefe rivers run through a rich country, abounding in extenfive, natural meadows,

dows, and numberless herds of buffaloe, deer, &c.

" The high grounds, juft mentioned, continue along the eaftern fide of the Kafkafkias river, at a fmall diftance from it, for the fpace of five miles and a half, to the Kafkafkias village; then they incline more towards that river, and run nearly parallel with the eaftern bank of the Miffiffippi, at the diftance of about three miles in fome parts, and four miles in other parts from it. Thefe are principally compofed of lime and free-ftone, and from 100 to 130 feet high, divided in feveral places by deep cavities, through which many fmall rivulets pafs before they fall into the Miffiffippi. The fides of thefe hills, fronting this river, are in many places perpendicular,—and appear like folid pieces of ftone mafonry, of various colours, figures, and fizes.

" The low land between the hills and the Miffiffippi, begins on the north fide of the Kafkafkias river, and continues for three miles above the River Mifouri, where a high ridge terminates it, and forms the eaftern bank of the Miffiffippi.—This interval land is level, has few trees, and is of a very rich foil, yielding fhrubs and moft fragrant flowers, which, added

to

to the number and extent of meadows and ponds difperfed through this charming valley, render it exceedingly beautiful and agreeable.

" In this vale ftand the following villages, viz. Kafkafkias, which, as already mentioned, is five miles and a half up a river of the fame name, running northerly and foutherly.—This village contains 80 houfes, many of them well built; feveral of ftone, with gardens, and large lots adjoining. It confifts of about 500 white inhabitants, and between four and five hundred negroes. The former have large ftocks of black cattle, fwine, &c.

" Three miles northerly of Kafkafkias, is a village of Illinois Indians (of the Kafkafkias tribe) containing about 210 perfons and 60 warriors. They were formerly brave and warlike, but are degenerated into a drunken and debauched tribe, and fo indolent, as fcarcely to procure a fufficiency of fkins and furs to barter for clothing.

" Nine miles further northward than the laft mentioned village, is another, called La prairie du Rocher, or the Rock meadows. It confifts of 100 white inhabitants, and 80 negroes.

" Three miles northerly of this place, on the

banks

banks of the Miſſiſſippi, ſtood Fort Chartres. It was abandoned in the year 1772, as it was rendered untenable by the conſtant waſhings of the River Miſſiſſippi in high floods.—The village of Fort Chartres, a little ſouthward of the fort, contained ſo few inhabitants, as not to deſerve my notice.

" One mile higher up the Miſſiſſippi than Fort Chartres, is a village ſettled by 170 warriors of the Piorias and Mitchigamias (two other tribes of the Illinois Indians). They are as idle and debauched as the tribe of Kaſkaſkias which I have juſt deſcribed.

" Four miles higher than the preceding village, is St. Philip's. It was formerly inhabited by about a dozen families, but at preſent is poſſeſſed only by two or three.—The others have retired to the weſtern ſide of the Miſſiſſippi.

" Forty-five miles further northwards than St. Philip's (and one mile up a ſmall river on the ſouthern ſide of it) ſtands the village of Cahokia. It has 50 houſes, many of them well built, and 300 inhabitants, poſſeſſing 80 negroes, and large ſtocks of black cattle, ſwine, &c.

" Four miles above Cahokia, on the weſtern

or

or Spanish side of the Mississippi, stands the village of St. Louis, on a high piece of ground. It is the most healthy and pleasurable situation of any known in this part of the country. Here the Spanish commandant and the principal Indian traders reside; who, by conciliating the affections of the natives, have drawn all the Indian trade of the Misouri;—part of that of the Mississippi (northwards), and of the tribes of Indians residing near the Ouisconsing and Illinois rivers, to this village. In St. Louis are 120 houses, mostly built of stone. They are large and commodious. This village has 800 inhabitants, chiefly French;—some of them have had a liberal education, are polite, and hospitable. They have about 150 negroes, and large stocks of black cattle, &c.

" Twelve miles below, or southerly of Fort Chartres, on the western bank of the Mississippi, and nearly opposite to the village of Kaskafkias, is the village of St. Genevieve, or Missire. It contains upwards of 100 houses, and 460 inhabitants, besides negroes. This and St. Louis are all the villages that are upon the western or Spanish side of the Mississippi.

" Four miles below St. Genevieve (on the western bank of the Mississippi), at the mouth of of a creek, is a hamlet, called the Saline. Here all the falt is made, which is ufed in the Illinois country, from a falt fpring that is at this place.

" In the feveral villages on the Miffiffippi, which I have juft defcribed, there were, fo long ago as the year 1771, twelve hundred and feventy-three fencible men.

" The Ridge which forms the eaftern bank of the Miffiffippi, above the Mifouri river, continues northerly to the Illinois river, and then directs its courfe along the eaftern fide of that river, for about 220 miles, when it declines in gentle flopes, and ends in extenfive rich favannahs. On the top of this ridge, at the mouth of the Illinois river, is an agreeable and commanding fituation for a fort, and though the ridge is high and fteep (about 130 feet high), and rather difficult to afcend, yet when afcended, it affords a moft delightful profpect. —The Miffiffippi is diftinctly feen from its fummit for more than twenty miles, as are the beautiful meanderings of the Illinois river for many leagues ;—next a level, fruitful meadow prefents itfelf, of at leaft one hundred miles in circuit on the weftern fide of the Miffiffippi, watered by feveral lakes, and fhaded by

fmall

fmall groves or copfes of trees, fcattered in different parts of it, and then the eye with rap-
ture furveys, as well the high lands bordering
upon the river Miffouri, as thofe at a greater
diftance up the Miffiffippi.—In fine, this charming ridge is covered with excellent grafs, large
oak, walnut-trees, &c. and at the diftance
of about nine miles from the Miffiffippi, up the
Illinois river, are feen many large favannahs,
or meadows abounding in buffalo, deer, &c.

" In afcending the Miffiffippi, Cape au Gres
particularly attracted my attention.—It is about
8 leagues above the Illinois river, on the eaftern fide of the Miffiffippi, and continues above
five leagues on that river. There is a gradual
defcent back to delightful meadows, and to
beautiful and fertile uplands, watered by feveral
rivulets, which fall into the Illinois river between 30 and 40 miles from its entrance into
the Miffiffippi, and into the latter at Cape au
Gres. The diftance from the Miffiffippi to the
River Illinois acrofs the country, is leffened or
increafed, according to the windings of the
former river ;—the fmalleft diftance is at Cape
au Gres, and there it is between four and five
miles. The lands in this intermediate fpace
between the above two rivers are rich, almoft
beyond

beyond parallel, covered with large oaks, walnut, &c. and not a ftone is to be feen, except
upon the fides of the river.—It is even acknowledged by the French inhabitants, that if
fettlements were only begun at Cape au Gres,
thofe upon the Spanifh fide of the Miffiffippi
would be abandoned, as the former would excite a conftant fucceffion of fettlers, and intercept all the trade of the upper Miffiffippi.

" The Illinois river furnifhes a communication with Lake Michigan, by the Chicago
river, and by two portages between the latter
and the Illinois river; the longeft of which
does not exceed four miles.

" The Illinois country is in general of a fuperior foil to any other part of North America
that I have feen. It produces fine oak, hickory, cedar, mulberry-trees, &c. fome dying
roots and medicinal plants ;—hops and excellent
wild grapes, and in the year 1769, one hundred
and ten hogfheads of well-tafted and ftrong
wine were made by the French fettlers from
thefe grapes,—a large quantity of fugar is alfo
annually made from the juice of the maple-tree ;
and as the mulberry-trees are long and numerous, I prefume the making of filk will employ
the attention and induftry of the fettlers, when
the

the country is more fully inhabited than it is at prefent, and efpecially as the winters are much more moderate, and favourable for the breed of filk worms, than they are in many of the fea coaft provinces.—Indigo may likewife be fuccefsfully cultivated (but not more than two cuttings in a year); wheat, peas, and Indian corn thrive well, as does every fort of grain and pulfe, that is produced in any of the old colonies. Great quantities of tobacco are alfo yearly raifed by the inhabitants of the Illinois, both for their own confumption, and that of the Indians; but little has hitherto been exported to Europe. Hemp grows fpontaneoufly, and is of a good texture; its common height is 10 feet, and its thicknefs three inches (the latter reckoned within about a foot of the root), and with little labour any quantity may be cultivated. Flax feed has hitherto been only raifed in fmall quantities. There has however been enough produced to fhew that it may be fown to the greateft advantage. Apples, pears, peaches, and all other European fruits, fucceed admirably. Iron, copper, and lead mines, as alfo falt fprings, have been difcovered in different parts of this territory. The two latter are worked on the Spanifh fide of

the

the Miſſiſſippi, with conſiderable advantage to
their owners. There is plenty of fiſh in the
rivers, particularly cat, carp, and perch, of an
uncommon ſize.—Savannahs, or natural meadows, are both numerous and extenſive ; yield-
ing-excellent grafs, and feeding great herds of
buffaloe, deer, &c.—Ducks, teal, geeſe, ſwans,
cranes, pelicans, turkies, pheaſants, partridges,
&c. ſuch as are feen in the ſea coaſt colonies,
are in the greateſt variety and abundance.—In
ſhort, every thing that a reaſonable mind can
deſire is to be found, or may, with little pains,
be produced here.

" Niagara Fort is a moſt important poſt. It
ſecures a greater number of communications
through a larger country than probably any
other pafs in interior America;—it ſtands at
the entrance of a ſtrait, by which lake Ontario
is joined to lake Erie, and the latter is connected with the three great lakes, Huron, Michegan,
and Superior. About nine miles above Fort
Niagara the carrying place begins. It is oc-
caſioned by the ſtupendous cataract of that
name. The quantity of water which tumbles
over this fall is unparalleled in America ;—its
heighth is not lefs than 137 feet. This fall
would interrupt the communication between
the

the lakes Ontario and Erie, if a road was not made up the hilly country that borders upon the ftrait. This road extends to a fmall poft eighteen miles from Fort Niagara. Here the traveller embarks in a battoe or canoe, and proceeds eighteen miles to a fmall fort at lake Erie. It may be proper alfo to add, that at the end of the firft two miles, in the laft-mentioned diftance of 18 miles, the ftream of the river is divided by a large ifland, above nine miles in length ; and at the upper end of it, about a mile from lake Erie, are three or four iflands, not far from each other ;—thefe iflands, by interrupting and confining the waters difcharged from the lake, greatly increafe the rapidity of the ftream; which indeed is fo violent, that the ftiffeft gale is fcarcely fufficient to enable a large veffel to ftem it; but it is fuccefsfully refifted in fmall battoes, or canoes, that are rowed near the fhore.

" Lake Erie is about 225 miles in length, and upon a medium about 40 miles in breadth. It affords a good navigation for fhipping of any burthen. The coaft, on both fides of the lake, is generally favourable for the paffage of battoes and canoes. Its banks in many places have a flat fandy fhore, particularly to the eaftward of

the

the peninfula, called Long Point, which extends into the lake, in a fouth-eaftern direction,
for upwards of 18 miles, and is more than five
miles wide in the broadeft part; but the ifthmus,
by which it joins the continent, is fcarcely 200
yards wide.   The peninfula is compofed of
fand, and is very convenient to haul boats out
of the furf upon (as is almoft every other part
of the fhore) when the lake is too rough for
rowing or failing; yet there are fome places
where, in boifterous weather (on account of
their great perpendicular height), it would be
dangerous to approach, and impoffible to land.
Moft of thefe places are marked in my map
with the letter X.

" Lake Erie has a great variety of fine fifh,
fuch as fturgeon, eel, white fifh, trout, perch,
&c.

" The country, northward of this lake, is in
many parts fwelled with moderate hills, but no
high mountains.   The climate is temperate,
and the air healthful.   The lands are well
timbered (but not generally fo rich as thofe
upon the fouthern fide of the lake), and for a
confiderable diftance from it, and for feveral
miles eaftward of Cayahoga river, they appear
quite level and extremely fertile; and except
where

where extenfive favannahs, or natural meadows intervene, are covered with large oaks, walnut, afh, hickory, mulberry, faffafras, &c. &c. and produce a great variety of fhrubs and medicinal roots.—Here alfo is great plenty of buffalo, deer, turkies, partridges, &c.

" Fort Detroit is of an oblong figure, built with ftockades, and advantageoufly fituated, with one entire fide commanding the river, called Detroit. This fort is near a mile in cir-cumference, and enclofes about one hundred houfes, built in a regular manner, with parallel ftreets, croffing each other at right angles. Its fituation is delightful, and in the centre of a pleafant, fruitful country.

" The ftrait St. Clair (commonly called the Detroit river) is at its entrance more than three miles wide, but in afcending it, its width per-ceptibly diminifhes, fo that oppofite to the fort (which is 18 miles from lake Erie) it does not exceed half a mile in width. From thence to lake St. Clair it widens to more than a mile. The channel of the ftrait is gentle, and wide, and deep enough for fhipping of great burthen, although it is incommoded by feveral iflands ; one of which is more than feven miles in length. Thefe iflands are of a fertile foil, and

from

from their fituation afford a very agreeable appearance.   For eight miles below, and the
fame diftance above fort Detroit, on both fides
of the river, the country is divided into regular
and well cultivated plantations, and from the
contiguity of the farmers houfes to each other,
they appear as two long extended villages.
The inhabitants, who are moftly French, are
about 2000 in number ; 500 of whom are as
good markfmen, and as well accuftomed to the
woods, as the Indian natives themfelves.   They
raife large ftocks of black cattle, and great
quantities of corn, which they grind by wind-
mills, and manufacture into excellent flour.—
The chief trade of Detroit confifts in a barter of
coarfe European goods with the natives for furs,
deer-fkins, tallow, &c. &c.

   " The rout from lake St. Clair to lake
Huron, is up a ftrait or river, about 400 yards
wide.   This river derives itfelf from lake Huron, and at the diftance of 33 miles lofes itfelf
in lake St. Clair.   It is in general rapid, but
particularly fo near its fource;—its channel,
and alfo that of lake St. Clair, are fufficiently
deep for fhipping of very confiderable burthen.
This ftrait has feveral mouths, and the lands
lying between them are fine meadows.   The
country

country on both fides of it, for 15 miles, has a
very level appearance, but from thence to lake
Huron, it is in many places broken, and covered with white pines, oaks, maple, birch, and
beech."

---

*Thoughts on the Duration of the American Com-
monwealth.*

THERE is a greater probability that the duration of the American commonwealth will be
longer than any empire that has hitherto exifted. For it is a truth, univerfally admitted, that
all the advantages which ever attended any of
the monarchies in the old world, all center in the
new; together with many others, which they
never enjoy. The four great empires, and the
dominions of Charlemaign, and the Turks, all
rofe by conquefts; none by the arts of peace.
On the contrary, the territory of the United
States has been planted and reared by a union of
liberty, good conduct, and all the comforts of
domeftic virtue.

All the great monarchies were formed by the
conqueft of kingdoms, different in arts, manners, language, temper, or religion, from the
conquerors; fo that the union, though in fome

cafes

cafes very ftrong, was never the real and intimate connection of the fame people; and this
circumftance principally accelerated their ruin,
and was abfolutely the caufe of it in fome.
This will be very different in the Americans.
They will, in their greateft extent and population, be one and the fame people; the fame in
language, religion, laws, manners, tempers, and
purfuits; for the fmall variation in fome diftricts, owing to the fettlement of Germans, is
an exception fo very flight, that in a few ages
it will be unknown.

The Affyrian and Roman empires were of
very flow growth, and therefore lafted the longeft; but ftill their increafe was by conqueft, and
the union of diffonant parts. The Perfian and
Macedonian monarchies were foon founded and
prefently overturned; the former not lafting fo
long as the Affyrian, nor a fixth of the duration
of the Roman; and as to the Maredonian, it lafted but fix years. This advantage of a flow
growth is ftrong in favour of the Americans;
the wonderful increafe of their numbers is the
natural effect of plenty of land, a good climate,
and a mild and beneficent government, in which
corruption and tyranny are wholly unknown.
Some centuries are already paft fince their firft
fettlement,

fettlement, and many more will pafs before their power appears in its full fplendour; but the quicknefs of a growth that is entirely natural will carry with it no marks of decay, being entirely different from monarchies founded by force of arms. The Roman empire perifhed by the hands of northern barbarians, whom the mafters of the world difdained to conquer; it will not be fo with the Americans, they fpread gradually over the whole continent, infomuch that two hundred years hence there probably will be nobody but themfelves in the whole northern continent; from whence therefore fhould their Goths and Vandals come? Nor can they ever have any thing to fear from the fouth; firft, becaufe that country will never be populous, owing to the poffeffion of mines: fecondly, there are feveral nations and languages planted and remaining in it: thirdly, the moft confiderable part of it lies in the torrid zone; a region that never yet fent forth nations of conquerors.

In extent the habitable parts of North America exceed that of any of the four empires, and confequently can feed and maintain a people much more numerous than the Affyrians or the Romans. The fituation of the region is fo advantageous

advantageous that it leaves nothing to be wifhed for; it can have no neighbours from whom there is a poffibility of attack or moleftation; it will poffefs all the folid advantages of the Chinefe empire without the fatal neighbourhood of the Tartars.

It will have further the fingular felicity of all the advantages of an ifland, that is, a freedom from the attacks of others, and too many difficulties, with too great a diftance, to engage in enterprifes that heretofore proved the ruin of other monarchies.

The foil, the climate, production, and face of the continent, is formed by nature for a great, independent, and permanent government : fill it with people who will of themfelves, of courfe, poffefs all forts of manufactures, and you will find it yielding every neceffary and convenience of life. Such a vaft tract of country, poffeffing fuch fingular advantages, becoming inhabited by one people, fpeaking the fame language, profeffing the fame religion, and having the fame manners ; attaining a population equal to that of the greateft empire; fprung from an active and induftrious nation, who have transfufed into them their own induftry and fpirit, and feen them worthy of their original ; inhabiting a foil not

dangeroufly

dangeroufly fertile, nor a clime generally conducive to effeminacy ; accuftomed to commerce : fuch a people muft found a commonwealth as indiffoluble as humanity will allow. Suffice it for England, that fhe will have been the origin of a commonwealth greater and more durable than any former monarchy ; that her language and her manners will flourifh among a people who will one day become a fplendid fpectacle in the vaft eye of the univerfe. This flattering idea of immortality no other nation can hope to attain.

And here let me make an obfervation that fhould animate the authors in the Englifh language with an ardour that cannot be infufed into thofe of any other nation ; it is the pleafing idea of living among fo great a people, through almoft a perpetuity of fame, and under almoft an impoffibility of becoming, like the Greek and Latin tongues, dead ; known only by the learned.—Increafing time will bring increafing readers, until their names become repeated with pleafure by above an hundred millions of people !

A STATE

A STATE OF THE COMMERCIAL INTERCOURSE
BETWEEN THE UNITED STATES OF AME-
RICA AND FOREIGN NATIONS. WRITTEN
IN THE MONTH OF JUNE 1792. BY THO-
MAS JEFFERSON, ESQ. SECRETARY OF STATE
TO THE SAID UNITED STATES.

THE countries with which the United States
have had their chief commercial intercourse,
are, Spain, Portugal, France, Great Britain, the
United Netherlands, Denmark, and Sweden,
and their American poffeffions ; and the articles
of export which conftitute the bafis of that
commerce, with their refpective amounts,
are—

	Dols.
Bread ftuff, that is to fay, bread-grains, meals, and bread, to the annual amount of - - - - - -	7,649,887
Tobacco - - - - - - -	4,349,567
Rice - - - - - - - - -	1,753,796
Wood - - - - - - - -	1,263,534
Salted fifh - - - - - - -	941,696
Pot and pearl afh - - - - -	839,093
Salted meats - - - - - -	599,130

Indigo

Dols.

Indigo - - - - - - - -	537,379
Horfes and mules - - - - -	339,753
Whale oil - - - - - - -	252,591
Flax feed - - - - - - -	236,072
Tar, pitch, and turpentine - -	217,177
Live provifions - - - - -	137,743
Ships	
Foreign goods - - - - - -	620,274

To defcend to articles of fmaller value than thefe, would lead into a minutenefs of detail neither neceffary nor ufeful to the prefent object.

The proportions of our Exports, which go to the nations before mentioned, and to their dominions, refpectively, are as follows:

Dols.

To Spain and its dominions - -	2,005,907
Portugal and its dominions - -	1,283,462
France and its dominions - - -	4,698,735
Great Britain and its dominions -	9,363,416
The United Netherlands and their dominions - - - - - -	1,963,880
Denmark and its dominions - -	224,415
Sweden and its dominions - -	47,240

Our Imports from the fame countries are—

Spain and its dominions - - -	335,110
Portugal and its dominions - -	595,763
	France

Dols.

France and its dominions - - 2,068,348
Great Britain and its dominions - 15,285,428
United Netherlands and their do-
    minions - - - - - - 1,172,692
Denmark and its dominions - - 351,394
Sweden and its dominions   - - 14,325

These Imports consist mostly of articles on which industry has been exhausted.

Our Navigation, depending on the same commerce, will appear by the following statement of the tonnage of our own vessels, entering into our ports, from those several nations, and their possessions, in one year, that is to say, from October 1789, to September 1790, inclusive, as follows:

Tons.

Spain - - - - - - - - 19,695
Portugal - - - - - - - 23,576
France - - - - - - - 116,410
Great Britain - - - - - - 43,580
United Netherlands - - - - 58,858
Denmark - - - - - - - 14,655
Sweden - - - - - - - - 750

Of our commercial objects, Spain receives favourably our bread stuff, salted fish, wood, ships, tar, pitch, and turpentine. On our meals, however, as well as on those of other foreign countries,

tries, when re-exported to their colonies, they have lately impofed duties of from half a dollar to two dollars the barrel, the duties being fo proportioned to the current price of their own flour, as that both together are to make the conftant fum of nine dollars per barrel.

They do not difcourage our rice, pot and pearl afh, falted provifions, or whale oil: but thefe articles being in fmall demand at their markets, are carried thither but in a fmall degree. Their demand for rice, however, is increafing. Neither tobacco nor indigo are received there. Our commerce is permitted with their Canary Iflands, under the fame conditions.

Themfelves and their colonies are the actual confumers of what they receive from us.

Our navigation is free with the kingdom of Spain; foreign goods being received there in our fhips, on the fame conditions as if carried in their own, or in the veffels of the country of which fuch goods are the manufacture or produce.

Portugal receives favourably our grain and bread, falted fifh and other falted provifions, wood, tar, pitch, and turpentine.

For

For flax-feed, pot and pearl afh, though not difcouraged, there is little demand.

Our fhips pay 20 per cent. on being fold to their fubjects, and are then free bottoms.

Foreign goods (except thofe of the Eaft Indies) are received on the fame footing in our veffels as in their own, or any others ; that is to fay, on general duties of from twenty to twenty-eight per cent. and confequently our navigation unobftructed by them.—Tobacco, rice, and meals, are prohibited.

Themfelves and their colonies confume what they receive from us.

Thefe regulations extend to the Azores, Madeira, and the Cape de Verd Iflands, except that in thefe meals and rice are received freely.

France receives favourably our bread ftuff, rice, wood, pot and pearl afhes.

A duty of five fous the kental, or nearly four and a half cents, is paid on our tar, pitch, and turpentine. Our whale oil pays fix livres the kental, and are the only foreign whale oils admitted. Our indigo pays five livres on the kental ; their own two and an half : but a difference of quality, ftill more than a difference of duty, prevents its feeking that market.

Salted

Salted beef is received freely for re-exportation, but if for home confumption, it pays five livres the kental. Other falted provifions pay that duty in all cafes, and falted fifh is made lately to pay the prohibitory one of twenty livres in the kental.

Our fhips are free to carry thither all foreign goods which may be carried in their own or any other veffels, except tobaccoes not of our own growth; and they participate with their's the exclufive carriage of our whale oils and tobaccoes.

During their former government, our tobacco was under a monopoly; but paid no duties, and our fhips were freely fold in their ports, and converted into national bottoms. The firft National Affembly took from our fhips this privilege : they emancipated tobacco from its monopoly, but fubjected it to duties of eighteen livres fifteen fous the kental, carried in their own veffels, and twenty-five livres carried in ours, a difference more than equal to the freight of the article.

They and their colonies confume what they receive from us.

Great Britain receives our pot and pearl afhes free, while thofe of other nations pay a duty of

two

two shillings and three-pence the kental. There
is an equal diftinction in favour of our bar iron,
of which article, however, we do not produce
enough for our own ufe. Woods are free from
us, whilft they pay fome fmall duty from other
countries. Our tar and pitch pay 11d. fterling
the barrel; from other alien countries they pay
about a penny and a third more.

Our tobacco, for their own confumption,
pays 1s. 3d. fterling the pound, cuftom and excife, befides heavy expences of collection. And
rice, in the fame cafe, pays 7s. 4d. fterling the
hundred weight; which rendering it too dear
as an article of common food, it is confequently
ufed in very fmall quantity.

Our falted fifh, and other falted provifions,
except bacon, are prohibited. Bacon and whale
oil are under prohibitory duties; fo are our
grains, meals, and bread, as to internal confumption, unlefs in times of fuch fcarcity as
may raife the price of wheat to 50s. fterling the
quarter, and other grains and meals in proportion.

Our fhips, though purchafed and navigated
by their own fubjects, are not permitted to be
ufed, even in their trade with us.

While

While the veffels of other nations are fecured by ftanding laws, which cannot be altered, but by the concurrent will of the three branches of the Britifh legiflature, in carrying thither any produce or manufacture of the country to which they belong, which may be lawfully carried in any veffels, ours, with the fame prohibition of what is foreign, are further prohibited by a ftanding law (12 Car. II. 28. §. 3) from carrying thither all and any of our own domeftic productions and manufactures. A fubfequent act, indeed, authorifed their executive to permit the carriage of our own productions in our own bottoms, at its fole difcretion; and the permiffion has been given from year to year by proclamation, but fubject every moment to be withdrawn on that fingle will, in which event our veffels having any thing on board, ftand interdicted from the entry of all Britifh ports. The difadvantage of a tenure which may be fo fuddenly difcontinued was experienced by our merchants on a late occafion, when an official notification that this law would be ftrictly enforced, gave them juft apprehenfions for the fate of their veffels and cargoes difpatched or deftined to the ports of Great Britain. The minifter of that court, indeed, frankly expreffed his

his perſonal conviction that the words of the
order went farther than was intended, and ſo he
afterwards officially informed us ; but the em-
barraſſments of the moment were real and great,
and the poſſibility of their renewal lays our
commerce to that country under the ſame ſpecies of diſcouragement as to other countries
where it is regulated by a ſingle legiſlator ; and
the diſtinction is too remarkable not to be no-
ticed, that our navigation is excluded from the
ſecurity of fixed laws, while that ſecurity is giv-
en to the navigation of others.

Our veſſels pay their ports 1s. 9d. ſterling per
ton, light and trinity dues, more than is paid
by Britiſh ſhips, except in the port of London,
where they pay the ſame as Britiſh.

The greater part of what they receive from
us is re-exported to other countries, under the
uſeleſs charges of an intermediate depoſit and
double voyage. From tables publiſhed in England, and compoſed, as is ſaid, from the books
of their cuſtom-houſes, it appears that of the
indigo imported there in the years 1773—4—5,
one third was re-exported ; and from a document of authority, we learn that of the rice
and tobacco imported there before the war,
four-fifths were re-exported. We are aſſured,
indeed,

indeed, that the quantities sent thither for re-exportation since the war, are confiderably dimiinifhed, yet lefs fo than reafon and national intereft would dictate. The whole of our grain is re-exported when wheat is below 50s. the quarter, and other grains in proportion.

The United Netherlands prohibit our pickled beef and pork, meals and bread of all forts, and lay a prohibitory duty on fpirits diftilled from grain.

All other of our productions are received on varied duties, which may be reckoned on a medium at about three per cent.

They confume but a fmall proportion of what they receive; the refidue is partly forwarded for confumption in the inland parts of Europe, and partly re-fhipped to other maritime countries. On the latter portion they intercept between us and the confumer fo much of the value as is abforbed by the charges attending an intermediate depofit.

Foreign goods, except fome Eaft India articles, are received in veffels of any nation.

Our fhips may be fold and naturalized there with exceptions of one or two privileges, which fomewhat leffen their value.

Denmark lays confiderable duties on our tobacco

bacco and rice carried in their own veffels, and half as much more if carried in ours ; but the exact amount of thefe duties is not perfectly known here. They lay fuch as amount to prohibitions on our indigo and corn.

Sweden receives favourably our grains and meals, falted provifions, indigo, and whale oil.

They fubject our rice to duties of fixteen mills the pound weight carried in their own veffels, and of forty per cent. additional on that, or 22,410 mills, carried in ours or any others. Being thus rendered too dear as an article of common food, little of it is confumed with them. They confume more of our tobaccoes, which they take circuitoufly through Great Britain, levying heavy duties on them alfo; their duties of entry, town duties, and excife, being 4 dols. 34 cents. the hundred weight, if carried in their own veffels, and of forty per cent. on that additional, if carried in our own or any other veffels.

They prohibit altogether our bread, fifh, pot and pearl afhes, flax-feed, tar, pitch, and tur-pentine, wood (except oak timber and mafts), and all foreign manufactures.

Under fo many reftrictions and prohibitions, our

APPENDIX.   **327**

our navigation with them is reduced almoſt to nothing.

With our neighbours, an order of things much harder preſents itſelf.

Spain and Portugal refuſe to thoſe parts of America which they govern, all direct intercourſe with any people but themſelves. The commodities in mutual demand between them and their neighbours muſt be carried to be exchanged in ſome port of the dominant country, and the tranſportation between that and the ſubject ſtate muſt be in a domeſtic bottom.

France, by a ſtanding law, permits her Weſt India poſſeſſions to receive directly our vegetables, live proviſions, horſes, wood, tar, pitch, and turpentine, rice, and maize, and prohibits our other bread ſtuff; but a ſuſpenſion of this prohibition having been left to the colonial legiſlatures in times of ſcarcity, it was formerly ſuſpended occaſionally, but latterly without interruption.

Our freſh and ſalted proviſions (except pork) are received in their iſlands under a duty of three colonial livres the kental, and our veſſels are as free as their own to carry our commodities thither, and to bring away rum and molaſſes.

Great

Great Britain admits in her iflands our vegetables, live provifions, horfes, wood, tar, pitch,
and turpentine, rice, and bread ftuff, by a proclamation of her executive, limited always to
the term of a year. She prohibits our falted
provifions : fhe does not permit our veffels to
carry thither our own produce. Her veffels
alone may take it from us, and bring in exchange, rum, molaffes, fugar, coffee, cocoa nuts,
ginger, and pimento. There are, indeed, fome
freedoms in the ifland of Dominica, but under
fuch circumftances as to be little ufed by us. In
the Britifh continental colonies, and in Newfoundland, all our productions are prohibited,
and our veffels forbidden to enter their ports ;
their governors however, in times of diftrefs,
have power to permit a temporary importation
of certain articles in their own bottoms, but
not in ours.

Our citizens cannot refide as merchants or
factors within any of the Britifh plantations,
this being exprefsly prohibited by the fame fta-
tue of 12 Car. II. C. 18, commonly called the
Navigation act.

In the Danifh-American poffeffions a duty of
five per cent. is levied on our corn, corn-meal,
rice, tobacco, wood, falted fifh, indigo, horfes,
                                        mules,

mules, and live ftock ; and of ten per cent. on our flour, falted pork and beef, tar, pitch, and turpentine.

In the American iflands of the United Ne- therlands and Sweden, our veffels and produce are received, fubject to duties, not fo heavy as to have been complained of ; but they are hea- vier in the Dutch poffeffions on the continent.

To fum up thefe reftrictions, fo far as they are important:

1ft. *In Europe—*

Our bread ftuff is at moft times under prohi- bitory duties in England, and confiderably du- tied on exportation from Spain to her colonies.

Our tobaccoes are heavily dutied in England, Sweden, and France, and prohibited in Spain and Portugal.

Our rice is heavily dutied in England and Sweden, and prohibited in Portugal.

Our fifh and falted provifions are prohibited in England, and under prohibitory duties in France.

Our whale-oils are prohibited in England and Portugal.

And our veffels are denied naturalization in England, and of late in France.

2d. *In*

2d. *In the West Indies.*

All intercourse is prohibited with the possessions of Spain and Portugal.

Our salted provisions and fish are prohibited
by England.

Our salted pork, and bread stuff (except
maize), are received under temporary laws only,
in the dominions of France, and our salted fish
pays there a weighty duty.

3d. *In the Article of Navigation.*

Our own carriage of our own tobacco is heavily dutied in Sweden, and lately in France.

We can carry no article, not of our own production, to the British ports in Europe.

Nor even our own produce to her American
possessions.

Such being the restrictions on the commerce
and navigation of the United States, the ques-
tion is, in what way they may best be removed,
modified, or counteracted?

As to commerce, two methods occur. 1. By
friendly arrangements with the several nations
with whom these restrictions exist: or, 2. By
the

the feparate act of our own legiflatures for
countervailing their effects.

There can be no doubt, but that of thefe
two, friendly arrangement is the moft eligible.
Inftead of embarraffing commerce under piles
of regulating laws, duties, and prohibitions,
could it be relieved from all its fhackles in all
parts of the world—could every country be
employed in producing that which nature has
beft fitted it to produce, and each be free to exchange with others mutual furpluffes for mutual
wants, the greateft mafs poffible would then
be produced of thofe things which contribute
to human life and human happinefs; the numbers of mankind would be increafed, and their
condition bettered.

Would even a fingle nation begin with the
United States this fyftem of free commerce, it
would be advifable to begin it with that nation;
fince it is by one only that it can be extended to all. Where the circumftances of either
party render it expedient to levy a revenue, by
way of impoft, on commerce, its freedom might
be modified, in that particular, by mutual and
equivalent meafures, preferving it entire in all
others.

Some nations, not yet ripe for free commerce,

in

in all its extent, might ftill be willing to mol-
lify its reftrictions and regulations for us in proportion to the advantages which an intercourfe
with us might offer. Particularly they may
concur with us in reciprocating the duties to be
levied on each fide, or in compenfating any excefs of duty, by equivalent advantages of another nature. Our commerce is certainly of a
character to entitle it to favour in moft countries. The commodities we offer are either
neceffaries of life, or materials for manufacture,
or convenient fubjects of revenue ; and we take
in exchange, either manufactures, when they
have received the laft finifh of art and induftry,
or mere luxuries. Such cuftomers may reafonably expect welcome, and friendly treatment
at every market ; cuftomers too, whofe demands, increafing with their wealth and population, muft very fhortly give full employment
to the whole induftry of any nation whatever,
in any line of fupply they may get into the habit of calling for, from it.

But fhould any nation, contrary to our wifhes,
fuppofe it may better find its advantage by continuing its fyftem of prohibitions, duties, and
regulations, it behoves us to protect our citizens,
their commerce, and navigation, by counter-
prohibitions,

prohibitions, duties, and regulations alfo. Free commerce and navigation are not to be given in exchange for reftrictions and vexations ; nor are they likely to produce a relaxation of them.

Our navigation involves ftill higher confiderations. As a branch of induftry, it is valuable ; but as a refource, effential.

Its value, as a branch of induftry, is enhanced by the dependence of fo many other branches on it. In times of general peace it multiplies competitors for employment in tranfportation, and fo keeps that at its proper level ; and in times of war, that is to fay, when thofe nations who may be our principal carriers, fhall be at war with each other, if we have not within ourfelves the means of tranfportation, our produce muft be exported in belligerent veffels at the increafed expence of warfreight and infurance, and the articles which will not bear that, muft perifh on our hands.

But it is a refource for defence that our navigation will admit neither neglect nor forbearance. The pofition and circumftances of the United States leave them nothing to fear on their land-board, and nothing to defire beyond their prefent rights. But on their fea-board, they are open to injury, and they have there, too,

too, a commerce which muſt be protected. This can only be done by poſſeſſing a reſpectable body of citizen-ſeamen, and of artiſts and eſtabliſhments in readineſs for ſhip-building.

Were the ocean, which is the common property of all, open to the induſtry of all, ſo that every perſon and veſſel ſhould be free to take employment wherever it could be found, the United States would certainly not ſet the example of appropriating to themſelves, excluſively, any portion of the common ſtock of occupation. They would rely on the enterprize and activity of their citizens for a due participation of the benefits of the ſeafaring buſineſs, and for keeping the marine claſs of citizens equal to their object. But if particular nations graſp at undue ſhares, and more eſpecially if they ſeize on the means of the United States to convert them into aliment for their own ſtrength, and withdraw them entirely from the ſupport of thoſe to whom they belong, defenſive and protecting meaſures become neceſſary on the part of the nation whoſe marine reſources are thus invaded, or it will be diſarmed of its defence; its productions will lie at the mercy of the nation which has poſſeſſed itſelf excluſively of the means of carrying them, and its politics may be influenced by thoſe who

command

command its commerce. The carriage of our own commodities, if once eftablifhed in another channel, cannot be refumed in the moment we may defire. If we lofe the feamen and artifts whom it now occupies, we lofe the prefent means of marine defence, and time will be requifite to raife up others, when difgrace or loffes fhall bring home to our feelings the error of having abandoned them. The materials for maintaining our due fhare of navigation are ours in abundance; and as to the mode of ufing them, we have only to adopt the principles of thofe who thus put us on the defenfive, or others equivalent and better fitted to our circumftances.

The following principles being founded in reciprocity, appear perfectly juft, and to offer no caufe of complaint to any nation.

1ft. Where a nation impofes high duties on our productions, or prohibits them altogether, it may be proper for us to do the fame by theirs, firft burthening or excluding thofe productions which they bring here in competition with our own of the fame kind; felecting next fuch manufactures as we take from them in greateft quantity, and which at the fame time we could the fooneft furnifh to ourfelves, or obtain from other countries; impofing on them duties lighter

lighter at firſt, but heavier and heavier afterwards, as other channels of ſupply open. Such
duties having the effect of indirect encouragement to domeſtic manufactures of the ſame
kind, may induce the manufacturer to come
himſelf into theſe ſtates; where cheaper ſub-
ſiſtence, equal laws, and a vent of his wares,
free of duty, may enſure him the higheſt profits from his ſkill and induſtry. And here it
would be in the power of the ſtate governments
to co-operate eſſentially, by opening the reſources of encouragement which are under their
controul, extending them liberally to artiſts in
thoſe particular branches of manufacture, for
which their ſoil, climate, population, and other
circumſtances have matured them, and foſtering
the precious efforts and progreſs of houſehold
manufacture, by ſome patronage ſuited to the
nature of its objects, guided by the local infor-
mations they poſſeſs, and guarded againſt abuſe
by their preſence and attentions. The oppreſ-
ſions on our agriculture in foreign ports would
thus be made the occaſion of relieving it from a
dependence on the councils and conduct of
others, and of promoting arts, manufactures, and
population, at home.

2d. Where a nation refuſes permiſſion to our
merchants and factors to reſide within certain
parts

parts of their dominions, we may, if it fhould be thought expedient, refufe refidence to theirs in any and every part of ours, or modify their tranfactions.

3d. Where a nation refufes to receive in our veffels any productions but our own, we may refufe to receive, in theirs, any but their own productions. The firft and fecond claufes of the bill reported by the committee are well formed to effect this object.

4th. Where a nation refufes to confider any veffel as ours which has not been built within our territories, we fhould refufe to confider as theirs any veffel not built within their territories.

5th. Where a nation refufes to our veffels the carriage even of our own productions to certain countries under their domination, we might refufe to theirs, of every defcription, the carriage of the fame productions to the fame countries. But as juftice and good neighbourhood would dictate, that thofe who have no part in impofing the reftriction on us, fhould not be the victims of meafures adopted to defeat its effect, it may be proper to confine the reftriction to veffels owned or navigated by any fubjects of the fame dominant power, other than

than the inhabitants of the country to which the faid productions are to be carried.—And to prevent all inconvenience to the faid inhabitants, and to our own, by too fudden a check on the means of tranfportation, we may continue to admit the veffels marked for future exclufion, on an advanced tonnage, and for fuch length of time only, as may be fuppofed neceffary to provide againft that inconvenience.

The eftablifhment of fome of thefe principles by Great Britain alone has already loft us, in our commerce with that country and its poffeffions, between eight and nine hundred veffels of near 40,000 tons burthen, according to ftatements from official materials, in which they have confidence. This involves a proportional lofs of feamen, fhipwrights, and fhip building, and is too ferious a lofs to admit forbearance of fome effectual remedy.

It is true we muft expect fome inconvenience in practice, from the eftablifhment of difcriminating duties. But in this, as in fo many other cafes, we are left to choofe between two evils. Thefe inconveniences are nothing when weighed againft the lofs of wealth and lofs of force, which will follow our perfeverance in the plan of indifcrimination.—When once it fhall
be

be perceived that we are either in the fyſtem
or the habit of giving equal advantages to thofe
who extinguiſh our commerce and navigation,
by duties and prohibitions, as to thofe who
treat both with liberality and juſtice, liberality
and juſtice will be converted by all into duties
and prohibitions. It is not to the moderation
and juſtice of others we are to truſt for fair and
equal accefs to market with our productions,
or for our due fhare in the tranfportation of
them; but to our means of independence, and
the firm will to ufe them. Nor do the inconveniencies of difcrimination merit confideration.
Not one of the nations before mentioned, perhaps not a commercial nation on earth, is
without them. In our cafe one diſtinction
alone will fuffice, that is to fay, between nations who favour our productions and navigation,
and thofe who do not favour them. One fet
of moderate duties, fay the prefent duties, for
the firſt, and a fixed advance on thefe as to
fome articles, and prohibitions as to others, for
the laſt.

Still it muſt be repeated, that friendly arrangements are preferable with all who will
come into them; and that we ſhould carry into

fuch

fuch arrangements all the liberality and fpirit of accommodation, which the nature of the cafe will admit.

France has, of her own accord, propofed negociations for improving, by a new treaty on fair and equal principles, the commercial relations of the two countries. But her internal difturbances have hitherto prevented the profecution of them to effect, though we have had repeated affurances of a continuance of the difpofition.

Propofals of friendly arrangement have been made on our part by the prefent government to that of Great Britain, as the meffage ftates; but, being already on as good a footing in law, and a better in fact, than the moft favoured nation, they have not as yet difcovered any difpofition to have it meddled with.

We have no reafon to conclude that friendly arrangements would be declined by the other nations with whom we have fuch commercial intercourfe as may render them important. In the mean while, it would reft with the wifdom of Congrefs to determine whether, as to thofe nations, they will not furceafe exparte regulations, on the reafonable prefumption that they

will

will concur in doing whatever juſtice and moderation dictate ſhould be done.

THOMAS JEFFERSON.

P. S. Since writing the above, ſome alterations of the condition of our commerce with ſome ſovereign nations have taken place. France has propoſed to enter into a new treaty of commerce with us, on liberal principles; and has, in the mean time, relaxed ſome of the reſtraints mentioned in the Report. Spain has, by an ordinance of June laſt, eſtabliſhed New Orleans, Penſacola, and St. Auguſtine, into free ports, for the veſſels of friendly nations having treaties of commerce with her, provided they touch for a permit at Corcubion in Gallicia, or at Alicant ; and our rice is by the ſame ordinance excluded from that country.

THE

THE FOLLOWING ARE SOME OF THE PRIN-
CIPAL ARTICLES OF EXPORTATION FROM
THE UNITED STATES OF AMERICA DUR-
ING THE YEAR ENDING IN SEPTEMBER
1792.

Three millions one hundred and forty thoufand two hundred and fifty-five buſhels of grain
(principally wheat).

One million four hundred and ſixty-nine
thouſand ſeven hundred and twenty-three barrels of flour, meal, biſcuit, and rice (reducing
caſks of various ſizes to the proportion of flour
barrels).

Sixty million ſix hundred and forty-ſix thoufand eight hundred and ſixty-one feet of boards,
plank, and ſcantling (inch board meaſure).

Thirty-one million ſeven hundred and ſixty
thouſand ſeven hundred and two ſtaves and
hoops.

Seventy-one million ſix hundred and ninety-
three thouſand eight hundred and ſixty-three
ſhingles.

Nineteen

Nineteen thoufand three hundred and ninety-one and a half tons of timber.

Eighteen thoufand three hundred and feventy-four pieces of timber.

One thoufand and eighty cedar and oak fhip knees.

One hundred and ninety-one frames of houfes.

Seventy-three thoufand three hundred and eighteen oars, rafters for oars, and handfpikes.

Forty-eight thoufand eight hundred and fixty fhook or knock down cafks.

One hundred and forty-fix thoufand nine hundred and nine barrels of tar, pitch, turpentine and rofin.

Nine hundred and forty-eight thoufand one hundred and fifteen gallons of fpirits, diftilled in the United States.

One hundred and fixteen thoufand eight hundred and three barrels of beef, pork, bacon, mutton, oyfters, &c. (reducing cafks of various fizes to the proportion of beef and pork barrels).

Two hundred and thirty-one thoufand feven hundred and feventy-fix barrels of dried and pickled fifh.

Seven thoufand eight hundred and twenty-three

three tons twelve cwt. and 4lb. of pot afhes and pearl afhes.

One hundred and twelve thoufand four hundred and twenty-eight hogfheads of tobacco.

Fifty-two thoufand three hundred and eighty-one hogfheads of flax feed.

Forty-four thoufand feven hundred and fifty-two horfes, horned cattle, mules, and fheep.

The preceding extract from the copy of an authentic official return of all the exports from the United States of America, within the year ending in September laft, conveys an idea of the wealth, importance, and progreffive profperity of that country, far furpaffing what has been heretofore entertained on the fubject.

P. S. From the 1ft of January 1793, to the 1ft of January 1794, there were exported from the port of Philadelphia 422,075 barrels of flour.

OF THE CIVIL LIST, AND REVENUE OF THE UNITED STATES.

Abftract of an Eftimate of the Expenditures of the Civil Lift of the United States, for the year

year 1793, reported by A. Hamilton, Secretary of the Treafury to the Houfe of Reprefenta-tives.

	Dollars.
Prefident's Salary	25,000
Vice-Prefident's ditto	5,000
Chief Juftice	4,000
5 Affociate Juftices	17,500
All the diftrict Judges,	21,700
Congrefs	143,591
Treafury Department	55,050
Department of State	6,300
Department of War	11,250
Commiffioners of old ac-counts	13,300
Loan Offices	13,250
Weftern Territory	11,000
Amount of Penfions	5,267
Contingencies	20,264
Total	352,466 or

In Britifh Money £.79,304.17.0 fterl.

THE REVENUE.

The American revenue, for 1793, is ftated to be 4,400,000 dollars, exclufive of what may

arife

arife from the fale of lands in the Weftern territory; there is likewife upwards of the value
of 5,000,000 dollars in bullion, lying in the
Bank of the United States.

ESTIMATE OF EXPENCE FOR THE YEAR 1794.

	Dols.	Cents.
The whole Civil Lift for 1794, is	397,201,	6
———— Extraordinaries for Public Works, Benevolences, &c. - - - -	147,693	43
———— Eftimate of the War expences for 1794 - -	1,457,936	1
Total	2,002,830	50

The Dollar is 4s. 6d. *fterling, and the Cent is
the hundredth part of a Dollar.*

The celebrated Mr. Thomas Paine, in his
letter to Mr. Secretary Dundas, publifhed in
London in the month of June, 1792, and who
on this fubject (without offending any party)
may be entitled to credit, gives a ftatement of
the expences of the American government in
the following words :

The expences of all the feveral departments
of the General Reprefentative Government of
the United States of America, extending over
a fpace

a fpace of country nearly ten times larger than
England, is two hundred and ninety-four thoufand five hundred and fifty-eight dollars, which
at 4s. 6d. per dollar, is 66,275 l. 11s. fterling,
and is thus apportioned :

Expence of the Executive Department.

	£.	s.
The Office of the Prefidency, at which the Prefident receives nothing for himfelf - -	5,625	0
Vice Prefident - - -	1,125	0
Chief Juftice - - -	900	0
Five affociate Juftices - -	3,937	10
Nineteen Judges of Diftricts and Attorney General - -	6,873	15

Legiflative Department.

Members of Congrefs at fix dollars (1 l. 7s.) per day, their Secretaries, Clerks, Chaplains, Meffengers, Door-keepers, &c. - -	25,515	0

Treafury Department.

Secretary, Affiftant, Comptroller, Auditor, Treafurer, Regifter, and Loan-Office-Keeper, in each State, together with all neceffary Clerks, Office-Keepers, &c. -	12,825	0

Department

Department of State, including Foreign Affairs.

Secretary, Clerks, &c. &c.   -   1,406   5

Department of War.

Secretary, Clerks, Paymafters, Com-
    miffioner, &c.   -   -   1,462 10

Commiffioners for fettling Old Accounts.

The whole Board, Clerks, &c.   -   2,598 15

Incidental and Contingent Expences.

For Fire Wood, Stationary, Print-
    ing, &c.   -   -   -   4,006 16
                                          _____
                         Total   66,275 11

F I N I S.